Sports Law in Switzerland

Sports Law in Switzerland

Fourth Edition

Lucien W. Valloni
Thilo Pachmann

This book was originally published as a monograph in the International Encyclopaedia of Laws/Sports Law.

Founding Editor: Roger Blanpain
General Editor: Frank Hendrickx
Volume Editor: Michele Colucci

Wolters Kluwer

Published by:
Kluwer Law International B.V.
PO Box 316
2400 AH Alphen aan den Rijn
The Netherlands
E-mail: international-sales@wolterskluwer.com
Website: www.wolterskluwer.com/en/solutions/kluwerlawinternational

Sold and distributed by:
Wolters Kluwer Legal & Regulatory U.S.
7201 McKinney Circle
Frederick, MD 21704
United States of America
E-mail: customer.service@wolterskluwer.com

ISBN 978-94-035-4132-7

e-Book: ISBN 978-94-035-4133-4
web-PDF: ISBN 978-94-035-4134-1

The Authors

Lucien W. Valloni, PhD, is a partner at VALLONI Attorneys at Law, a law firm focusing on dispute resolution in Zurich.

He is known as one of the best sports lawyers in the Swiss market with an emphasis on sports litigation and arbitration and he is ranked as leading sports lawyer in leading legal directories. He has successfully represented clients in numerous high profile cases in the field of sport, especially CAS proceedings and other fields. His practice focuses on litigation and arbitration, sports, media and entertainment law, labour law as well as commercial law. He has vast experience in CAS proceedings and with appeals of CAS decisions to the Swiss Federal Supreme Court and the European Court for Human Rights.

Lucien W. Valloni is a frequent lecturer at sports law conferences and has published various articles. Furthermore, he is the President of the Swiss Association of Football Players (SAFP), the President of the World Association of Icehockey Players' Unions (WAIPU) and a Board Member of FIFPRO. He is also a lecturer at Paris Sorbonne University, Abu Dhabi, where he is head of the sports law module of the FIFA/CIES Executive Programme.

Thilo Pachmann, PhD, is a partner at Pachmann attorneys at law, a boutique style law firm in the heart of Zurich, Switzerland which has been ranked among the leading sports law firms in Switzerland during the last years. His practice focuses on litigation and arbitration, especially in the field of sports law, intellectual property rights, commercial, entertainment law and IT law. In the past, Thilo Pachmann has successfully represented several Olympic gold medal winners in proceedings in front of the Court of Arbitration for Sport. Moreover, he has vast experience with appeals to the Swiss Federal Tribunal and the European Court for Human Rights.

Thilo Pachmann has published various articles on sports and corporate law, in particular his doctoral thesis on 'Sports Associations and Corporate Governance'. Furthermore, he is a frequent speaker at international conferences on sports law and a lecturer at Zurich University, Switzerland and Seoul National University, South Korea.

The Authors

Thilo Pachmann is a former top athlete and a former Vice President of the Swiss Judo Federation (SJV) and was responsible for its Olympic delegation. Furthermore, he is a member of the International Association of Young Lawyers (AIJA) and was the President of its sport law commission.

Table of Contents

List of Abbreviations

AD	Anno Domini
AIJA	International Association of Young Lawyers
ASA	Swiss Arbitration Association
ATP	Federal Act on Therapeutic Products of 15 December 2000
BASPO	Federal Ministry of Sport
BGE	Decision of the Swiss Federal Tribunal (leading case)
Bull.	Bulletin
C.	Consideration
CartA	Federal Act on Cartels and other Restraints of Competition of 6 October 1995
CAS	Court of Arbitration for Sports
CCMJPD	Conference of Cantonal Ministers of Justice and Police Directors
CEO	Chief Executive Officer
CFI	Court of First Instance of the European Communities
CFSC	Code on the Federal Supreme Court of 17 June 2005
CHF	Swiss Franc(s)
CIAS	Conseil International de l'Arbitrage en matière de Sport
CIES	Centre International d'Etude du Sport
CIS	International Skiing Commission
CoA	Concordat on Arbitration of 27 March 1969
Coll.	Collection
CPC	Swiss Civil Procedure Code of 19 December 2008
CSC	Federal Constitution of the Swiss Confederation of 18 April 1999
DNA	Deoxyribonucleic acid
DSL	Digital Subscriber Line
EAA	European Athletic Association
EC	European Community

List of Abbreviations

ECHR	European Convention on Human Rights of 4 November 1950
ECJ	European Court of Justice
ECR	European Court Reports
ELAV	Eidgenössischer Leichtathletikverband
ESA	Employment Services Act of 6 October 1989
EU	European Union
EUR	Euro
FAN	Federal Act on Narcotics of 3 October 1951
FAS	Federal Act on Furthering of Sports of 17 June 2011
FC	Football Club
Fedpol	Federal Police Department
FEI	Fédération Équestre Internationale
FENS	Federal Act on Measures to Ensure National Security of 21 March 1997
FG	Federal Gazette
FIBA	Fédération Internationale de Basketball
FIFA	Fédération Internationale de Football Association
FIFPRO	Fédération Internationale des Associations de Footballeurs Professionnels
FIS	Fédération Internationale de Ski
FIVB	Fédération Internationale de Volleyball
FSA	Federazione Svizzera d'Atletica Leggera
GISS	Geneva International School of Soccer
IAAF	International Association of Athletics Federations
ICAS	International Council of Arbitration for Sport
IIHF	International Ice Hockey Federation
IOC	International Olympic Committee
JAR	Jahrbuch des Schweizerischen Arbeitsrechts (yearbook of Swiss labour law)
LBA	Federal Lotteries and Commercial Betting Act of 8 June 1923
lit.	Litera
N	Margin Numbers
NjW	Neue Juristische Wochenschrift
OC	Olympic Charter of 7 July 2007
PILA	Private International Law Act
PJA	Pratique juridique actuelle
PR	Public Relations

R	Rule
RDS	Revue de droit suisse
Rep.	Repertorio di giurisprudenza patria
RJB	Revue de la société des juristes bernois
RPS	Revue pénale suisse
RSJ	Revue suisse de jurisprudence
RTVG	Federal Act on Radio and Television of 24 March 2006
SAFP	Swiss Association of Football Players
SAIP	Swiss Association of Icehockey Players
SARB	Schweizerisches Arbeitsrecht
SC	Systematic Compilation of the Federal Legislation
SECO	State Secretariat for Economic Affairs
SFL	Swiss Football League
SFV	Swiss Football Association
SJV	Swiss Judo Federation
SLV	Schweizerischer Leichtathletik-Verband
SpuRt	Zeitschrift für Sport und Recht
TAS	Tribunal Arbitral du Sport/Court of Arbitration for Sport
UCI	Union Cycliste Internationale
UCL	Swiss Unfair Competition Law of 19 December 1986
UEFA	Union of European Football Associations
USD	United States Dollar
VAT	Value Added Tax
WADA	World Anti-Doping Agency
WAIPU	World Association of Icehockey Player Unions
ZGB	Swiss Civil Code of 10 December 1907

List of Abbreviations

Acknowledgements

Talent wins games but teamwork and intelligence win championships.[1]

This publication would not have been possible without the support and the assistance and the contribution of many of our colleagues working in the sports law department of our firms. Special thanks goes to Patrice Züger who helped updating this new edition.

Lucien W. Valloni & Thilo Pachmann
Zurich, 23 June 2021

1. Michael Jordan, American basketball player, widely considered as the greatest player ever.

Acknowledgements

General Introduction

§1. Introduction

1. Organized sport is of paramount importance in Switzerland. Many important bodies organize worldwide sports from Switzerland. Fédération Internationale de Football Association (FIFA), International Olympic Committee (IOC), Union of European Football Associations (UEFA), Fédération Équestre Internationale (FEI) Fédération Internationale de Basketball (FIBA), Fédération Internationale de Volleyball and International Ice Hockey Federation (IIHF) are all incorporated in Switzerland. It is no coincidence that these sports organizations have all chosen the legal form of a Swiss association pursuant to Articles 60 et seq. Swiss Civil Code. Apart from its neutrality, political stability and moderate taxation, a Swiss association offers a legal form that gives maximum flexibility to the organization. A Swiss association has to comply with the entire Swiss legal system; however, there is very good protection against too much influence by the State or courts. The right to gather in an association is a constitutional right in Switzerland.

2. The World Anti-Doping Agency (WADA), a foundation incorporated in Switzerland (Lausanne), whose secretariat is in Canada (Montreal), is leading the fight against doping in sport. WADA's organization and its rules are, hence, based on Swiss law. Similarly organized is the International Testing Agency (ITA) which is also a Swiss foundation having its head office in Lausanne.

3. The Court of Arbitration for Sport (CAS) which is set up by the International Council of Arbitration for Sport (ICAS), a foundation incorporated in Switzerland, is the leading body for the resolution of sporting disputes. Its awards are subject to judicial review by the Swiss Federal Supreme Court. Swiss law is therefore very important at CAS level. The CAS Code provides in respect of ordinary arbitration that in the absence of a choice of law by the parties, the dispute shall be decided in accordance with the rules of the involved sports organization, alternatively in accordance with Swiss law (N45). The CAS decides appeal procedures in accordance with the regulations of the sports organization and the chosen law or the law of the country in which the sports organization is domiciled or the rules of law which the panel deems appropriate if no national law has been chosen (N58). In the third division of the CAS, the CAS Anti-doping Division (CAS ADD), the disputes are decided pursuant to the applicable ADR and in the absence thereof or any agreement by the parties according to Swiss law.

4. The importance of Swiss law for sport is considerable; there are many scenarios in which Swiss law applies to worldwide-organized sport. According to Articles 1 and 155 lit. f Swiss Private International Law Act (PILA), Swiss law on associations is applicable between the association and its foreign members.[2]

5. Despite the fact that Switzerland is not a Member State of the European Union (EU), in the past few years, European law has had a growing impact on international sports organizations incorporated in Switzerland. These organizations, which are usually monopolies of a certain sport, are forced more and more to adapt their regulations not only to Swiss but also to European law, including competition law and the rules on free movement of employees. Even WADA has been subjected to European law in the field of fighting doping.

6. A variety of Swiss law rules, including employment law, competition law, law on associations, privacy laws and contract law apply to organized sport, often in combination with specific regulations of the sports organization; specific regulations of sports organizations only apply to sportspersons who exercise their sport under the supervision of the organization. There are not many Swiss law rules that are specific for sport. A comprehensive sports law with special rules considering the characteristics of sport does not exist in Switzerland.[3]

7. The importance of law for sports has increased due to increased professionalism and economic importance as well as interest of media and therefore sponsors. Given the massive turnovers for football world cups, football European championships and Olympic Games, which may amount to several billions US dollars, there is more and more need for a legal framework. In addition, there are more and more regulations in the area of sport.

8. Sport, in particular professional sport, has become more important in Swiss society over the last couple of years, both for education and as a value. Diverse cultures and nations can be integrated through sport and sports teams, and grass-roots sport is an important element in improving health. Sports politics has become more important due to the commercialization of sport. Politicians have become more aware of the importance of sport. Big events, such as Euro 2008 or the Ice Hockey World Championships 2009 as well as the world skiing championships in St. Moritz 2016 are used more and more for political purposes.

---

2. Cf. to the whole issue RIEMER, Sportrechtsweltmacht Schweiz – Internationale Sportverbände und schweizerisches Recht, 106 et seq.
3. The applicable rules are basically found in normal legal acts. Only the Federal Act on Furthering of Sports of 17 Jun. 2011 (as well as the corresponding Federal Ordonnance on Furthering of Sports) enacted certain special rules for sports.

§2. Statistics

9. According to a study[4] of the Federal Ministry of Sport (BASPO), 70% of the Swiss population are doing at least one sport per week. 51% of the Swiss population exercise more than three hours per week. These numbers have significantly increased over the last couple of years. More and more women and elderly people are into sport. However, there are differences between the language regions. Swiss-Germans generally do more sports than Italian or French-speaking Swiss. There are also social differences, which have an impact on sports. The higher the education, the better the job and the higher the income, the more active are the people. The reasons given for doing sports include in particular health and fun, which is more important for most participants than competing. The favourite sports include walking/hiking, cycling/mountain biking, swimming and skiing.

§3. Institutions

10. Switzerland distinguishes between public law and private law sports organizations.[5]

11. At Federal level, the most important public law sports organizations include the Federal Sports College in Magglingen and the BASPO, which is also domiciled in Magglingen.[6] At Cantonal level, there are further Cantonal sports offices and sports schools.

12. BASPO is Switzerland's centre of competence for Swiss Sport. It is currently under the supervision of Federal Minister Guy Parmelin. Within the Federal sports plan, BASPO shall further sport and its values for all ages and capabilities, across all social and cultural boundaries and shall develop and co-create national sports politics. BASPO evaluates goals and strategies to further sports in close cooperation with private law sports organizations. BASPO and its institutions are thus a service, education and training centre for Swiss sport. BASPO also offers a very good environment for sport infrastructure of national importance.

13. The most important private law sports organizations include Swiss Olympic, the national sport associations and Sport Toto Society. Swiss Olympic is the national umbrella organization for sport as well as the National Olympic Committee at the same time. As an umbrella organization Swiss Olympic combines 106 member organizations (81 national sports associations and 25 partner organizations) with

---

4. Study 'Sport Schweiz 2020' of BASPO.
5. Concept of the Swiss Federal Council for sports politics in Switzerland of 30 Nov. 2000.
6. *See* thereto http://www.baspo.admin.ch/ .

more than 18,000 clubs and around 2 million members.[7] The national sport federations organize their respective sport. The Sport Toto Society, i.e., the national sports lottery, is the most important sponsor for Swiss sport, providing approximately CHF 50 million per year.[8]

§4. Sports Governance: Autonomy and Specificity

14. Swiss legislation grants sports organizations far-reaching autonomy in organizing their sport and their structures. However, sports organizations are part of society and are legal organizations, which means they must comply with national and international legal frameworks.

15. The ongoing commercialization of sport has led to a vast increase of legal rules in sport. The commercial interests at stake have become paramount. It is therefore only natural that legal aspects become more and more important. The laws of the game, the starting point of legal rules in sports, have become less and less important. Employment law, free movement of persons, competition law and doping proceedings are legal aspects, which have considerably changed sport and will continue to change it.

16. The inclusion of 'specificity of sport' in the (failed) European Constitution and the Treaty of Lisbon shows that the EU is becoming increasingly involved in sports issues and only allows specific rules for sports if the specificity of sport actually requires such rules. There is the tendency that sport loses its vast autonomy to State interventions due to its increasing economic power and popularity. Sport's increasing importance has motivated politicians to use their influence on sport via politics. In Switzerland, the autonomy of sports is, however, still rather well protected due to the introduction of sports arbitration which applies rather strictly the sporting rules and whose awards may only be reviewed by the Federal Tribunal under exceptional circumstances.

17. Having said that, Swiss law grants international sports organizations an ideal legal framework. In particular, the Swiss legal form of association offers sports organizations considerable flexibility in organizing and managing such bodies. Sports, in particular, team sports, regularly serve as an example for the integration of sportspersons from diverse backgrounds. Sports has become a medium for dissemination of ideas and political issues.[9]

18. Despite all these challenges with which sport is faced, it is important that sport keeps its autonomy, particularly in view of the principle of 'specificity of

7. *See* http://www.swissolympic.ch.
8. *See* thereto http://www.sport-toto.ch. In addition to the funds of the Sport Toto Society, there are the funds of the Cantonal Sport-Toto-Funds in the amount of more than CHF 100 million.
9. *See* for instance http://www.showrespect.ch or 'Show Rasicsm the Red Card' http://www.srtrc.org or, for example, Fare http://www.farenet.org.

sport'. It is important that solutions can be found within the framework of the social dialogue between the social partners which can be integrated into the existing legal framework, taking into account the principle of 'specificity of sport', in order to limit the influence of state bodies to a required minimum and to preserve the autonomy of sports organizations. Autonomy of sport can be preserved by integrating the most important persons in sports organizations, ensuring equal influence of athletes' organizations on decision-making within sports organizations, as well as, the state-of-the-art organization and decision-making mechanisms. However, such autonomy may under no circumstances create a space where the generally accepted legal rules and mandatory Swiss law does not apply. Otherwise, there is not enough legal control to contain the sports federations which have become major economic players.[10]

10. The vast autonomy of the sports federations has in the end led to substantial governance problems not only in FIFA but also other sports federations. Such governance problems may only be prevented if the sports federations do not operate without being subject to legal rules and legal review.

Part I. Organization of Sport

Chapter 1. Sports Governance

§1. Basic Principles

I. The Sporting Pyramid

19. Characteristically for the organization of sport is the hierarchic structure. At the base of the pyramid are the athletes that are regularly bound to the clubs either as a member or by a contract. These clubs are members of a national federation that is on its part member of the continental federation and the international federation. In each geographic area there is only one competent sports federation.

Figure 1 The Sporting Pyramid

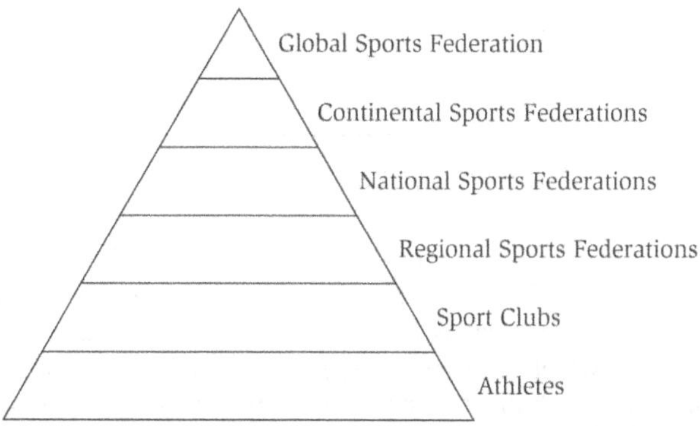

20. The control over the sport organization is in principle carried out by this basis. However, the higher the hierarchy, the weaker is the control by the athletes. The influence and control of the athletes over the International Sports Federations is therefore factually extremely weak.

II. One-Place Principle

21. From the Sporting Pyramid it becomes obvious that just one organizational unit is responsible for the administration of sports on every hierarchic and geographical level. This principle is called the one-place principle. Therefore, the sport organization has a quasi-monopolistic position towards the athletes and clubs. However, inside the sporting pyramid and also between the different sporting pyramids there is a big competition. The clubs compete to become national champions, the national sports federations want to become world champions, and the different sports want to raise the most funds possible for themselves.

III. Double Memberships

22. Besides the Sporting Pyramid especially the double membership is an important element to understand the worldwide sports organization. The national sports associations are members of their – in the Sporting Pyramid superior – continental and international sports federations as well as a member of the National Olympic Committee respectively in the national federation.

Figure 2 Double Memberships

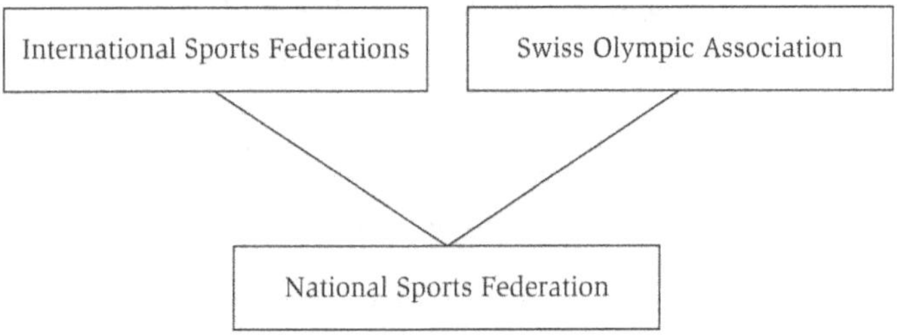

23. Therefore, the national sports federations in general control the National Olympic Committee as well as the superior sports federations (bottom up). However, this possibility of control is factually the other way around (top down). Because of the funds, which are transferred from the top to the bottom, and because of their monopolistic position, the superior sports federations have an extensive influence down to the bottom. As a consequence, smaller national sports federations in Switzerland heavily depend on Swiss Olympic, and the international sports associations of minority sports heavily depend on the IOC.

IV. Governance of the International Sport Organization

24. The principles of the double membership, the pyramidal hierarchic sport organization and the one-place principle are the most important basic principles in order to understand the functionality of international sport. There is a close network between all sport organizations because of the double membership. The pyramidal sport organization permits to organize the sport worldwide. At last the one-place principle gives the power to the sport associations to enforce their rules towards the athletes. Consequently, the athletes are accompanied by a quasi-monopoly organization. They are integrated in this organization and are a part of it. The result is an extraordinary global position of power of the international sport organization which is based in Switzerland.

§2. National Federations

I. Swiss Olympic

A. Formation

25. Swiss Olympic resulted in 1997 from the merger between Schweizerischer Landesverband für Sport, Schweizerisches Olympisches Komitee and Nationales Komitee für Elite Sport.

26. Following this merger Swiss Olympic is both the Swiss National Olympic Committee and the national governing body for sports. As a governing body, Swiss Olympic furthers sports in society as a contribution to the quality of life and health. Swiss Olympic furthers the motivation of the population to exercise regularly. At the same time Swiss Olympic furthers international competitive sports representing the interests of private law sports of Switzerland vis-à-vis the public, authorities and national and international organizations. As National Olympic Committee, Swiss Olympic furthers and protects the Olympic movement and its aims in Switzerland, as well as, its promotion in schools and universities.[11]

B. Organization

27. Swiss Olympic's bodies include the sports parliament, the executive council, the disciplinary chamber for doping cases and the auditors.[12]

28. The sports parliament, Swiss Olympic's supreme body, consists of the following members with voting rights: delegates of all the member federations (in proportion to the number of their members), Swiss IOC members and three to five athletes' representatives. The executive council, the executive managing body of Swiss Olympic, comprises the president and the vice president, ten members including two representatives of the government and one representative of a non-Olympic member organization, and the two Swiss IOC members.[13]

11. Article 1.2 of the articles of association of Swiss Olympic.
12. Article 3.1 of the articles of association of Swiss Olympic.
13. Article 5.1 of the articles of association of Swiss Olympic.

29. The member organizations are obliged to comply with the articles and regulations as well as the decisions of the sports parliament and the executive council of Swiss Olympic.[14] It follows that the power of Swiss Olympic,[15] as National Olympic Committee and umbrella organization of the eighty-one national sports organizations (Aero Club of Switzerland, Auto Sport Switzerland, Cricket Switzerland, Federal Crossbow Shooters Association, Swiss Hornusser Association, Federal Schwinger Federation, Federation of Motorcyclists of Switzerland, Pentathlon Suisse, PluSport Disabled Sports Switzerland, SWISS SQUASH - Swiss Squash Association, SWISSCURLING ASSOCIATION, Swiss Alpine Club, Swiss Paraplegics Association, Swiss Rugby Federation, Swiss Shooting Sports Association, Swiss Tug of War Association, Swiss Underwater Sports Association, Swiss Water Driving Association, Swiss Life Saving Association, Swiss Amateur Weightlifting Association, Swiss American Football Association, Swiss Billiards Federation, Swiss Boccia Federation, Swiss Boules Federation, Swiss Casting Association, Swiss Curling Association, Swiss Corporate and Recreational Sports Federation, Swiss Football Association, Swiss Handball Federation, Swiss Hang Gliding Association, Swiss Inline Hockey Association, Swiss Judo & Ju-Jitsu Federation, Swiss Kickboxing Association, Swiss Pontooning Federation, Swiss Pétanque Federation-Swiss Rowing Federation, Swiss Chess Federation, Swiss Bowling Federation, Swiss Public Transport Sports Association, Swiss Gymnastics Federation, Swiss Twirling Bâton Federation, Swiss Equestrian Sports Association, Swiss Water Ski and Wakeboard Association, Swiss Aquatics, Swiss Athletics, Swiss Baseball and Softball Federation, Swiss Basketball, Swiss Canoe, Swiss Cycling, Swiss DanceSport Federation, Swiss Disc Sports Association, Swiss Fencing, Swiss Golf, Swiss Hockey, Swiss Ice Hockey Federation, Swiss Ice Skating, Swiss Karate Federation, Swiss Minigolf, Swiss Orienteering, Swiss Sailing, Swiss Skate, Swiss Skateboard Association, Swiss Sliding, Swiss Snow Bike, Swiss Street Hockey, Swiss Surfing Association, Swiss Table Tennis, Swiss Tablesoccer Federation, Swiss Taekwondo, Swiss Tchoukball, Swiss Tennis, Swiss Triathlon, Swiss University Sports, Swiss Volley, Swiss Wrestling Federation, Swiss Wushu Federation, Swiss-Ski, SwissArchery Association, SwissBoxing, Swiss Badminton, Swiss Unihockey) is vast. Ultimately, Swiss Olympic decides how the subsidies of the federations are distributed. Swiss Olympic has issued rules according to which the subsidies are allocated. However, the members (the national sports organizations) remain autonomous for their respective sports.[16]

C. *Finances*

30. Swiss Olympic is primarily financed by Sport Toto Society and the Swiss state. The legal basis for such funding is Article 4 Federal Act on Furthering of

---

14. Article 2.2.2 para. 2 of the articles of association of Swiss Olympic.
15. Organized as an association pursuant to Arts 60 et seq. Swiss Civil Code and with its registered office in Bern. Swiss Olympic is a politically independent, confessionally neutral, non-profit organization (Art. 1.1. of the articles of association of Swiss Olympic).
16. Article 2.2.2 para. 1 of the articles of association of Swiss Olympic.

Sports (FAS). Due to Swiss Olympic's position as umbrella sports organization Swiss Olympic is entrusted with several tasks by the Swiss state and financed accordingly. Further, revenues are created through sponsors.[17] The financial means are primarily used for member organizations, direct payments to athletes, special projects and administration.[18]

II. Swiss Football Association

A. *Formation*

31. The Swiss Football Association (SFV) was formed in 1895 by eleven associations located in Lausanne, Ouchy, Neuchâtel, Yverdon, Zurich, St. Gallen, Basel, Geneva and Lausanne. SFV in turn was one of the seven national organizations that created the world football organization FIFA in 1904. At the beginning, there was a separate league in the French-speaking part of Switzerland. When further associations from the French-speaking towns La-Chaux-de-Fonds, Biel and Geneva joined in 1900, SFV managed to establish itself in the French-speaking part of Switzerland where it started to organize championship games.[19]

32. Today, SFV is the umbrella organization of Swiss football. SFV has three divisions, the Swiss Football League (SFL),[20] the first league, and the amateur league, counting 1,389 associations, 14,206 teams and 273,644 players. SFV divisions have their own legal personality. Seat of SFV is the House of Swiss Football in Muri. Dominique Blanc has been president since 1 July 2019.

B. *Purpose*

33. SFV's main purpose is furthering physical exercise by the youth, women and men promulgating football as well as the promotion, regulation and control of football in Switzerland, fair play and the educational, cultural and integrative power of football shall be given special consideration.[21] SFV also regulates the relationships between the divisions and organizations belonging to them and represents common interests in other organizations in Switzerland and abroad.[22]

---

17. In 2015, CHF 27.6 million came from the Sport Toto Society, CHF 12.2 million from the State and CHF 2.7 million from sponsors; *see* annual report of Swiss Olympic 2015.
18. In the year 2015 CHF 24.8 million were utilized for the member organizations, CHF 1 million for athletes, CHF 1.4 million for Olympic missions and special projects on behalf of the Swiss state CHF 2.5 million; *see* annual report of Swiss Olympic 2015.
19. For more information *see* http://www.football.ch/sfv/de/Geschichte_SFV.aspx?vNews=1&newsID =1.
20. For members of the Super League of the Swiss Football Association, the legal form of the corporation is mandatory (Art. 9 of the articles of association of the Swiss Football Association).
21. Article 2 lit. a and b of the articles of association of the Swiss Football Association.
22. Article 2 lit. e and f of the articles of association of the Swiss Football Association.

C. Organization

34. SFV's bodies are the assembly of delegates, the council, the central board, the legal bodies and the finance commission.[23]

35. The assembly of delegates,[24] the supreme body of SFV, comprises of the three divisions, each of which may delegate a number of delegates: twenty-eight delegates of SFL, twenty-six delegates of first league and forty-seven delegates of amateur league. Each delegate has one vote, resulting in the amateur associations dominating. The assembly of delegates is convened by the central board and normally takes place every two years in February. Extraordinary assemblies of delegates are convened by the central board if it is considered necessary or if a division or one-fifth of the members requires it so.

36. The central board,[25] the executive body, comprises of the central president, the three-division presidents and a member of each division. The assembly of delegates elects the central president and a member of each division. The division presidents are ex officio members of the central board. A member of the Executive Committee of FIFA/UEFA proposed by SFV is an ex officio member of the central board from the day of his or her election until he or she retires. The central board represents SFV vis-à-vis third parties and supervises all of SFV's activities. The central board has the power to do everything, which is not delegated to a different body by law or in the articles of association.

37. The council[26] comprises of twenty-five members, including the seven members of the central board and the six members of each division. It is in charge of making special strategic decisions as well as the interpretation of the articles of association. The central board convenes council meetings. Each year at least two ordinary meetings take place (one in spring and one in autumn). The central board may convene an extraordinary meeting if necessary or if requested by a division committee.

38. The Control and Disciplinary Commission[27] comprises of one president and twelve members. The members are elected by the assembly of delegates. For the rest the commission constitutes itself (among other things the election of a president and two vice presidents). The different tasks of the commission are regulated in Article 35 paragraph 2 of the articles of association. That includes among other things the dealing with all disciplinary cases, as long as they are not assigned to another institution or authority of the SFV.

23. The corporate bodies of the Swiss Football Associations and their composition and function are governed by Art. 20 of the articles of association of the Swiss Football Association.
24. Articles 25 et seq. of the articles of association of the Swiss Football Association.
25. Articles 31–35 of the articles of association of the Swiss Football Association.
26. Article 30 of the articles of association of the Swiss Football Association.
27. Article 36 of the articles of association of the Swiss Football Association.

39. The appellate court[28] comprises of the president, three vice presidents, twenty-one judges and six to nine clerks. The members of the appellate court are elected by the assembly of delegates upon nomination by the central board. The appellate court is responsible for the treatment of appeals against decisions of the Control and Disciplinary Commission, the Technical Department and the Referees Committee, as far as it is not a final decision.

40. The finance commission[29] comprises of the president and five members who are elected by the assembly of delegates. Each division nominates two experienced members. The finance commission constitutes itself.

III. Swiss Ice Hockey Federation

A. Formation

41. The Swiss Ice Hockey Federation, is an association in accordance with Articles 60 et seq. Civil Code, with its domicile in Zurich. Since 1 June 2011, it is the successor of the Swiss Ice Hockey Association, that was incorporated on 27 September 1908 and itself the successor of the *Ligue de hockey sur glace de la Suisse romande*, which had been incorporated in 1904.

42. Creating revenues of more than CHF 60 million, the Swiss Ice Hockey Federation is one of the most important sports organizations in Switzerland.[30]

43. The Swiss Ice Hockey Federation is a member of the IIHF, which is also located in Zurich.

B. Purpose

44. The Swiss Ice Hockey Federation aims at promulgating and furthering ice hockey in Switzerland.[31] The Swiss Ice Hockey Federation also represents Swiss Ice Hockey nationally and internationally. Furthermore, the Swiss Ice Hockey Federation gives the eligibility to play, that entitles to participate in the championship.

C. Organization

45. The Swiss Ice Hockey Federation is similarly organized as a company limited by shares. Its bodies are the General Assembly, the board of directors, which delegates the operative business to the managers, and the auditors. It includes the

28. Articles 38 and 38*bis* of the articles of association of the Swiss Football Association.
29. Article 39 of the articles of association of the Swiss Football Association.
30. See Annual Report SIHF 19/20.
31. Article 2 of the articles of association of the Swiss Ice Hockey Association.

National League Assembly, the Regional Assembly, the delegates for young and amateur sport, the Competitive Sports Committee and the Youth and Amateur Sports Committee.

46. The top body of the Swiss Ice Hockey Federation is the General Assembly, which meets annually at the Ice Hockey Congress. The General Assembly comprises of the NL-Assembly and the delegates of Youth and Amateur Sports. Both have an equal voting power in the General Assembly. The General Assembly's main competences are the arrangement of frame conditions (e.g., arrangement and modification of the articles of association), personnel-related decisions (e.g., electing the members of the board of directors) and further decisions (e.g., approving the business report).

47. The board of directors[32] consists of six to ten members, split up equally between the NL-Assembly and the delegates for the Youth and Amateur Sport. The board of directors manages the Swiss Ice Hockey Federation and represents it vis-à-vis third parties.

48. The legal bodies of the Swiss Ice Hockey Federation include the Association Sports Court, a single judge for disciplinary matters in competitive sport and for the Youth and Amateur Sport, the general manager of the Youth and Amateur Sport, a single judge for transfers in the competitive sport and for transfers in youth and amateur sports as well as the combined Appeals Section for transfers.[33]

IV. Swiss Ski Federation (Swiss-Ski)

A. Formation

49. Swiss-Ski was established on 20 November 1904 in Olten and is comprised of the divisions: Ski Alpine, Ski Nordic, Snowboard and Grass-Roots Sport.

50. Today, Swiss-Ski comprises and looks after the following disciplines; Ski Alpine, Cross Country, Ski Jumping, Ski Nordic Combination, Biathlon, Snowboard, Freestyle and Telemark. Swiss-Ski is a member of the Fédération Internationale de Ski (FIS), Swiss Olympic Association and Swiss Snow sports. Twelve regional associations and the two professional associations Swiss Grass Ski and Swiss Speed Ski are sub-organizations of Swiss-Ski. Swiss-Ski is incorporated in Muri near Bern.

32. Articles 26–35 of the articles of association of the Swiss Ice Hockey Association.
33. Article 101 et seq. of the articles of association of the Swiss Ice Hockey Association.

B. Purpose

51. The aim of Swiss-Ski is to be the leader in professional, grass-roots and youth sport. Swiss-Ski shall also promote ski and snowboard sports.[34] Furthermore, Swiss-Ski creates the foundations for successful sport by furthering clubs, professional athletes, young athletes and employees.[35] However, the primary concern of Swiss-Ski is professional sport. Swiss-Ski shall further the best development of athletes. Specific measures are being taken to further young athletes. By offering contemporary opportunities for sports, grass-roots snow sports shall be furthered and the young shall obtain the first opportunity to participate in competitions. By offering a broad range of opportunities, the health of the population shall improve and all ages, classes and regions shall be encouraged to engage in ski sports.[36]

C. Organization

52. Swiss-Ski's supreme body is the assembly of delegates. Apart from extraordinary meetings the assembly of delegates meets once a year. It comprises representatives of club members and single members, clubs and collective members and associations.[37]

53. The conference of presidents comprises of the President of Swiss-Ski, the six members of the Executive Committee, the presidents of the regional associations, the presidents of the professional associations, the presidents of the member organizations, as well as other members designated by the Executive Committee. The conference of presidents is a consultative body, which is updated by the President and management of Swiss-Ski at least twice a year and generally discusses ideas.[38]

54. The Executive Committee is responsible for strategically leading Swiss-Ski and comprises seven members.[39] The management implements the strategy at an operational level.[40] Furthermore, the director can establish task forces for specific tasks.[41] The articles of association provide for auditors, if Swiss-Ski is legally obliged to have auditors according to Article 69 Swiss Civil Code/Article 727 Swiss Code of Obligations.[42]

34. Article 3.1 of the articles of association of Swiss-Ski.
35. Article 3.2 of the articles of association of Swiss-Ski.
36. Cf. concept of Swiss-Ski.
37. Articles 29 et seq. of the articles of association of Swiss-Ski.
38. Articles 36 et seq. of the articles of association of Swiss-Ski.
39. Articles 41 et seq. of the articles of association of Swiss-Ski.
40. Article 42.1 of the articles of association of Swiss-Ski.
41. Articles 45 et seq. of the articles of association of Swiss-Ski.
42. Articles 46 et seq. of the articles of association of Swiss-Ski.

D. Finances

55. Swiss-Ski is financed by member contributions, contributions by private persons and public authorities, contributions by associations, revenues from sponsors, revenues from training and other operational revenues. Swiss Ski generates annual revenues of approximately CHF 50 million. [43] The biggest part is revenues from advertising (CHF 34 million), amounting to 69% in the business year 2015.[44]

E. Membership in International Sports Organizations

56. Swiss-Ski is a member of the FIS. The President of FIS, Gian-Franco Kasper, is an honorary member of Swiss-Ski.

V. Swiss Athletics

A. Formation

57. Swiss Athletics resulted from a merger between SLAV and Eidgenössischer Leichtathletikverband (ELAV). Since 1 November 2006, it acts under the name Swiss Athletics. The names *Schweizerischer Leichtathletik-Verband (SLV), Fédération Suisse d'Athletisme und Federazione Svizzera d'Atletica Leggera* are still in use; however, the abbreviations SLV and Federazione Svizzera d'Atletica Leggera (FSA) have been abandoned.

58. Swiss Athletics' seat is in the House of Sports in Ittigen, Berne.

B. Purpose

59. Swiss Athletics is the Swiss professional association for track and field athletics. It furthers and disseminates athletics and enhances the profile of this sport within all sports. Swiss Athletics cooperates with other organizations engaged in athletics. Swiss Athletics furthers professional sport, training of young athletes and the development of grass-roots sports. Swiss Athletics represents the interests of its members and offers various services.[45]

---

43. Annual Report Swiss-Ski 19/20, 9.
44. Annual Report Swiss-Ski 15/16, 52.
45. Article 2 of the articles of association of Swiss Athletics.

C. Organization

60. The assembly of delegates, the supreme body of Swiss Athletics, meets once a year.[46]

61. The central board of directors manages Swiss Athletics, represents it vis-à-vis third parties and supervises other bodies. It also defines Swiss Athletics' politics.[47]

62. The central board of directors is being advised by the advisory committee, consisting of not more than twelve prominent figures of athletics.[48]

63. Swiss Athletics has its own tribunal, which is another of its bodies. The tribunal has three members. All members of Swiss Athletics and their members as well as the regional assemblies submit all disputes related to Swiss Athletics to the tribunal.

D. Finances

64. In 2020, Swiss Athletics generated total earnings of CHF 13.3 million. Most revenues come from sponsoring, membership contributions and contributions by assemblies generate further revenues. Swiss Athletics also receives money from private benefactors and public authorities. In addition, Swiss Athletics generates revenues by organizing events and training.[49]

E. Relationship Between International Sports Organizations

65. Swiss Athletics is a member of the European Athletic Association (EAA) and the International Association of Athletics Federations (IAAF).

§3. International Federations

I. Introduction

66. The most important international sports federations and sports organizations are incorporated in Switzerland. The IOC is domiciled in Lausanne, like many other international sports federations. FIFA is domiciled in Zurich and UEFA in Nyon.

46. Article 21 of the articles of association of Swiss Athletics.
47. Articles 35 et seq. of the articles of association of Swiss Athletics.
48. Article 43 of the articles of association of Swiss Athletics.
49. Annual Report Swiss Athletics 2020, 38 et seq.

67. Switzerland offers international sports federations its legal system based on which their rules are enacted. For purposes of private international law, international sports federations are subject to the competence-competence of Switzerland. They are governed by Swiss law because they are organized in accordance with Swiss law.[50] Switzerland is thus often referred to as world power of sports law.[51]

68. All international sports federations are associations pursuant to Articles 60 et seq. Swiss Civil Code. Despite the fact that international sports federations often consider themselves to be supranational organizations, they have no special legal status. Only the IOC has an international public law status. In 1981, the Swiss Federal Council recognized the IOC's legal personality. In 2000, a treaty was signed with the IOC, according to which the IOC is exempt from direct federal taxes and to a large extent from Value Added Tax (VAT), and has received additional privileges for international transactions.[52]

II. International Olympic Committee

A. Formation

69. After the antique Olympic Games were abolished in 393 AD by the Roman Emperor Theodosius in the course of Christianization, the Frenchman Pierre de Coubertin took up the idea again in the nineteenth century. In 1892, he founded a club together with seven other people aimed at reviving the Olympic Games and educating youth by means of sports.

70. In 1915, Pierre de Coubertin decided to transfer the IOC's seat to neutral Switzerland due to the political situation (up to then the seat had rotated between the various organizing cities of the Olympic Games). Lausanne thus became the Olympic capital.

71. During the following years, the IOC became the most important international sports organization. Due to increasing economic importance of the Olympic Games, the members of IOC increasingly became targets of attempted corruption, cumulating in the Salt Lake City corruption scandal where the children of IOC members received funding, the political campaigns of IOC members were financed and the members first class return tickets, which could be exchanged for cash at the airport. A profitable 'inspection tourism' evolved for IOC members.

72. Following these events, the IOC's organization and the mechanism for granting Olympic Games was changed. A maximum term for the IOC members was

50. Article 154 PILA (so-called principle of incorporation).
51. Riemer, Sportrechts-Weltmacht Schweiz, 106 et seq.
52. Agreement between the Swiss Federal Council and the IOC regarding the statute of the IOC in Switzerland, SC 0.192.122.415.1.

introduced, they were prohibited from visiting candidate cities and members were chosen taking into account the most important stakeholders.

B. Organization

73. The IOC is governed by the Olympic Charter (OC).

74. The Session is the general meeting of the members of the IOC comprising of a maximum of 115 natural persons elected by co-optation, resulting in a maximum of 70 independent members, 15 active athletes and 15 executive members each of international sports organizations and national Olympic committees. Due to the election based on co-optation, the members are not true representatives of their organizations. This means that the IOC is legally not directly incorporated into the sporting pyramid. Therefore, the IOC is legally still completely independent from its most important stakeholders. The Session's most important tasks are electing the host city of the Olympic Games, determining the sports and electing the Executive Board.

75. The Executive Board assumes the general overall responsibility for the administration and the management and monitors the observance of the Olympic Charter.[53] It consists of the president, four vice presidents and ten ordinary members. There are also various advisory commissions.[54]

76. The Olympic Games are organized by the organizing committee consisting of representatives of the National Olympic Committees and the host city. In this regard the IOC has no financial responsibility.

77. Neither the international sports organizations responsible for organizing their sport at the Olympic Games nor the national Olympic committees selecting the athletes for the Olympic Games are direct members of the IOC. For this reason the athletes are being submitted under the Olympic Charter by entry forms which allow them to participate in the Olympic Games. Precondition for a participation in the Olympic Games is, however, the indirect membership in the international sports federations and the results achieved which make the athletes eligible to be nominated by their national Olympic committees.

78. Despite any direct connection between the National Olympic Committees and International Sports Federations on the one hand and the IOC on the other hand, the National Olympic Committees and International Sports Federations are given very important tasks under the Olympic Charter. It is, hence, possible to look at the National Olympic Committees and International Sports Federations as being legal organs of the IOC,

53. Article 19 OC.
54. Article 21 OC. Currently, there are 29 different commissions for amateur sports, solidarity, sports and law, sports and environment, etc.

79. The National Olympic Committees' important role is to promote and develop the fundamental principles and values of Olympianism in the world.[55] The majority of the members must be the international Olympic sports organizations and the IOC members of the respective countries must have a seat in the executive.[56] All nations apply these rules when organizing their national Olympic committees.

C. *Finances*

80. IOC owns the rights to the Olympic Games.[57] The IOC's revenues derive from the Olympic Games. Main revenues come from selling TV rights to broadcast the Olympic Games. Additional revenues are derived from sponsoring contracts, ticket sales and licence fees. About 90% of the revenues are distributed to the organizing committee, the international sports organizations and the national Olympic committees according to an agreed formula. The remaining 10% are used for administration within the IOC. The athletes do, however, not receive any direct subsidies and compensation.

III. FIFA and UEFA

A. *Formation*

81. FIFA was founded on 21 May 1904 in Paris by the Dutchman Carl Anton Wilhelm Hirschmann and the Frenchman Robert Guérin. Other founding members included the national football associations of Switzerland, Denmark, France, Holland, Belgium and Sweden. Some of the founding members, however, were different from the associations existing today, such as Real Madrid. Germany joined FIFA on the founding day by telegram. During the following years, further members joined; nowadays FIFA has 208 national associations as members. The first major international football competition took place during the Olympic summer games of 1908 in London. The World Football Association was incorporated in Zurich.

82. UEFA was founded on 15 June 1954 in Basel, following discussions between the associations of France, Belgium and Italy. According to the founders' minutes, of the thirty-one associations from Europe who were members of FIFA, twenty-five were present and two were represented. By the time of the first UEFA congress in March 1955, the others had also joined, and Turkey was admitted to the congress. UEFA's seat used to be in Paris until it moved to Berne in 1959. Since 1995, the management seat has been in Nyon.

55. Article 27 OC.
56. Article 28.1 and Art. 28.3 OC.
57. Article 7 OC.

B. Purpose

83. FIFA's mission is to constantly improve the game of football and promote it globally in the light of its unifying, educational, cultural and humanitarian values, particularly through youth and development programmes, organizing international competitions and drawing up regulations and provisions and ensuring their enforcement. FIFA also aims at preserving the integrity of games and competitions.[58]

84. UEFA deals with all questions relating to European football, promoting football in Europe in the spirit of peace, understanding and fair play. UEFA also organizes and conducts international competitions and tournaments, preventing all methods or practices, which might jeopardize the regularity of matches or competitions or give rise to the abuse of football. UEFA further ensures that sporting values always prevail over commercial interests by redistributing revenues generated by football in accordance with the principle of solidarity, and supports reinvestment in favour of all levels and areas of football, especially the grass roots of the game. UEFA also maintains good relations and cooperates with FIFA and the other confederations recognized by FIFA. UEFA shall enhance Europe's position in world football. UEFA shall seek to achieve its objectives by implementing any measures it deems appropriate, such as setting out rules, entering into agreements or conventions, taking decisions or adopting programmes.[59]

C. Organization

85. FIFA's supreme and legislative body is the Congress.[60] The Ordinary Congress is held every year; the Council may convene Extraordinary Congresses at any time.[61]

86. The Council is the strategic and oversight body.[62] The Council consists of thirty-seven members: one president (elected by the Congress), eight vice presidents and twenty-eight other members.

87. The General Secretariat is FIFA's executive body.[63] The General Secretariat shall perform its tasks under the direction of the Secretary General.[64] The Secretary General is the Chief Executive Officer (CEO) of FIFA.[65]

88. The President legally represents FIFA. He or she is primarily responsible for implementing the decisions passed by the Congress and the Executive Committee

58. Article 2 of the articles of association of the FIFA.
59. Article 2 of the articles of association of the UEFA.
60. Article 24 para. 1 of the articles of association of the FIFA.
61. Articles 25 et seq. of the articles of association of the FIFA.
62. Article 24 para. 2 of the articles of association of the FIFA.
63. Article 24 para. 3 of the articles of association of the FIFA.
64. Article 36 para. 1 of the articles of association of the FIFA.
65. Article 37 para. 1 of the articles of association of the FIFA.

through the General Secretariat. He or she also supervises the work of the General Secretariat and maintains relations between FIFA and the confederations, members, political bodies and international organizations.[66]

89. FIFA also has a number of standing committees dealing with finances, audit, major sports events and internal affairs such as marketing, media.[67] Recently the ethics committee was founded and also became active due to bribery of members of the Executive Committee in connection with the election of the FIFA World Cups 2016 and 2020.

90. UEFA's bodies are the Congress, the Executive Committee, the President and various bodies for the administration of justice. The Congress is UEFA's supreme body. An Ordinary Congress is held every year and its decisions are binding on all member associations.[68] The Executive Committee consists of the president and fifteen other members elected by the Congress. The Executive Committee has the overall control of UEFA and has the power to give all directions necessary for this purpose.[69] The President of UEFA represents UEFA vis-à-vis third parties.[70] The bodies for the administration of justice include the Control and Disciplinary Body, the Appeals Body, the Ethics and Disciplinary Inspector and the Club Financial Control Body. The jurisdiction and proceedings are governed by the Disciplinary Regulations.[71]

D. Finances

91. FIFA splits its revenues into three main categories: Television broadcasting rights, marketing rights and licensing rights. The most important of these categories is revenue from TV broadcasting rights. In 2019, revenues from broadcasting amounted to 45% of the total revenues of USD 766 million. The second most important category are revenues from marketing and licensing rights. These revenues each contribute approximately 21 % of the total revenues of FIFA. Other revenues contribute 12%.[72] In the year 2015, FIFA has suffered severe losses due to the investigations into the allegations of the corruption affair. In 2015, FIFA suffered a loss of USD 122 million despite increasing revenues. All of this led to only 74% of the revenues being directly invested into football.[73]

92. UEFA's main source of income is media rights, amounting to 85.4% of the total revenues of EUR 3,038.2 million. Commercial rights contribute 13.7% to the

66. Article 35 of the articles of association of the FIFA.
67. Article 39 of the articles of association of the FIFA.
68. Articles 12 et seq. of the articles of association of the UEFA.
69. Articles 21 et seq. of the articles of association of the UEFA.
70. Article 29 of the articles of association of the UEFA.
71. Articles 32 et seq. of the articles of association of the UEFA.
72. FIFA Annual Report 2019, 17.
73. FIFA Financial Report 2015, 14.

total revenues. According to the consolidated annual accounts, ticket sales contribute 0.1% and other revenues 0.8% of the total revenues.[74]

IV. International Ice Hockey Federation

A. *Formation*

93. IIHF was founded on 15 May 1908 in Paris as *Ligue international de hockey* by representatives from Belgium, England, Switzerland and France. Representatives from Germany and Russia were also invited but they did not take part in the founders' meeting. Germany joined one year later. Later the same year Bohemia joined as the fifth member and it is sometimes listed as one of the founding members. Russia only joined in 1952 as the Soviet Union. Today the IIHF has eighty-one member national associations. The IIHF's seat is Zurich.

B. *Purpose*

94. The IIHF's mission is to promote ice hockey throughout the world and to lead the ice hockey movement as recognized by the International Olympic Committee. [75]

C. *Organization*

95. IIHF's legislative body is the Congress. IIHF distinguishes between the General Congress, which takes place every four years, the Annual Congress, the Semi Annual Congress and any Extraordinary Congress.[76]

96. IIHF's executive body is the Council consisting of the president, one senior vice president (in force as of September 2021) three vice presidents, nine other members of which at least two must be female and at least two must be male. Amongst other things, the Council is responsible for observing and enforcing the statutes, by-laws and regulations and for executing decisions of the Congress.[77]

97. Other bodies of the executive are the Director and the IIHF Office.[78]

74. UEFA Financial Report 2019/2020.
75. Statute 4 of the articles of association of the IIHF.
76. Statute 14 of the articles of association of the IIHF.
77. Statute 15 of the articles of association of the IIHF.
78. Statutes 16 & 17 of the articles of association of the IIHF.

98. In addition, there is a Finance Committee, an Ethics Board, Operational Committees and two Internal Auditors.[79] Audit Committee monitors financial matters and advises other bodies.[80] Besides, there are judicial bodies such as the Disciplinary Board and the Appeal Board and Appeal Panels. The Disciplinary Committee avenges breaches of the disciplinary regulations of IIHF.[81]

D. *Finances*

99. IIHF's annual report for 2019/2020 states total revenues of CHF 26,652,712 with a negative result of CHF 4,011,109. The budgeted result was a loss of CHF 8,371,520. According to IIHF the difference between the actual result and the budgeted loss reflects the management of the IIHF Insurance Contract and the payment of the insurance for the cancelled World Championship 2020 in Switzerland.[82] In 2018, a revenue of CHF 50,722,163 was achieved due to marketing income and income from the Olympic Games. IIHF normally generates approximately half of the revenues from marketing . About 2% come from sponsoring and suppliers, the remaining come from contributions for the Olympic Games, championship incomes and not-further-specified sources. Due to Covid-19, 86% of the revenue in 2019/2020 stemmed from insurance reimbursement.[83] The IIHF has negotiated and implemented an event cancellation insurance which due to the pandemic covered the missing income out of the marketing contract in the amount of CHF 22,850,000.

V. Fédération Équestre Internationale

A. *Formation*

100. FEI was founded in Paris on 24/25 November 1921 by Belgium, Denmark, France, Italy, Japan, Norway, Sweden and the US. Germany joined in 1927. With Bahamas, Mongolia and Côte d'Ivoire recently joining in 2019, as of today 136 countries are members of FEI.

101. The FEI is the patron for all international tournaments organized by its members. FEI establishes the regulations for the World Equestrian Games and the Olympic Games. It is also in charge of medical support and doping tests at international tournaments. FEI's seat is in Lausanne.

79. Statute 18 of the articles of association of the IIHF.
80. Article 18.2.4 of the articles of association of the IIHF.
81. Statute 20.1 of the articles of association of the IIHF.
82. IIHF Annual Report 2019/2020, 7.
83. IIHF Annual Report 2019/2020, 27.

B. Purpose

102. FEI appears to be the only organization for international events for equestrian disciplines. FEI establishes regulations, and coordinates and supervises them. FEI's mission is to advance fair competition between athletes from different nations at international events. FEI is also concerned with the welfare of the horse and the natural environment, which it aims to protect, by a code of conduct.[84]

C. Organization

103. FEI's supreme body is the General Assembly. It is held yearly, taking decisions with regard to amending the statutes, approving of long-term strategies and budgets. The General Assembly governs the overall direction, the development and management of FEI's disciplines throughout the world for the coming year.[85]

104. The Bureau is FEI's executive body. It is composed of the president, two vice presidents, the chairs of the technical discipline committees, the chairs of the regional groups, the audit and compliance groups and the chair of the Athletes Committee. The Bureau is responsible for all matters not confined to the General Assembly or any other body.[86]

105. The President is responsible for ensuring that the purposes and principles of FEI are observed and represents FEI vis-à-vis third parties.[87] The President, together with the vice presidents and two technical chairs, form the Executive Board.

106. Another important body of FEI are the Headquarters. The Head of the Headquarters and at the same time Chief Executive Officer (CEO) of FEI is the Secretary General. He or she reports to the President and through the President to the Bureau and the General Assembly.[88]

107. Other bodies of FEI include the Regional Groups. They promote and coordinate the development and activities of equestrian sport and represent the national federations of their groups within FEI. There are also a number of committees, among others for the respective technical disciplines.[89]

---

84. Article 1 of the articles of association of the FEI.
85. Article 9 of the articles of association of the FEI.
86. Articles 19 et seq. of the articles of association of the FEI.
87. Article 22 of the articles of association of the FEI.
88. Articles 28 et seq. of the articles of association of the FEI.
89. Articles 30 et seq. of the articles of association of the FEI.

108. Another body of FEI is the FEI Tribunal. It decides all cases submitted to it by or through the Secretary General concerning infringements of the statutes, sport rules and procedural rules.[90]

D. *Finances*

109. FEI's main revenues derive from marketing and other commercial activities, amounting to over 50% of the total revenues. Approximately 37% of all revenues come from operational activities. Another source of revenue are the contributions from the IOC and other funds. In 2019, FEI generated revenues totalling CHF 54,448,471.[91]

VI. Union Cycliste Internationale

A. *Formation*

110. UCI was founded in Paris on 14 April 1900 by the Belgium, French, Italian, Swiss and US national federations. As of today, 170 national and five continental federations are members of UCI. UCI's seat is in Aigle.

B. *Purpose*

111. As the umbrella organization of the national cycling federations, UCI's main purpose is to direct, develop, regulate, control and discipline cycling in all forms worldwide. UCI promotes cycling publicly and organizes competitions in all countries of the world. UCI shall carry out its activities in compliance with the principles of non-discrimination, furthering the spirit of sport and fairness. UCI is the official representative of cycling vis-à-vis IOC.[92]

C. *Organization*

112. UCI's supreme body is the Congress. It is held annually and comprises of representatives of the recognized national federations.[93]

113. The Congress elects the Management Committee, which manages UCI on behalf of and under the authority of the Congress. The Management Committee has

90. Article 38 of the articles of association of the FEI.
91. FEI Financial Report 2019.
92. Article 2 UCI-Constitution.
93. Articles 28 et seq. UCI-Constitution.

fifteen members and meets three times a year. As executive body, the Management Committee is allowed to take all necessary measures.[94]

114. Routine or urgent business is dealt with by the Executive Committee. It consists of the president and three vice presidents.[95]

115. The President of UCI chairs the Congress as well as the meetings of the Management Committee and Executive Committee. He or she also represents UCI vis-à-vis third parties, including in legal disputes in which UCI is a claimant or a defendant.[96]

116. The Administrative Service is the operative body of UCI comprising of three former athletes as well as experts who meet in commissions and execute decisions of the Management Committee.[97]

D. Finances

117. In the business year 2019, UCI achieved revenues amounting to CHF 40.7 million. Approximately 24% of the revenue came from media rights and distribution, 26% from host city fees, 22% of the revenue was created from other commercial rights and the rest of the revenue stems from registration fees (18%) and other revenues (12%).[98]

VII. Fédération Internationale de Ski

A. Formation

118. International Skiing Commission (CIS) was founded on 18 February 1910 in Christiania (Norway) by delegates from ten countries. Approximately one year later, in March 1911, the first regulations with international effect were passed. On 2 February 1924, during the first Olympic Games in Chamonix, thirty-six delegates from fourteen countries decided to establish FIS, the successor of CIS.

119. As of today, FIS has 135 member associations. FIS' seat is in Oberhofen at Lake Thun.

94. Articles 46 et seq. UCI-Constitution.
95. Articles 59 et seq. UCI-Constitution.
96. Articles 62 et seq. UCI-Constitution.
97. Article 69 UCI-Constitution.
98. UCI Annual Report 2019.

B. Purpose

120. FIS' main purpose is to promote the sport of skiing and to supervise and direct the development of all skiing activities. FIS shall also establish and maintain friendly relations with and between the member associations. FIS also organizes competitions such as the world ski championships, world cups and continental cups. FIS also establishes rules for all ski competitions and monitors their compliance and enforcement, including the fight against doping in the sport of skiing.[99]

C. Organization

121. The Congress is the supreme body of FIS. Apart from establishing and modifying the statutes and the international ski competition rules, the Congress also elects the Council and decides on admissions and expulsions of members and the calendar for competitions.[100]

122. The Council, which is elected by the Congress, is the supreme authority of FIS. It appoints organizers of world ski championships and prepares proposals to be submitted to the Congress. The Council is the representative of the Congress; decisions taken by the Council are only valid until the next Congress. Other participants of the Congress are the Executive Board, the Secretary General and the Doping Panel.[101]

123. The President of FIS is also a member of the Council. He or she represents FIS in all important matters, in particular in negotiations with the IOC and other international organizations. The President also directs the Congress and the Council Meetings.[102]

124. FIS' judiciary bodies include the FIS Court, the Competition Juries and the Appeals Commission. The FIS Court has jurisdiction for disputes between the member associations and regarding appeals against sanctions imposed by the Council. The Council may also request that the FIS Court decide other cases. The respective competition juries decide breaches against the competition rules. They may refer grave breaches to the Appeals Commission. The Appeals Commission decides cases, which are referred by competition juries as well as appeals against decisions of competition juries.[103]

99. Article 3 of the articles of association of the FIS.
100. Article 13 of the articles of association of the FIS.
101. Articles 24 et seq. of the articles of association of the FIS.
102. Article 35 of the articles of association of the FIS.
103. Articles 43 et seq. of the articles of association of the FIS.

125. The Council may also appoint Committees, Sub-Committees and Working Groups. The Committees advise the Council and are responsible for technical and other specified activities of FIS. Further bodies of FIS are the Auditors and the General Secretariat.

D. Finances

126. In the business year 2018/2019, FIS generated total revenues of CHF 50,054,822. Approximately 90% of the revenues were created by selling marketing rights for major events such as the Olympic Games, the World Ski Championships, World Cups and other events. Around 9% of the revenues derive from membership contributions, calendar fees and registration fees as well as homologations. About 1% of the revenues derive from further means of income.[104]

§4. International Sport Institutions

I. WADA

127. At the first World Conference on Doping in Sport organized by the IOC in 1999, the sport organizations and the national states achieved a consensus regarding the WADA (and the WADA Code), which has since been reviewed and amended several times.

128. WADA, a foundation under Swiss law incorporated in Switzerland (Lausanne) whose headquarters are in Canada (Montreal), was established to enforce the Anti-doping Code. WADA has regional offices in Europe (Lausanne, Switzerland), Asia/Oceania (Tokyo, Japan), Africa (Cape Town, South Africa) and Latin America (Montevideo, Uruguay).[105]

129. The Foundation Board is composed equally of representatives from the Olympic movement and national governments. WADA is equally financed by the sports organizations and the national states in order to secure WADA's independence and to bring the fight against doping to an international level. WADA ensures that the sports organizations impose harmonized fines. WADA has, for example, developed the standards for the Athlete Biological Passport. It is obvious that the sportspersons themselves are not adequately represented within WADA and that their position within the WADA rules and the WADA organization must be improved. Apart from that the main role of WADA is to guarantee the correct application of the WADA Code. Hence, WADA is supposed to take a neutral role concerning this task. However, the way WADA is using its granted appeal right does

104. FIS annual financial report 2018/2019, 2.
105. *See* thereto also http://www.wada-ama.org.

shows as if WADA is appealing only to obtain further convictions of an athlete. Appeals of WADA in favour of athletes allegedly violating the WADA Code are not known or not made public.

130. Since WADA's establishment, the tasks of the sports organizations have substantially changed. The fight against doping is no longer for the national sports organizations; it is now for national doping agencies to fight doping. In Switzerland, the fight against doping is led by the Foundation Anti-doping Schweiz, which is equally funded by the Swiss state and Swiss Olympic.

131. Such development has been significantly furthered by the UNESCO International Convention against Doping in Sports. The Convention represents the first time that governments around the world have agreed to apply the force of international law to anti-doping, and to ensure the effectiveness of the World Anti-Doping Code (the Code). As the Code is a non-government document that applies only to members of sports organizations, the Convention provides the legal framework under which governments can address specific areas of the doping problem that are outside the domain of the sports movement. As such, the Convention helps to formalize global anti-doping rules, policies and guidelines in order to provide an honest and equitable playing environment for all athletes. The governments have certain flexibility over how the effect is given to the Convention, either by way of legislation, regulation, policies or administrative practices. Even though the Convention does not make the Code directly applicable in the countries, the signatory governments are required to take specific action to:

- Restrict the availability of prohibited substances or methods to athletes including measures against trafficking.
- Facilitate doping controls and support national testing programs.
- Encourage producers and distributors of nutritional supplements to establish 'best practice' in the labelling, marketing and distribution of products which might contain prohibited substances.
- Support the provision of anti-doping education to athletes and the wider sporting community.

132. Entered into force on 1 February 2007 the Convention has become the most successful convention in the history of UNESCO in terms of rhythm of ratification after adoption and is ratified by almost all countries.

II. International Testing Agency (ITA)

133. The ITA was founded by the IOC in 2018 to separate the anti-doping testing from the policy making body (WADA). In theory, this should make the anti-doping control system more independent and reliable. However, the close factual connections to its founding organisation as well as the IOC put these goals into doubt.

134. The Board of ITA is composed of four independent/neutral members and three members representing: (a) athletes, (b) the International Olympic Committee and National Olympic Committees and (c) international sports federations. The ITA Board is responsible for the appointment of the ITA Director General who should be autonomous.

III. Court of Arbitration for Sport (CAS)

135. CAS was established in 1983 by IOC to create a specialized arbitral tribunal for sports-related disputes. In the last couple of years CAS's importance continuously increased due to almost all international sports organizations choosing CAS as their official arbitral tribunal and also because CAS operates an ad hoc tribunal during the Olympic Games (as well as other major sports events). CAS has decentralized offices all over the world. The seat of the arbitral tribunal is, however, usually in Switzerland.

136. CAS's supreme body is the ICAS, which is composed of representatives of sports organizations. ICAS determines the organization of CAS, decides the budget and appoints arbitrators and the secretariat.

137. CAS has three divisions. The Ordinary Arbitration Division decides disputes submitted to CAS. The Appeals Arbitration Division decides disputes resulting from final-instance decisions taken by sports organizations. The Anti-doping Division replaces the anti-doping tribunals of international sports federations. It is also possible to submit legal questions to CAS and to ask CAS to mediate disputes.

138. In 1993, the Swiss Federal Supreme Court decided that CAS is an arbitral tribunal independent from the international sports organizations in the sense of Articles 176 et seq. PILA, despite a limited list of arbitrators and Conseil International de l'Arbitrage en matière de Sport (CIAS's) domination.[106] However, more and more people seem to question whether CAS is really independent, given the list of arbitrators and the strong connections to sports organizations.[107] The main reason for such criticism comes from the composition of the ICAS which is dominated by the sports organizations.[108]As the ICAS has wide-reaching powers by appointing the arbitrators on the closed list of arbitrators, by appointing the President of the panel, and by being able to remove arbitrators from the closed list of arbitrators (S6 CAS Code) the independence of CAS Panels may be questionable in certain cases.[109] Even though, that until today the Swiss Federal Tribunal has always confirmed the independence and impartiality of the CAS Panels, there is a need for

106. BGE 119 II 271 et seq.
107. Heini & Scherrer in Honsell & Vogt, Zivilgesetzbuch, N 30 to Art. 75 Swiss Civil Code.
108. Valloni, CAS Structure and Procedure p. 38.
109. Valloni, CAS Structure and Procedure p. 39.

future changes to ensure the maintenance of the CAS.[110] CAS proceedings are also very costly which makes it often impossible for athletes have their case heard. CAS's pro bono counsel system does not ensure a balanced procedure for the athletes as the pro bono counsels lack experience and founding.

§5. Structure and Governance of Sport Federations

I. The Meaning of Switzerland for the Worldwide Governance of Sports

139. As already mentioned, the most significant international sport federations and sporting institutions, i.e., the IOC, the CAS and the WADA, have their domicile in Switzerland. In order to find out how the governance of world sports operates, it is fundamental to understand the sporting network. The network of the sport organizations operates not only from the basis of the sporting pyramid through the exertion of voting rights (bottom up), but also the other way around, as the sport federations on the top of the hierarchy control their subordinated sport federations through their contributions and rules (top down). This interdependence and interconnection are crucial to understand the worldwide functionality of sports.

II. Corporate Governance of Sport Federations

A. Term of the Corporate Governance

140. Corporate Governance literally means governance of the corporate body. Consequently, the definition goes beyond the agency relation between athletes and functionaries. Subject to Corporate Governance are the entire governance and administrative structures of a company, in short the entire corporate constitution. The Corporate Governance of sport federations therefore consists of the internal and external governing structure of the corporate body. The internal governing structure is about the interaction of the organs and establishment of the governing body. The external governing structure is about control mechanisms like the market and the transparency.

B. The Application of the Corporate Governance Theories on Sport Federations

141. Sport federations are generally Non-Profit Organizations. Therefore, their goal is the maximization of the ideal purpose and not the maximization of the profit. Top priority has the promotion of the sport. Therefore, the Corporate Governance simply has the goal to maximize the promotion of the sport. The sport federation –

110. In his article, Valloni (CAS Structure and Procedure, pp. 42 et seq.) proposes several possibilities to ensure such maintenance.

in highly simplified terms – has to maximize the benefit of everybody that is interested in its sport. As a result, good Corporate Governance has to secure that the sport federations act in the best possible way to further sports.

142. Sport federations have a lot of stakeholders, i.e., athletes, clubs and referees just to name a few, which are highly dependent on the sport federations. They have a real interest to exercise the necessary control in the sport federations. To ensure a functioning governance structure with effective control mechanisms, these stakeholder groups have to be granted effective influence and control possibilities.

III. Economical Characterization

A. National Sports Federations as Cooperatives to Reach the Ideal Purpose

143. The national sports federations basically have to be qualified as 'fake' non-profit organizations. The members of the national federations have joined together to support each other (similar to a cooperative) with conjoint factual self-help. The sport clubs, as members of the national sports federations, contribute together so that the sport is in an optimal way enhanced.

144. From the economic point of view sport clubs, as members of the national sports federations are in a position similar to an owner, because they exercise the residual control. The legal form of the clubs as associations secures that all the investments of the members are mandatorily used for the sport. This effect exists as well regarding sponsors and patrons. The promotion of the sport through the national sports federations is a profit for the other athletes that exercise a certain sport as well. Therefore it is important for the national sports federations to spread the costs for the creation of the sports competitions and regulations as wide as possible, for which reason a de facto compulsory membership is established through the necessity of the licence.

B. International Sports Federations are Between Cooperatives and Real Non-profit Organizations

145. The mission of the international sports federations is the worldwide promotion of their sport. In this context the international sports federations fulfil sports development tasks worldwide. The international sports federations do not self-finance themselves anymore through membership fees. They finance themselves through the realization of the rights on their sporting events, which is what makes them financially strong companies.

146. The control is basically exercised by the national sports federations. However, their possibilities of influence are not as big as on the national level. In many cases a functional control is not possible because of the great number of members and the missing knowledge about the activity of the international sports federations.

Moreover, the small members which have the majority have quite a different agenda than the bigger members. Therefore the international sports federations are by trend rather real non-profit organizations. They not only promote the interests of their own members through conjoint self-help, but also perceive, detached from the members, the interests of third parties.

147. The self-interests of the functionaries rise with the decreasing inducement of control by the members. Through their position of power, which they can exercise by the allocation of the financially lucrative sporting events, the danger of agency problems rises. Because the direct personal contact and the reciprocal social control of the federation's functionaries, that works well on the national level, gets weaker, the danger of opportunistic actions rises too. Therefore good governance has to secure that the possible selfish interests of the board of directors do not proceed at the expense of the organization.

C. International Olympic Committee as Real Non-profit Organization

148. The IOC is finally a 'real' non-profit organization. That means the members are not addressees of the club's activity. The interests of the world of sports are indeed pictured in the member's structure of the IOC, but these sport organizations are not able to exercise direct influence on the IOC. At most 115 individuals that are elected through co-optation are members of the IOC. That makes the IOC a small and elitist structure, in which the members participate neither directly nor indirectly in the residual income. However, they are in charge of the allocation of the most important sporting event worldwide, for which reason there is a danger that they could utilize their position. Concerning this matter there is still a deficit concerning Corporate Governance.

149. Nevertheless the organizational form of the IOC has significant advantages: Would a profit-oriented organization have the rights of the Olympic Games, the earnings would not completely flow back into the sport. This is one reason why the athletes are willing to participate almost for free in the Olympic Games (and until recently without being allowed to market themselves during the Olympic Games). They know that all the financial means flow back into the sport, whereupon they profit again themselves.

150. Furthermore there is a greatly reduced inducement of control, because the members do not get a direct benefit from their actions. Through the co-optation of the members the IOC secures that the members keep the major focus on the promotion of the sport objective. The payment of the money to the international sports federations and the national Olympic committees leads to a top-down dependency between the IOC and the international sports federations, the National Olympic Committees and to some extent the host cities of the Olympic Games. The forbiddance of payout, that is provided in the law of associations for non-profit organizations, favours the formation of the reciprocal dependency. In the ideal case this money should be completely reinvested on all levels down to the athletes.

D. Implementation of a Good Corporate Governance

151. The organization of the associations as non-profit organizations has proved of value in the past. However, it requires efficient safeguarding mechanisms. It is necessary that the forbiddance of payout (i.e., the non-distribution constraint) of the association form is maintained and enforced on all levels. In particular an avoidance of the forbiddance of payout through exorbitant expenses has to be stopped.

152. The pressure from the members and the superior sports federations on the hierarchically lowest sports federations to implement good Corporate Governance is high. In recent years the control on the level of the national sports federation decreased because of the increase of professionalism and the lack of transparency, what in addition accent in the international sports federations. Therefore the sports federations have tried to grant more rights of co-determination to the especial dependent-involved parties, using committees and special representatives to set up an efficient control. However, these internal safeguard mechanisms only function to a certain extent.

153. For the guarantee of a good Corporate Governance in sport associations it is necessary that there is not just an internal, but also a public control. However, this control can just be guaranteed if there is transparency. Therefore, a certain regulatory action of the state is basically desirable.

154. A competition of location concerning the domicile of the international sports associations comes more and more between the national states. The sports organizations basically prefer the location which has few mandatory legislations and gives the sports associations more autonomy. Therefore, there is a risk that it comes to a regulatory 'race to the bottom'. The national state with the fewest regulations wins the competition of location. Should Switzerland want to improve the Corporate Governance of the sports federations, this basically has to be done by the sports federations themselves or at least under their voluntary cooperation.

Chapter 2. Public Regulation

§1. Introduction

155. According to Article 68 paragraph 1 of the Swiss Constitution, the Federation is entitled to promote sport in general, in particular sport education. In parallel, the Cantons have the same competence. The Federation is therefore not entitled to regulate all aspects of sport, for example, to make exercise compulsory for adults. The competence to regulate the conditions for training teachers and trainers remains with the Cantons and the sports organizations. Based on Article 68 paragraph 1 of the Swiss Constitution, the Federation has enacted the Federal Act on Sports of 17 June 2011[111] and the Federal Ordinance on Sports of 23 May 2012.[112]

156. According to these rules the Swiss State furthers sports by means of subsidies or deficit guarantees, teacher training, providing material and procuring infrastructure.

157. Regarding elite sports the State complies with the principle of subsidiarity. The State only provides a framework and merely furthers elite sports where elite sports cannot obtain means on the open market.

158. In addition to the Cantons, the Federation subsidizes in particular the Youth & Sport programme.[113] The Youth & Sport programme mainly subsidizes grassroots sports. Only recently, the Youth & Sports programme also provides funding for high level sports. According to Article 4 paragraph 1 FAS the Federation supports financially the national umbrella sports federation, i.e., Swiss Olympic. Swiss Olympic is entrusted with the task to further high level sports by supporting professional athletes, the education of coaches and the hiring of trainers for elite sports.[114] Furthermore, the Federation helps in organizing big sports events[115] of worldwide or at least pan-European importance, mainly by granting deficit guarantees.[116] The Federation also furthers the construction of national sports fields.[117]

159. The Federation runs the Federal Sports School in Magglingen, and its affiliated Centro sportivo nazionale della gioventù in Tenero.[118] This sports school is a

111. SR 415.0 (hereinafter FAS).
112. SR 415.01 (hereinafter FOS).
113. Article 6 FAS.
114. Article 4 FAS and Art. 16 FAS.
115. For example, the Olympic Winter Games or the European Football Championship 2008 in Switzerland.
116. Article 17 FAS.
117. Article 5 FAS. For example, the football stadiums in Bern, Basel and Geneva, the bobsled track in St. Moritz, the ski jumping centre in Kandersteg, or the ice rink in St. Léonard Freiburg.
118. Articles 14 and 26 FAS.

training and course centre. It engages in basic and applied research in the fields of medicine, physiology, sports traumatology, sports sociology, sports psychology and sports education.[119]

160. It follows from the rather limited competence of the Federation, which more or less focuses on furthering sports, that Switzerland does not intend to limit national and international sports organizations in their freedom to regulate sports by internal rules.

§2. Regulation of Sports Organizations

I. Introduction

161. Most sports organizations in Switzerland are associations pursuant to Articles 60 et seq. Swiss Civil Code. They are autonomous legal entities. The form of association gives sports organizations a lot of freedom for their internal organization, and allows its members to further sports without any personal liability of the members.

162. It is only in exceptional circumstances that sports organizations require clubs to organize themselves as a joint-stock company (*Aktiengesellschaft*) or as a limited liability company (*GmbH*). Professional sports organizations tend to organize themselves as corporations, mainly companies limited by shares. All football clubs of the Super League are organized as companies limited by shares for professional football. In the Challenge League, thirteen football clubs are organized as companies limited by shares and three clubs as associations. The same is true for the clubs of the Swiss Ice Hockey league. They are generally organized as joint-stock companies which allow the investors to acquire shares, and to invest in the teams. However, all national and international sports organizations are organized as associations.

II. Autonomy of Associations

163. The autonomy of associations is an emanation of the human right to self-determination and is firmly anchored in Swiss law, giving the right to determine the articles of association as well as the right to self-manage.

164. Each association is free within the framework of Swiss law to legislate for itself and its members, to apply and to enforce such rules. There is also a constitutional right to found associations, to become a member, to be a member and to participate in its activities.

119. Article 14 FAS.

165. Sports organizations make use of their autonomy when establishing, applying and enforcing their articles and regulations, as well as to uniformly regulate their respective sport.

166. It follows from the autonomy of associations that an association is not allowed to completely submit itself to third-party decisions. According to the Swiss Federal Supreme Court, a provision in articles of association giving third parties a veto right concerning all decisions of the General Assembly is in breach of *bona mores* and ultimately not compliant with the principle of autonomy of associations, meaning that the respective provision in the articles of association was considered to be void.[120]

167. The principle of autonomy of associations is particularly limited when it comes to judicial review because each member of an association has a compulsory right to appeal against decisions of the association.[121] This appeal is a means to review all decisions of associations as to whether they comply with the law and the articles of association. Under Swiss law the courts are basically only allowed to annul the decision of the association. Afterwards, it is up to the association to decide again autonomously. However, the application of such principle is limited in sports cases. The rules of the Court of Arbitration for Sport (R57) enable the Court of Arbitration for Sport to decide *de novo*, i.e., issuing a completely new decision.

168. An important element of organizing an association is the legal prerequisite that the association has to pursue an ideal purpose, rather than an economic purpose.[122] However, it is possible to pursue non-economic purposes with economic means. Therefore the fact that some sport associations make billions in revenues is not relevant for the evaluation of the legitimacy of the association form from a legal point of view.

169. Economically, the ideal purpose basically contains a non-distribution constraint. This means that all the funds which an association generates need to be used to further sports (i.e., the ideal purpose of the sports association). In case, a sports association misuses its funds, for example, by paying unjustified bonuses to its functionaries such payments may be reclaimed due to the violation of the necessity to use all funds for the ideal purpose.

---

120. BGE 97 II 108 et seq. For this reason, the Court of Arbitration for Sport is basically not allowed to decide de novo on a decision of the association's General Assembly. The highest power within an association remains with its General Assembly. In such cases, the Court of Arbitration for Sport is only allowed to annul the decision.
121. Article 75 Swiss Civil Code.
122. Article 60 para. 1 Swiss Civil Code. Regarding problems of distinguishing between pursuance of non-economic and economic purposes *see* BGE 100 III 19 et seq., further in detail BERETTA, Wirtschaftliche Vereine, 3 et seq.; BERETTA, Wirtschaftliche Vereine und Corporate Governance, 1 et seq.

III. Articles of Association

170. Together with the statutory rules, the articles of association form the corporate constitution of the sports organization. They form a starting point for the regulations and the decisions of the bodies of the association. The articles of association are complemented by the association's internal continuing practice. The articles, regulations and decisions are binding due to the collective consent when the association is founded or a member is joining the association.

171. Views regarding the legal nature of articles of associations differ. Articles of association are neither an objective law nor a contract; they are a private law institution, a contractual regulation of the associations' legal affairs. According to a majority view, articles of association are contractual in nature.[123] The interpretation of articles of associations follows the principle of good faith.[124] However, the purpose of the association and the interests of the members are important when interpreting the articles of associations. The limitations to the legal content of articles of associations are identical to those of contracts. These limitations are statutory law, public policy, privacy laws and *bona mores*.[125]

172. Associations have to comply with the hierarchy of laws. In case of contradictory rules mandatory statutory law always prevails, followed by the articles of association and continuing practices (Article 36 paragraph 2 Swiss Civil Code), followed by non-mandatory statutory law (Article 63 paragraph 1 Swiss Civil Code). It is not clear whether autonomous rules of an association at a lower level, such as regulations which are set up by other bodies than the General Assembly, can prevail over non-mandatory statutory rules. This is in any case only possible if the articles of associations contain the foundation for such regulation.[126] Regulations and other rules of the association are therefore in principle at the bottom of the hierarchy.[127]

173. Articles of associations may have an effect outside the respective organization. Some sports organizations' articles of association explicitly refer to the articles of association of umbrella sports organizations or the umbrella sports organization obliges its members to comply with its own rules (so-called dynamic references). Articles of associations of umbrella organizations may have effect in the subordinated sports organization. However, in order for the rules of the umbrella organization to be binding, it is necessary that the articles of association of the subordinated organization refer to those rules.[128] The issue as to whether the articles of

123. BGE 140 V 81 with further reference.
124. BGE 126 III 380. Other authors propagate, for good reasons, the analogous application of the principle of the interpretation of law at least with regard to large associations; PORTMANN, N 73.
125. Cf. Art. 19 para. 2 Swiss Code of Obligations in connection with Art. 7 Swiss Civil Code; BGE 80 II 132; BGE 97 II 113.
126. Cf. for example, HEINI, PORTMANN & SEEMANN, Grundriss des Vereinsrechts, N 58; Basler Kommentar-RIEMER, Art. 63 N 52.
127. Cf. for example HEINI, PORTMANN & SEEMANN, Grundriss des Vereinsrechts, N 58.
128. Pachmann, Corporate Governance, 231; HEINI & SCHERRER, N 13 et seq. to Art. 64 Swiss Civil Code; dissenting opinion Basler Kommentar-RIEMER, N 508.

association in force at a specific date or the current articles of association are applicable (so-called dynamic reference), is decided by interpreting the reference in accordance with the principle of good faith.[129] Due to the enormous consequences dynamic references may have on the legal position of one party such dynamic references need to be accepted only very restrictively. Dynamic references in preambles of regulations, for example, need to be considered as non-binding as preambles are generally not binding.

IV. Rules of the Game and Rules of Law

174. In the past, some Swiss legal scholars were of the opinion that the rules of the game and the respective rights and duties are legally irrelevant. The distinction between the rules of the game and the rules of law goes back to an article by Max Kummer,[130] which was influential way beyond Switzerland and was adopted by the Swiss Federal Supreme Court.[131] According to this theory, sports organizations autonomously and finally decide about the rules concerning the game itself and their application; these rules of the game are not subject to judicial review. The only exception concerns rules that have an impact beyond the game as such and impact the privacy rights of sportspersons.

175. Scholars from newer schools of thought criticize that it is inherently difficult to distinguish between the rules of the game and the rules of law, because any breach of a rule of the game always may have an impact beyond the game. Furthermore, it is possible, they argue, to include rules of the game in the legal system assuming lawlessness would contravene the rule of law.[132]

176. Acknowledging lawlessness broadens the power of organizations. If the power of organizations is broadened, the balance of interest contained in non-mandatory law will be lost. The moral decisions of the Swiss legal system are negated. It follows that there should be no difference between the rules of the game and the rules of law as this contravenes the mandatory rule of Article 75 Swiss Civil Code.[133]

177. Also, according to the CAS jurisprudence, it is established that a referee or umpire does not enjoy free discretion in his or her control of the game; he or she must comply with the rules of the game. A deviation by a referee or an umpire from

129. PACHMANN, Corporate Governance, 231 et seq.
130. KUMMER, Spielregel und Rechtsregel, Bern 1973.
131. BGE 103 IA 412A, according to which the decisions of association bodies on the entitlement of athletes to play are acts that cannot be reviewed under civil law; for the newer developments have a look at the *Sion* case under N 302 et seq., where the courts directly intervened into the game.
132. JAQUIER, La qualification juridique des règles autonomes des organisations sportives, N 314 et seq.; PORTMANN, Das Schweizerische Vereinsrecht, N 291 et seq.; PACHMANN, Corporate Governance und Sportverbände, 233 et seq.
133. In this sense, and also for the reviewing of game decisions HEINI, PORTMANN & SEEMANN, Grundriss des Vereinsrechts, Zurich 2009, N 246.

a mandatory rule of the game undermines the utility of the rule and, moreover, may affect the outcome of the game or the tournament.[134] Every rule and its application are, therefore, in principle subject to legal review. CAS however limits the legal review only to cases of fraud and severe violations of personality rights.

178. The possibility of judicial review depends on the extent to which the sports organization has used its autonomy and the extent to which it grants the rights of appeal. It also depends on the rights granted in the articles of association and the statutory rights of the people who are affected by rules of the game. However, the rules of the game and their application can never exceed the given frame of the mandatory law.

179. It follows that the umpire may have vast discretion due to the game having to continue. If the umpire violates the discretion, this results in a decision that is subject to judicial review. The decision as well as the proceedings leading to the decision can be reviewed.[135] Before the decision can be appealed against in courts outside the organization, it is necessary to exhaust the possibilities within the organization.

180. A decision may also be subject to judicial review if it lies within the discretion given to the umpire, and the umpire exceeded its discretion or did not apply the discretion given to him. Rules of the game and their application may potentially infringe the privacy rights of the respective person. In this case, it has to be decided whether the infringement can be justified.

V. Relations Between Organizational Rules and State Law

181. Sports organizations often impose a duty on their members to comply with their rules, which sometimes may be sanctioned. Contracts between members (such as transfer contracts) or between athletes and the sports federations (such as entry forms) refer to these rules and declare them to be applicable. Swiss law, therefore, has to decide whether in international constellations such references to rules of a private institution are legal in accordance with Article 116 paragraph 1 and Article 187 PILA ('the contract is governed by the law chosen by the parties').

182. According to the Swiss Federal Supreme Court, rules of private organizations do not have the same quality as rules of state law. The rules of private associations are in general subordinated to state law and therefore just applicable as far as state law leaves space for an autonomous regulation. They are not 'law' pursuant

134. CAS 2001/A/354, C. 1, 17.

135. If umpires are bribed, their independence is no longer given and the outcome of the game is predetermined. The decision can be challenged. However, the further course of a multistage competition often prevents a replay. Compensation or a subsequent cancellation of the result are the only solutions.

to Article 116 paragraph 1 and Article 187 PILA and cannot be recognized as 'lex sportiva transnationalis', as some authors argue.[136]

183. It is however recognized that contractual parties may include the rules of sports organizations in their contracts, usually in combination with contractual rules they have created themselves, thus agreeing to include such rules as contractual provisions. This is possible.

184. However, the rules of an organization are lower in the hierarchy of laws than state statutes. Before a state court a reference to rules of an organization is only relevant, provided state law allows an autonomous rule and does not provide for mandatory legal rules.[137] As mentioned above, an agreement deviating from the non-mandatory law requires at least a foundation in the articles of association.[138]

185. The situation is different in the area of international arbitration. There it is possible to refer to non-state rules (Article 187 PILA). This is very important given that many international sports organizations and their members have subjected themselves to international arbitration, in particular CAS.[139] Through the CAS Code which is applied in sports arbitrations the rules of the sports organizations are applied which factually excludes the application of state law.

186. The relation between applicable rules of organizations and Swiss law pursuant to R45 and R58 CAS Code is not entirely clear and CAS Panels do often not apply Swiss law when applying the federations' rules and regulations. However, in order to avoid lawlessness, CAS would have to apply mandatory Swiss law when applying the rules of an organization (as these rules are set up within the limits of Swiss law). Furthermore, non-mandatory Swiss statutory law needs to be applied on the lower rules and regulations of an association. This principle obviously needs to be applied as the federation's rules are set up within the limits of the associations' autonomy given by the Swiss law. Such autonomy is always limited by the mandatory Swiss law and for regulations on a lower level by the non-mandatory Swiss law. Swiss law sets, hence, the frame within which the CAS may apply the federations' rules.

---

136. Cf. BGE 132 III 285, according to which the rules of international sports associations are only applicable as an agreement between two private parties, which is subordinated to state law.
137. BGE 132 III 285 et seq. *In casu* there was a provision in a player-transfer agreement, according to which the transfer agreement should be subordinated to the FIFA rules and the laws of Switzerland.

138. Heini, Portmann & Seemann, Grundriss des Vereinsrechts, Zurich 2009, N 58.
139. *Jenny, Verbandsregularien v. staatliches Recht*, 492–494.

VI. Limits of Autonomy of Organizations

187. Despite the law on associations being mostly not compulsory, there are a few mandatory rules, which have an impact on the autonomy of sports organizations.[140] These include a duty to treat all members equally, except if there are factual reasons to treat them differently.[141]

188. Many important limits to the autonomy of organizations are based on unwritten laws.[142] Members of an association have a fiduciary duty. Before internal disciplinary measures can be taken, the members have to be granted the right to be heard. The principles of equal treatment, legality and proportionality all follow from the principle that rights must not be abused:[143]

- According to the principle of equality, a sports organization has to treat its members equally, both in an absolute and in a relative sense when issuing rules and using discretion.
- According to the principle of legality, all duties, which sports organizations impose on their members, must be based on a provision in the articles of association. According to the articles of association, the person imposing such duties must at least be competent to define members' duties within a given framework.
- The principle of proportionality is one of the most important principles of the Swiss company law. Sports organizations have to act in a way which least infringes the rights of their members. Any infringement has to be appropriate and necessary and the reason and the result have to be balanced.

189. Further compulsory rules follow from private law in general,[144] public policy and *bona mores*.[145] Sports organizations may in particular be restricted to act with regard to sportspersons by Article 21 Swiss Code of Obligations exploitation.[146] Any excessive binding of the sportsperson by the sports organization is a violation of Article 27 Swiss Civil Code.[147]

190. Amongst the most important limits are privacy rights and competition law, which will be discussed in detail below.

---

140. Article 63 para. 2 Swiss Civil Code.
141. Article 67 para. 1 Swiss Civil Code.
142. Basler Kommentar-Riemer, N 39 et seq., and N 41 to Art. 63 Swiss Civil Code, N 42 and N 52 to Art. 72 Swiss Civil Code.
143. Fuchs, Rechtsfragen Der Vereinsstrafe, 110 et seq.
144. Cf. thereto *inter alia* BGE 132 III 285, in which the shortening of the enforceability in accordance with the relevant FIFA Regulations was considered to be a breach of the mandatory limitation period of (elected) Swiss substantive law (*see* Art. 127 and Art. 129 Swiss Code of Obligations). Consequently, the relevant provision was not applicable in the case at hand.
145. Article 19 para. 2 Swiss Code of Obligations.
146. The sports organization shall only require services of an athlete that are in proportion to the contribution. Thus, when concluding an athlete's agreement this balance must be assured, provided there is an obligation to contract.
147. Decision of the Federal Supreme Court 4A_558/2011 dated 27 Mar. 2012 (Matuzalem case).

VII. Judicial Review: Appeal, Nullity of Decisions and Provisional Measures

A. Judicial Review

191. The most important corporate remedy to safeguard the rights of members is the right to appeal pursuant to Article 75 Swiss Civil Code. Not only can members fight against breaches of law, but this right also guarantees that corporate life in general complies with the law and that the association is managed in accordance with statutory law and the articles of association.[148]

192. According to Article 75 of the Swiss Civil Code, decisions[149] that breach statutory law[150] or the articles of association can be challenged before a court by each member who has not given his or her consent within one month from when the member has become aware of the decision. However, CAS has reduced this mandatory statutory time limit to file the Appeal Statement to twenty-one days (R49 CAS Code); it foresees, however, an extendable deadline to give the reasoning in the appeal brief. The appeal can refer to any breach of statutory law or the articles of association that in fact have an impact on the decision. This includes all explicit and implied rules of law, as well as all internal rules, including rules of the association and rules of the game.[151] This includes in particular decisions referring to the right of the members or the privacy rights under Articles 27 and 28 Swiss Civil Code.[152] However, mere declarations by a director or an employee of the organization cannot be the subject of an appeal. It needs to be a declaration which is interpreted as the final decision of the organization.

193. Contrary to the wording of Article 75 Swiss Civil Code, not only direct members of an association but also indirect members, i.e., the sportsmen that are members of a club which is a member of a sports federation, have a right to appeal. The reason given for this by the courts is the special relationship between indirect members and the organization[153] on which they depend.

194. If an appeal is granted, the court will cancel the decision without replacing it.[154] The association is bound by the judgment; however, it can still exercise its autonomy within the limits of the decision. However, CAS proceedings include the

148. BGE 108 II 18.
149. Although the law only mentions the resolutions of the general meeting of an association, other resolutions by organs of an association may also be challenged through the courts if they cannot be challenged within the association and if they concern the rights of members of an association; BGE 108 II 18 et seq.; BGE 118 II 17 et seq.
150. Cf. hereto *inter alia* decision of the District Court of VIII Bern-Laupen of 13 Jun. 2008. *In casu* the court held that the 'foreigner provision' (restriction on the number of foreign players allowed to participate in the competition) of Swiss Athletics contravenes the Agreement with the EU on the Free Movement of Persons.
151. PORTMANN, Schweizer Vereinsrecht, N 279.
152. BGE 120 II 369 et seq. Cf. SCHERRER, Aktuelle Rechtsfragen bei Sportvereinen, 46 et seq.
153. BGE 119 II 271 et seq.
154. In principle, the judge has no authority to intervene in the order of jurisdiction of the association. Dissenting opinion HANDSCHIN & TRUNIGER, 142 et seq.

so-called de novo rule. Under R56 CAS Code CAS may replace the decision. This infringes the right to autonomy of the organization. Due to the limited grounds for appeals to the Swiss Federal Supreme Court this violation could so far not be challenged.

B. Nullity of Decisions

195. A decision by an association that is formally or with regard to its content, gravely tainted, is void. This is the case if the decision breaches the mandatory rules of law, public policy, *bona mores* or the privacy rights or if it is 'impossible'. In these cases, the claimant may at any time request that the court declare the decision void. However, the decision is only partially void insofar as the violated rule requires it to be void. There is no time limitation for this claim, but the claimant has to prove a sufficient interest.

196. The directors of the association are liable contractually and non-contractually for any direct loss they cause by an international negligent act. According to Article 55 paragraphs 2 and 3 of the Swiss Civil Code, a claim may be directed against either the director or the association.

C. Provisional Measures

197. Provisional measures are very important in sports law. A recent decision[155] has clarified some open issues. According to the court, the state courts are mandatorily competent to issue provisional measures even if there is a clause for arbitration. This is necessary due to the fact that the state has the monopoly of power. Therefore, provisional measures are the only way to break out of the appeal system which was built by the sports federations. This legal situation has not changed with the new Swiss Civil Procedure Code (CPC) (*see* Article 374), even though it is basically possible that provisional measures are also granted by the arbitral tribunals (as long as the requirements of Article 6 European Convention on Human Rights (ECHR) are fulfilled). At least the state courts are parallelly in charge. Turning to state courts for provisional measures is, hence, still possible under the newly introduced CAS Code according to which the parties waive their right to seek legal recourse from the state courts (R37).[156] Furthermore, it was confirmed that all internal rights of appeal have to be exhausted first (this is also the case for claims under

155. Decision of the District Court of the Canton of Lucerne of 25 Jan. 2010.
156. Order of the District Court Lausanne dated 29 Jan. 2014 which was later even confirmed by the Cantonal Court of the Canton of Vaud on 24 Jul. 2014.

Article 75 Swiss Civil Code), except if the provisional measures shall protect privacy rights. Such claims may be brought before a state court as soon as privacy rights have been infringed or even if such infringements are merely imminent.[157]

§3. Sport and Tort Law

I. Introduction

198. Liability in tort in sports is characterized by the interplay between rules of sports and state law. State law provides the grounds for civil and criminal law liability.

199. Criminal law focuses on punishing the sportsperson, whereas private law liability focuses on making the sportsperson pay damages. Disciplinary liability of sportspersons within a sports organization takes an intermediate role, primarily using bans and fines.

200. The sports rules of the respective organizations defining the permitted and non-permitted behaviour, ultimately enacted to avoid major injuries of all participants, are paramount when judging the behaviour of sportspersons, both for criminal and private law purposes. In Switzerland, no specific rules exist defining the behaviour and liability of sportspersons when exercising professional sports. This shows that the state assumes that regulating the basic behaviour of sportspersons is for the respective sports organizations.

201. The Swiss Federal Supreme Court therefore applies the respective rules when defining the tolerated behaviour when exercising a sport, such as skiing[158] or ice hockey.[159] If the sports organizations have not enacted any written rules regarding accepted behaviour, the court applies those general security requirements, which are generally recognized for the respective sport.[160] If there are no such rules, the behaviour of the sportsperson will be judged against a security rule defined by the court, taking into account the behaviour of a reasonable person.[161] International sports organizations enact rules of the game regulating participants' behaviour during a competition, which are recognized rules of behaviour for the respective sport. Such rules may also have an impact on people who exercise the sport outside the

157. *In casu*, a basketball player was prohibited from wearing a headscarf during the official games. The player then announced she would file an action for personal injury against her basketball organization, but requested preliminary measures in order to continue to take part in the official games. The court affirmed its competence in this case (despite the existence of an arbitration agreement), but it dismissed the request for preliminary measures, since the interests of the sports organization to conduct the official games according to the international rules takes precedence and the player also accepted the corresponding rules of the organization; decision of the District Court of the Canton of Lucerne of 25 Jan. 2010.
158. BGE 122 IV 20 C. 2b aa; BGE 106 IV 352 C. 3a.
159. BGE 121 IV 254 C. 3a bb.
160. BGE 122 IV 20 C. 2b aa; BGE 122 IV 147 C. 3b aa; BGE 121 IV 211 C. 2a.
161. BGE 122 IV 21 C. 2b bb.

framework of an association or sports organization. For example, FIS rules apply to all people who exercise the sport of skiing.[162] However, these rules are very general. All these rules not only regulate the sport/game, but they also aim at protecting the physical integrity of sportspersons as far as possible within a certain sport.

202. There are neither special rules regarding liability in certain risky sporting trends nor special rules regarding the behaviour of sportspersons during competitions. However, due to a severe canyoning accident Switzerland enacted a law regarding the regulation of companies offering risky sports such as bungee jumping, canyoning, river rafting, mountain guiding, and snow sports outside the slopes.[163] Such companies need to show their expertise and need a special licence.

203. The rules of sports are in particular relevant when judging the degree of fault and the degree of accepted risk.

II. Private Liability for Sports Accidents

204. According to a majority view, sports accidents fall within Article 41 Swiss Code of Obligations. The prerequisites for liability are therefore an intentional or a negligent act, which causes a certain loss that is unlawful. A loss will be unlawful if the physical integrity of the claimant is infringed. In case of mere financial loss there will only be damages awarded if a rule has been breached which provides for damages. The degree of fault will be judged against the applicable sports rules.

205. The starting point for deciding whether an unlawful act has been committed is the imminent danger and risk potential of the respective sport. A sportsperson exercising a sport assumes such risks and gives his or her consent to the dangers and risks. According to the principle of individual responsibility, the sportsperson is primarily responsible for accidents and harm done. There will only ever be a sanction if the loss was caused by behaviour that is not acceptable in the respective sport. Sports rules are rules for general behaviour.

206. When determining whether the breach of a sports rule leads to liability, the purpose of the sports rule has to be taken into account. The purpose of the sports rule implies the relevant criteria. As a principle, rules regarding the organization of the sport event are irrelevant. Rules regarding equal opportunities may be relevant when judging financial loss. The most important rules for tort are those that aim at protecting the health of sportspersons and avoiding accidents.[164] Furthermore, the

162. BGE 122 IV 21 C. 2b bb.
163. Act for Mountain Guides and the Offering other Risky Activities; SR 935.91.
164. For example: FIS-Code of Conduct for Skiers and Snowboarders.

dictate of fair play implies guidelines for acceptable behaviour within a certain sport.[165] Individual agreements between sportspersons prevail over official sports rules.

III. Criminal Liability for Sports Accidents

A. *Introduction*

207. A sportsperson injuring another sportsperson during a competition may not only be liable under private law, but also under criminal law. Despite such injuries being relatively frequent, criminal proceedings are an exception. This may be because sportspersons are reluctant to file a complaint against their colleagues. Many sports organizations are keen to establish breaches of sports rules themselves and to apply sanctions in order to avoid state courts being involved. State courts often only get involved if the injured person hopes to obtain considerable damages, which may be easier to get if a criminal court has established the defendant's negligence.[166]

208. In order to establish whether a sportsperson is liable, the criminal laws must be applied. There are no specific sports criminal law rules, except the disciplinary rules of the sports organizations for example regarding doping. This means that the behaviour of the sportsperson will be judged against normal criminal law rules. It follows that the behaviour must fulfil the *actus reus*, must be against the law and must have been committed with *mens rea*. The main criminal offences are assault and manslaughter. An important issue is whether the behaviour can be justified, for example, because the injured sportsperson has given his or her consent by accepting certain risk when taking part in a sports competition. However, such consent may only be construed insofar the sportsperson did not blatantly violate the rules of the game. The Swiss Federal Supreme Court has dealt with this question in a number of cases concerning ice hockey and skiing.

B. *Sportspersons Being Subject to Criminal Law*

209. During the ice hockey match between HC Davos and ZSC Lions, Kevin Miller fouled Andrew McKim so badly that the latter had to end his professional career. According to the Swiss Federal Supreme Court, Kevin Miller's behaviour amounted to intentional assault as well as reckless grievous bodily harm under Articles 123 and 125 Swiss Penal Code.[167] The Swiss Federal Supreme Court thus

165. Fair play is the highest, generally unwritten, rule in all sports and can be described as a duty to perform sports in good faith. It serves as a means of concretizing and interpreting what is proper sporting behaviour. Cf. in detail THALER, Sportregeln und zivilrechtliche Haftung' 142 et seq.
166. Cf. SCHERRER, Strafrechtliche Sanktionen nach Sportverletzungen, 31 et seq.
167. BGE 134 IV 26 et seq. The problem of (too) serious fouls in football in Switzerland is known from the case Chapuisat/Favre. The defender Chapuisat was convicted of negligent grievous bodily harm

confirmed the earlier judgment Antisin/Malkow where Mike Antisin was found guilty of reckless bodily harm.[168] The Swiss Federal Supreme Court accepts that a sportsperson may give their consent to an injury as long as the sportsperson injuring another sportsperson could not have avoided breaching the sports rules aimed at avoiding accidents.[169]

210. When assessing foul play in team sports for criminal law purposes, the Swiss Federal Supreme Court also looks at the rules of the game. The more blatantly the rules of the game aimed at protecting the physical integrity of the players are breached, the more it is justified to instigate criminal proceedings against the player. A sportsperson intending a common assault, or acknowledging that such may happen, as well as causing grievous bodily harm, commits both crimes of intentional simple assault and reckless grievous bodily harm.

211. In a recent case, the Federal Supreme Court upheld a decision of the Cantonal Court St. Gallen, in which a goalkeeper was found not guilty of assault through negligence by injuring the knee of an opponent during a defensive action (fracture in the area of the tibial plateau).[170] In first instance, the district court had found the goalkeeper guilty.

212. In its decision, the Federal Supreme Court stated that in determining the permissible conduct and the duties of care to be respected in the game of football, in addition to the general principle of 'neminem laedere',[171] the laws of the game laid down by the International Football Association Board (IFAB) must be observed in particular.[172] The Federal Supreme Court added that the 'normal' fouls that inevitably occur in team sports competitions involving physical contact are part of the basic risk of playing football. Merely misconduct that can be judged as gross justifies judging that the limits of the player's tacit consent to the risk of injury to have been exceeded and imposing a criminal sanction.[173] The Federal Supreme Court concluded that the actions of the goalkeeper do not constitute a violation of the rules that would justify a criminal sanction.

213. From a legal as well as from a sporting point of view, it is preferable that courts deal with assault cases in sporting contexts in a restrained manner. Injuries unfortunately are part of the game in many sports. It would have a negative impact on sports if filing complaints against opponents became the rule. Yet, this does not mean that gross fouls excessively exceeding the limits of the game shall not be criminally punished.

---

after he had stopped the striker Favre by stretching out his leg and Favre suffered a serious knee injury as a result; decision of the Geneva Police Tribunal of 11 Jun. 1987.

168. BGE 121 IV 249 et seq.
169. BGE 121 IV 247 C. 4.
170. Decision of the Federal Supreme Court 6B_1060/2019 dated 15 Jan. 2020.
171. Principle of not causing harm to others.
172. Decision of the Federal Supreme Court 6B_1060/2019 dated 15 Jan. 2020, para. 3.2.2.
173. Decision of the Federal Supreme Court 6B_1060/2019 dated 15 Jan. 2020, para. 3.2.2, with reference to BGE 134 IV 26 E. 3.2.5.

214. In a different case, the Swiss Federal Supreme Court applied the FIS rules when assessing the duty of care with which a skier has to comply when entering the waiting area in front of the skiing station. A skier who did not adjust his speed to these circumstances and who passed too close to a group of standing people, injuring one person, was in breach of the rules of the game and was found guilty of a criminal offence.[174]

C. *Justifications*

215. From a theoretical point of view, it is not quite clear how criminal offences in sports may be justified. Some scholars assume that the injured person has given his or her consent, others assume that the *actus reus* is missing because the behaviour is socially adequate or because an allowed risk is being taken or because everybody is responsible for their own behaviour.

216. The Swiss Federal Supreme Court puts special emphasis on the aspect of self-endangering. A sportsperson does not give his or her consent to a potential injury inflicted by another sportsperson, but only to the risk which is inherent in the behaviour conforming with the rules.[175] The consent of the injured person can therefore not be assumed as justification. Consent justifying the injury is only possible in sports disciplines in which even behaviour conforming with the rules of the game will have an impact on the physical integrity of the participants.[176] However, it is not clear how far such consent may go. Is it right that the rules of a sport allow that participants may regularly suffer grave injuries or death when everybody complies with the rules?

IV. Liability of the Organizers of Sports Events

217. Organizers of sport may become liable in private law and criminal law if they make mistakes. In private law, organizers may become liable in contract or tort.

218. In the context of sports events, most contractual breaches concern breaches of custodial duties and duties of care. The organizer has to take adequate protective measures, which are reasonable for the type of event. However, the participant has to bear the residual risks.[177]

219. The organizer is liable in tort pursuant to Article 41 Swiss Code of Obligations. The precautions, which the organizer has to take often, result from the principle that somebody creating a dangerous situation has to bear the resulting risks

174. BGE 106 IV 350 et seq.
175. For example, football, handball, etc.
176. For example, boxing.
177. ARTER & SCHWEIZER, Verantwortlichkeit des Veranstalters von Sportanlässen, 31.

and take adequate measures.[178] Furthermore, the organizer may become liable pursuant to Article 58 Swiss Code of Obligations if any buildings are structurally or technically not fit for use.

220. Apart from the liability of the organizer foreseen in the Swiss law the sports organizations have set up a liability of the organizer to have the sporting event held without any interference. Football clubs are, for example, held responsible for the behaviour of their fans. Interestingly, such liability does usually not depend on any negligence or fault.

V. Lost Profit of Competitors Due to a Breach of Rules

221. In order to win a competition sportspersons have to go to the limits of what is permitted under the rules. Aiming at perfection is part of sports. If a sportsperson infringes the rules, thus winning against a competitor, the issue arises whether the competitor can claim compensation. Using illegal performance-enhancing substances by one sportsperson may lead to the loss of prize money and future marketing revenues by another sportsperson.

222. As far as we are aware, there is no case law in Switzerland regarding this subject. Liability may however be constructed pursuant to Article 41 Swiss Code of Obligations, a special liability based on trust between sportspersons, privacy laws or anti-competition laws.[179]

223. Under Article 41 Swiss Code of Obligations, the infringed sports rules would have to be aimed at financial compensation. The special relationship required for liability based on trust can be seen in the fact that both sportspersons subject themselves to the same values. Between professional sportspersons, sports competition may be seen as economic competition, which has to be undertaken without engaging in unfair, illegal or misleading practices.

VI. Sports Organizations' Liability for Licensing Procedures

224. Many legal disputes in sport concern licences. Apart from the sports organization as licensor and the competitors, licensing decisions frequently have an impact on third parties (e.g., competitors, sponsors, owners of media rights, organizers and others). Direct and indirect financial losses often occur. Given the number of people involved, a mistake in granting licences may lead to a number of potential claimants.

225. In 2003, Football Club (FC) Sion, which had applied for a licence to compete in the SFL, was not granted such licence. This led to a legal dispute in front of

178. To the duty to secure roads around a ski piste cf. BGE 117 IV 415 et seq.; BGE 115 IV 189 et seq.
179. THALER, Sportregeln und zivilrechtliche Haftung, 156 et seq.

state courts. According to the Cantonal Court of the Canton of Valais, the SFL had breached a number of duties, including breach of the right to be heard and acting outside the scope of discretion. FC Sion only joined the league a month after the beginning of the season when the court granted a provisional measure against the SFL.[180]

226. The President of FC Sion filed a number of claims against SFL. Among other things he claimed that one of the players had a contract with a fixed transfer sum of EUR 1 million, however, since FC Sion was not granted a licence the player was transferred to the German Bundesliga without obtaining a transfer sum. He further alleged that the spaces for publicity in the stadium could only be sold for six instead of twelve months and that there were lost profits from sponsoring.[181]

§4. Sports and Hooligans

I. Introduction

227. Hooligans and hooliganism[182] are recognized phenomena in modern sports, which have become acute in Switzerland since the turn of the millennium. In recent times, hooliganism no longer only concerns the top leagues, or just football and ice hockey. Foreign hooligans appear more and more at Swiss sports events and Swiss hooligans often act as vandals abroad.

228. Typical hooligan behaviour is caught by the Swiss criminal law, including crimes against physical integrity (Articles 111 et seq. Swiss Penal Code), against property (Articles 137 et seq. Swiss Penal Code), liberty (Articles 180 et seq. Swiss Penal Code), *ordre public* (Articles 258 et seq. Swiss Penal Code) and public authority (Articles 285 et seq. Swiss Penal Code) as well as racial discrimination (Articles 261*bis* Swiss Penal Code).[183] There is no single crime of hooliganism in Switzerland.

229. However, Swiss criminal law alone is not adequate. Switzerland has therefore introduced a number of additional statutory measures in order to give state

180. Decision of the Cantonal Court of the Canton of Vaud of 20 Oct. 2003.
181. Cf. Heermann, Haftungsrisiken des Sportverbandes bei Lizenzierungsverfahren im Ligasport, 184 et seq.
182. The term 'hooliganism' is documented only since the beginning of the twentieth century and the origin of the word 'hooligan' remains unknown. The initial term for a 'violent criminal' was transformed over time to a term for violent, rude people and was getting progressively closer to the term 'rowdy'. Today, the term 'hooliganism' stands, in general, for violence at sporting events; Thaler, Hooliganismus und Sport, 245 et seq.
183. Cf. also the elements of crime listed in Art. 2 para. 2 of the Concordat on Measures against Violence at Sporting Events.

security organizations and organizers adequate measures against the increasing number of incidents, and provide increased readiness to the violent and increasing internationalism of hooliganism.[184]

II. Anti-hooligan Legislation

A. *Federal Act on Measures to Ensure National Security (FENS)*

230. On 24 March 2006,[185] the parliament updated the FENS[186] and gave authorities new measures against violence at sports events.[187] The provisions of the new law section 5a, include measures to repress hooligans such as bans from certain areas (Article 24b FENS), limitations on travelling out of Switzerland (Article 24c FENS), duties to report (Article 24d FENS) as well as the possibility to take people into preventive custody for a maximum of twenty-four hours (Article 24e FENS). Furthermore, Article 24a FENS created an electronic information system containing data regarding people who committed violence at sports events in Switzerland and abroad.

231. However, even while the act was still in parliament, three of the five new measures (bans from certain areas, duty to report and custody) caused great controversy because they may not comply with the Swiss Constitution. The issue is whether hooliganism is a danger for the security of Switzerland in general. If not, it would be for the Cantons to legislate in this area.[188] Parliament therefore limited these three measures until the end of 2009. At the same time, it instructed the Federal Government to ensure that these measures could continue thereafter without interruption.[189] For this reason, in 2012 the FENS was slightly amended in the light of the Swiss Constitution, and allowed the Federal Government to continue with the legal measures.

B. *Inter-cantonal Treaty Regarding Measures Against Violence During Sports Events*

232. On 15 November 2007, the Conference of Cantonal Ministers of Justice and Police Directors (CCMJPD) signed an inter-cantonal treaty regarding measures against violence during sports events, in order to ensure the continuation of the three limited measures provided for in the FENS. The treaty entered into force on 1 January 2010. All Cantons have since joined the treaty.

184. Cf. overview in the Federal Council Dispatch regarding the constitutional provision about the combat against violence at sporting events (hooliganism) and regarding amendment of the Federal Act on Measures to Ensure National Security (FENS) of 29 Aug. 2007, FG Nr. 39, 2007.
185. OC 2006, 3703.
186. Federal Act of 21 Mar. 1997 on Measures to Ensure National Security (FENS), SC 120.
187. In this context, the media and the vernacular speak about the 'Hooligan-Act'.
188. Scherrer et al., Sportrecht, 146.
189. Federal Council Dispatch, FG Nr. 39, 2007, 6466.

233. The treaty also contains further measures that had been controversial. According to Article 10 of the treaty, the police may recommend to sports organizations and owners of stadiums whom to exclude from the stadium. This measure is mainly aimed at people who committed violence outside a stadium in connection with a sports event. Such information shall be shared through the hooligan database created in accordance with Article 24a FENS. Furthermore, according to Article 2 paragraph 2 of the treaty, transporting pyrotechnic items when travelling to or from a sports event qualifies as behaviour showing readiness for violence.

C. Hooligan Database 'HOOGAN'

234. Article 24a FENS provides the legal grounds for creating an information-sharing system regarding personal data of people committing violence at sports events in Switzerland and abroad. The information-sharing system 'HOOGAN' is run by the Federal Police Department (fedpol). 'HOOGAN' may be accessed by fedpol departments in charge of applying FENS, cantonal police authorities, the Swiss Central Authority for Hooliganism, as well as, customs officials.

235. In addition to the FENS, there is also a Regulation regarding Police Measures and Information Systems of the Federal Authority for Policing of 4 December 2009.[190] Furthermore, the Federal Department for Justice and Policing has issued a regulation regarding the information system HOOGAN,[191] as well as, guidelines for using and processing of HOOGAN data by organizers of sports events and their security officers.[192]

236. Personal data may be included in the electronic information system if either: (a) such measure is ordered by a court or has been confirmed, (b) such measure was ordered due to a criminal offence for which charges have been filed with the competent authority, or (c) such measure is necessary for maintaining security for people or sports events and this can be made credible.[193]

III. Criticism of the Legislation

237. The inter-cantonal treaty and FENS were at the beginning quite controversial. It was not clear whether the information system 'HOOGAN' complies with

190. SC 120.52.
191. Accessible under: http://www.ejpd.admin.ch/content/dam/data/pressemitteilung/2006/pm_2006_12_29/. bearbeitungsreglementhoogand.pdf.
192. Accessible under: http://www.ejpd.admin.ch/content/dam/data/sicherheit/hooliganismus/richtlinie-d.pdf.
193. Cf. Art. 24a para. 2 FENS.

data protection standards.[194] The main issues raised were that there was no distinction between violent hooligans and those who pose no danger, or between organized and incidental violence. Furthermore, the criteria for data to be included in the information system were controversial as well as the rights to access, maintain, control, correct and use the data.[195]

238. It was for these reasons that a number of appeals had been filed[196] with the Swiss Federal Supreme Court against several Cantons joining the treaty and a number of referenda have been taken. These appeals mainly concerned breaches of human rights and breaches of the principle of proportionality. However, the issue of whether the Federation may introduce such measures is also raised in the appeals. After the FENS had been reviewed in 2012 pursuant to different legal opinions the public criticism ended.

194. SCHERRER ET AL., Sportrecht, 146.
195. THALER, Hooliganismus und Sport, 298.
196. Lucerne, Zurich, Canton of Basel-Land, Canton of Basel-Stadt and Ticino.

Part II. Employment and Sport

Chapter 1. Athletes' Position

§1. Overview

239. Sportspersons are without any doubt the most important subjects of sports law. As a general rule, they are part of the sports network through their membership in a club, which in turn is a member of a sports organization.

240. Even without such links, there may be a contractual or a quasi-contractual relationship between the sportsperson and the club or the organization. Sportspersons have to take out licences or enter into contracts (so-called entry forms) to participate. Professional sportspersons in team sports usually enter into regular employment contracts with their clubs.

241. Depending on how a sport is organized, there may be a corporate and/or contractual relationship between sportspersons and the sports organization. The corporate relationship may exist either due to direct membership in a sports organization or through membership in a club, which in turn is a member of a sports organization (so-called indirect membership).

§2. Contracts with Athletes

242. Sports organizations often enter into contracts with athletes to submit them to their rules and to tie them to the organization. In general, such contracts take one of the following three forms:[197]

- 'Individual contracts' are negotiated with a specific star athlete.
- 'Athletes' contracts' are standard-form contracts allowing for a contractual relationship between squad athletes and the sports organization.
- 'Athletes' declarations' (also licences or entry forms) consist of the sportsperson's consent to the admission to competitions of the sports organization.

243. Such contracts may deal with aspects such as image rights, submission to a doping regime, a certain arbitration clause or the limitation of liability by the

197. Thaler, in *Sport und Recht*, ed. Arter & Baddeley Bern 2007, 21.

sports organization. In addition, the parties often enter into a contract according to which the athletes submit to certain rules. The sportspersons undertake to recognize the articles of association of the sports organization, thus ensuring that the sport is uniformly exercised and the chances of all participants are equal.

§3. Legal Qualification of Athletes' Contracts and Athletes' Declarations

244. So-called dynamic references, that is, references in contracts with athletes referring to other rules of organizations in their current form frequently pose issues. Such dynamic references are basically possible as long as the athlete has easy access to the rules and as long as these rules do not contain anything unusual.[198] Whether 'easy access' just means that the rules need to be available or whether this also means that the rules need to be written in a language the athlete speaks has not been decided yet. In our opinion the 'easy access' must be understood in a broad sense to give the athletes the possibility to actually be able to understand to what they submitted themselves.

245. National squad athletes are often bound to athletes' agreements and are obliged to take part in squad meetings and training camps and to compete in competitions. The sports organization obtains the rights to the image and the name of the athlete. Athletes also waive certain sponsorship rights. The sports organization in turn undertakes the responsibility to further the athletes' development by providing infrastructure for training and national coaches, scientific coaching and help to plan the athletes' career. The agreement may also provide for financial compensation.

246. Athletes' agreements are not explicitly regulated in the Swiss Code of Obligations. It follows that those statutory rules apply which are closest to the various contractual aspects.

247. A characteristic of athletes' agreements is the fact that athletes are compelled to sign such agreements due to the monopoly of sports organizations. Athletes' agreements often have to be signed as a whole, which has to be taken into account when interpreting such contracts, meaning that unclear issues are interpreted against the federation and unusual issues do not have any legal effect.

248. There is often a conflict of interest between the sports organization and the athlete. The sports organization's autonomy (Articles 60 et seq. Swiss Civil Code/ Article 23 Swiss Constitution) and the athlete's personality rights (Article 28 Swiss Civil Code) and the right to choose a profession (Article 27 Swiss Constitution) have to be weighed against each other. In view of the monopoly of the sports organization, cartel laws must be complied with, meaning that the rights and duties

198. According to the Swiss Federal Supreme Court, dynamic references are also applicable to arbitration clauses; decision of the Swiss Federal Supreme Court 4A_460/2008 of 9 Jan. 2009.

always have to be reasonable and balanced. However, if the athlete has a real choice whether to sign, the athletes' agreement, and the athlete is able to negotiate the athletes' agreement the contractual rules have to be strictly complied with.

Chapter 2. Labour Law

§1. Legal Basis

249. In comparison to other European legal regimes, Swiss employment law is very liberal. Establishing and terminating an employment relationship is relatively easy.

250. Swiss law contains no specific rules for employment contracts with sportspersons. The legal relationship is defined by the employment contract between the sportsperson, the club/sports organization, the general statutory rules of Articles 319 et seq. Swiss Code of Obligations, and the Labour Law Statute. The legal relationship is further defined by the regulations of the club, provided they do not contravene compulsory statutory law.

251. The protection provisions of the Swiss Labour Law Statute also apply to sportspersons who are employees, although the general submission of employment contracts with sportspersons under the Labour Law Statute does not always seem to be appropriate. So far, sportspersons have not been excluded from the protection provisions in accordance with Article 27 Labour Law Statute. The Labour Law Statute therefore also applies to competitions and training sessions on weekends and in the evenings. However, in actual fact the flexible working hours of sportspersons are not disputed in Switzerland.

252. Swiss courts determine the applicable law in accordance with the rules of the PILA. As a general rule, employment contracts are governed by the law of the state in which the employee normally works (Article 121 paragraph 1 PILA). If the employee works in more than one state, the employment contract is governed by the law of the state in which the employer is incorporated (Article 121 paragraph 2 PILA). According to Article 121 paragraph 3 PILA, the parties may also choose the law of the state in which the employee normally resides or in which the employer is incorporated.

§2. Definition of Employment Contracts

253. There are many different ways in which sportspersons exercise their profession. There are no clear limits between sport as a hobby, amateur sports and professional sports. Team sports are different from non-team sports.

254. In order to be an employment contract under Swiss law, the parties must have the intent to enter into a contract and to be bound by it.

255. Every employment contract has four elements:

(1) the performance, which has to be personal;
(2) the time frame during which work has to be performed;

(3) financial compensation; and
(4) the employee is subordinated to the employer.

256. Not all contracts with sportspersons are employment contracts. Each contract has to be analysed specifically. In professional team sports, employment contracts are common. In non-team sports, sportspersons are often not party to an employment contract but are self-employed.

§3. Duties of Care of the Sportsperson

257. According to Article 321a paragraph 1 Swiss Code of Obligations the employee has a duty of care when performing the work and has to take into consideration the legitimate interests of the employer. The sportsperson has to use his or her entire physical and psychological capacity to achieve success. Sportspersons who are employees must not only give their best during working hours but also lead appropriate private lives in order to achieve top results and to avoid jeopardizing their work through dangerous sports or unhealthy lifestyles. However, no employee owes a specific success, such as scoring a specific goal, but only due performance (kicking a ball in such a way as to enhance the chances of scoring a goal). Inadequate results are therefore no justification for terminating the contract. Even the exclusion from the training due to inadequate results or even inappropriate behaviour may be challenged by the sportsperson if the training is, for example, necessary to keep the sporting level. The personality rights of the sportspersons give the legal grounds (Article 328 Swiss Code of Obligations). Based on this provision several football players have successfully fought their way back into the training with the first team after the coach had excluded them due to an (allegedly) bad influence.[199]

258. As a counterpart of the employer's duty of care, the sportsperson has a fiduciary duty. The sportsperson must behave adequately at all times and protect the employer's interests when dealing with the media and the sponsors. However, the fiduciary duty is limited by the employee's own interests.

259. According to Article 27 paragraph 2 Swiss Civil Code, a sportsperson cannot commit oneself in an excessive way. Sportspersons must not be exposed to too much strain; they are obliged to follow their employer's medical recommendations and instructions. However, the sportsperson's personal doctor is bound by confidentiality, which the sportsperson has to waive explicitly to enable the doctor to inform third parties about the sportsperson's health. This is necessary for the coaches to adequately decide on the capability to play, and in transfer matters to allow the potential new club to check the physical capabilities of the sportsperson.

260. Depending on the sport, it may be necessary to include a non-competition clause according to which the sportsperson is not allowed to work for a different

199. *See* below in more detail §7 Personality Rights of the Employees.

employer. However, the sportsperson must be allowed to earn money on the side, provided there is no conflict with the interests of the main employer.

261. Sportspersons have to follow their employer's instructions (Article 321d paragraph 1 Swiss Code of Obligations). Such instructions may relate to organizing the work, preparation for competitions and the behaviour of the sportsperson. However, the sportsperson only has to comply with instructions that are legal.

262. The employer's duty of care is not explicitly stated in Swiss law, but it is generally recognized.[200] A number of the employer's obligations derive from its duty of care.

§4. Legal Consequences of Breaches of Duty

263. It is very difficult to sanction insufficient effort. Sanctions against a sportsperson can only be taken in case of serious breaches of the duty to work and the fiduciary duty. Sanctions include termination without notice, denying or reducing the salary, penalties, damages and insisting on specific performance, which is however, not a practical solution because the sportsperson's motivation is paramount.

264. Particularly serious breaches by the employee may justify terminating the contract without notice, provided the circumstances be such that it is no longer reasonable for the employer to continue the employment relationship (Article 337 paragraph 2 Swiss Code of Obligations). Minor breaches may justify termination without notice if they occur repeatedly, and a warning had been issued beforehand.[201] Repeated refusal to work, such as not attending training despite warnings or accepting bribes, may justify a termination. However, in general, inadequate achievements alone do not justify termination without notice.

265. If the sportsperson does not comply with his or her duty to work and this is not justified, the employer may refuse to pay the salary. However, if the work is merely insufficient the employer may not reduce the salary.[202]

266. The most useful measures in practice are contractual penalties. Minor breaches are sanctioned by warnings, serious breaches by fines or bans. However, all these measures require legal grounds and are subject to review in accordance with Articles 160 et seq. Swiss Code of Obligations. The amount of contractual penalties must be determinable, the breach must be clearly defined and the penalty must not be excessive. If the penalty contains an element of compensation, it also falls

200. But cf. Art. 328 para. 2 Swiss Code of Obligations, according to which the employer is obliged to take measures to ensure the safety of life, health and personal integrity of the employee.
201. BGE 129 III 380 et seq. C. 2.1.
202. Aebi-Müller & Rüfenacht, in *Sport und Recht*, ed. Arter & Baddeley, Bern 2007, 135 et. seq.

under Article 321e Swiss Code of Obligations.[203] Despite contractual penalties, the employer must continue to bear the operational risk. Hence, the employer, for example, cannot retain a certain amount of an agreed salary to cover a loss of the employers' business.

§5. Arbitrability of Labour Disputes

267. In the decision 4A_7/2018 of April 18, 2018, the Federal Supreme Court addressed the issue of whether the claims of an employee covered by Article 341 paragraph 1 Swiss Code of Obligations are arbitrable in internal arbitration proceedings.[204]

268. In terms of the facts of the case, an employment contract between a football coach and a club contained a dispute resolution clause that set forth that the parties in a first step shall seek to settle any disputes before the monitoring and Disciplinary Commission of the Swiss Football Association. If no settlement was reached, the parties agreed to resolve any dispute under their contract by arbitration before the CAS. After the club terminated the contract with immediate effect, the coach filed a claim for damages and compensation to the civil court. The civil court awarded damages and compensation to the coach. The cantonal court of appeal dismissed a following appeal by the club. Eventually, the club appealed to the Federal Supreme Court to set aside the decision due to lack of jurisdiction.

269. The Federal Supreme Court confirmed the decision of the cantonal courts. The court held that the arbitrability must be determined under Article 354 Civil Procedure Code. Hence, contrary to international matters – where pursuant to Article 177 paragraph 1 PILA all disputes involving monetary interests are arbitrable – in domestic disputes merely claims over which the parties may freely dispose may be subject to an arbitration agreement. The court further found that in the case of claims covered by Article 341 Code of Obligations, not only is a waiver by the employee during the term of the employment relationship and one month after its termination excluded, but a settlement between the contracting parties is also exclusively permissible under certain material restrictions for the protection of the employee. Accordingly, substantive private law grants the employing party special protection due to the dependency relationship inherent in the employment relationship. Following this reasoning, the Federal Supreme Court rendered the claim to be not arbitrable.

270. A problematic thereof – as the Federal Supreme Court likewise stated – lies within the fact that the limited arbitrability of claims under labour law entails the

203. Pursuant to Art. 321e Swiss Code of Obligations the employee is responsible for damage intentionally or negligently caused to the employer in breach of his duty to work and his fiduciary duty. If the non-fulfilment of the obligation to work results from an unjustified non-appearance or an unjustified leaving of the working place the liability to pay damages will be in accordance with Art. 321d Swiss Code of Obligations.

204. Decision of the Federal Supreme Court 4A_7/2018 of 18 Apr. 2018.

risk of a separation in the legal process for mandatory and non-mandatory claims arising from the employment relationship. If, in order to resolve a dispute, it is necessary to bring one claim before a state court and the other before an arbitration court, this is unsatisfactory from a practical point of view as parallel proceedings occur. The Federal Supreme Court clarified this problematic by stating that the will of a party to waive state jurisdiction in favour of an arbitral tribunal is not lightly assumed, which is why a restrictive interpretation is required in cases of doubt.

271. Hence, domestic labour disputes are generally not arbitrable under Article 354 Civil Procedure Code in conjunction with Article 341 Code of Obligations. International labour disputes are arbitrable according to Article 177 paragraph 1 PILA.

§6. Doping and Employment Contracts

I. Overview

272. If an employed sportsperson uses illegal substances, the employer has several options. The employer may refuse to select the sportsperson for competitions for a certain period of time, thus waiving the work offered by the sportsperson.[205] Even if one assumes that the sportsperson has the right to be kept occupied, the employer cannot be forced to use the sportsperson who is in danger of elimination.[206] Not being able to use the employee is in general no ground for termination without notice.[207]

II. Extraordinary Dismissal

273. The employer may also try to terminate the contract without notice. However, one has to bear in mind that, according to the Swiss Federal Supreme Court, only very serious breaches justify a termination without notice. In doping cases the employer may consider termination without notice in accordance with Article 337 paragraph 1 Swiss Code of Obligations (breach of fiduciary duty). If positive results were obtained during internal checks or if there are external positive doping results, which cannot foreseeably be rebutted, it is possible to assume a breach of contract and a breach of fiduciary duty.[208] If the breach is so serious that the employer cannot reasonably continue working with the sportsperson for the duration of the termination period (Article 334 Swiss Code of Obligations), the employer is entitled to terminate the contract without notice (Article 337 paragraph 1 Swiss Code of

205. Dissenting opinion: decision of the Swiss Federal Supreme Court 4A_352/2009 of 13 Oct. 2009, where an internal positive urine assay was not considered an important reason for the termination of the contract.
206. Valloni, in *Sport und Recht*, ed. Arter & Baddeley, Berne 2007, 217.
207. JAR 2002, 252; JAR 1991, 141.
208. Valloni, in *Sport und Recht*, ed. Arter & Baddeley, Bern 2007, 219.

Obligations).[209] However, the employer has to await confirmation of the A-test by a second B-test. It is therefore, in general, not possible to terminate the contract without notice before the A-test has been confirmed by a B-test. Once the results of the B-test are available, the employer who is aware of a reason for terminating without notice has to react immediately and has a few days only[210] to decide whether or not to do so. The right to terminate without notice expires if this deadline is not met.[211]

274. Contrary to the view of the majority of scholars, it is possible under certain circumstances to terminate a contract without notice merely based on suspicions.[212] Termination without notice may still be justified if the suspicion is objectively serious and the suspected employee cannot rebut the suspicion within reasonable time or if the sportsperson even hinders the employer investigating the case. However, mere suspicions are not sufficient evidence; the employer still has to prove that the facts are objectively true.[213] If the employer terminates the contract based on mere suspicions, he or she bears the financial risk. If the suspicion is confirmed later, the termination without notice is justified. If the suspicion is cleared, the employer has to bear the financial consequences of an unjustified termination without notice.[214]

275. If the employer is not entitled to terminate the contract without notice, he or she has to pay a penalty of up to six-month salary. Furthermore, the employer is obliged to continue paying the salary during the notice period, even if the sportsperson does not have to continue performing his or her duties. If the employee cannot work for personal reasons, which he or she has not caused negligently, the employer has to continue paying the salary for a certain time (Article 324a Swiss Code of Obligations). The burden of proof that the employee was not negligent lies with the employee.[215] The employer can only cease to pay the salary if the employee acted with gross negligence. If the employee knowingly and intentionally uses illegal substances leading to internal or external bans, the salary has no longer to be paid.[216]

209. VALLONI, in *Sport und Recht*, ed. ARTER & BADDELEY, Bern 2007, 219; BGE 129 III 380 C.2.1 and 3.1; BGE 127 III 351 C.4a; BGE 116 II 142 C.5c; BGE 112 II 41 C.3a; BGE 108 II 444 C.2.; dissenting opinion: Decision of the Swiss Federal Supreme Court 4A_352/2009 of 13 Oct. 2009.
210. Two to three working days, in exceptional cases one week, are generally considered a reasonable time (BGE 130 III 28 C.4.4, BGE 93 II 19). Legal persons whose decision on termination falls within the competence of a multi-member body shall be provided with a period of time of one week due to the longer decision-making process (BGer 13 Aug. 2001; JAR 2002, 267; BGer 21 Jun. 1995; SARB 1997, 24).
211. VALLONI, in *Sport und Recht*, ed. ARTER & BADDELEY, Berne 2007, 217. BGE 123 III 86 C.2a; BGE 112II 41 C.3; BGE 97 II 142 C.2a.
212. VALLONI, in *Sport und Recht*, ed. ARTER & BADDELEY, Bern 2007, 217.
213. Decision of the BGer dated 22 Aug. 1997; JAR 1998, 218.
214. VALLONI, in *Sport und Recht*, ed. ARTER & BADDELEY, Bern 2007, 221.
215. Article 8 Swiss Civil Code; BGE 125 III 76 C.3c.
216. VALLONI, in *Sport und Recht*, ed. ARTER & BADDELEY, Bern 2007, 222.

III. Indemnity Claim

276. The employee is liable to the employer for the financial loss caused intentionally or negligently (Article 321e Swiss Code of Obligations, Article 337b Swiss Code of Obligations in case of termination without notice). The elements of Article 321e Swiss Code of Obligations are: breaches of contract (non-performance or bad performance, for example, breach of a duty of care, breach of a fiduciary duty, breach of the duty to obey). The sportsperson is to refrain from illegal or otherwise unacceptable behaviour, and is not allowed to take any illegal substances. Another element is that the sportsperson has to act intentionally or negligently. Furthermore, there has to be a causal nexus between the breach and the financial loss. In case of doping, the employer may suffer damage to image, lose the sportsperson's manpower, suffer from a team being disqualified, have licensing problems and the relationship with the sponsors may be affected. There are a number of exceptions to the general principle of liability. If the sportsperson acted negligently but in an excusable manner (e.g., contaminated dietary supplements) damages may be reduced or even waived. If the employer has given his or her consent to the act of doping there is no breach of contract and the sportsperson is not liable. It is also clear that an employer who administered illegal substances without the sportsperson being aware of it cannot claim any compensation. If the employer participated, there will be either no liability or only a limited liability of the sportsperson. The burden of proof for the breach of contract, the financial loss and the causal nexus lie with the employer. The employee has to prove that he or she did not act negligently or intentionally.[217]

277. The extent to which the employee can claim financial compensation from the employer depends on the breach. The type and amount of compensation is determined in accordance with Article 97 or Article 41 Swiss Code of Obligations. In case of an unjustified termination without notice (e.g., acquittal from doping suspicion after termination without notice), the sportsperson can claim damages from the time of termination (Article 337 Swiss Code of Obligations).[218] The employer must put the sportsperson financially in a position as if the termination had not happened by paying an equivalent amount to the salary (including price money) the sportsperson would have earned upon expiry or ordinary termination of the employment contract.[219] According to the Swiss Federal Supreme Court, an additional compensation of a maximum of six months of salary is owed, except in exceptional circumstances (Article 337c paragraph 3 Swiss Code of Obligations).[220] The additional compensation will be determined taking into account the circumstances of the case.[221] In case of termination without notice, the employee has to prove the causal nexus between the loss and the unjustified termination. The employer has to prove valid reasons and reasons for reducing the compensation. The employer cannot

217. Article 98 para. 2 Swiss Code of Obligations; VALLONI, in *Sport und Recht*, ed. ARTER & BADDELEY, Berne 2007, 231.
218. BGE 103 II 274; VALLONI, in *Sport und Recht*, ed. ARTER & BADDELEY, Berne 2007, 232.
219. BGE 117 II 270 C.3b; BGE 111 II 357.
220. BGE 121 III 64 C.3c; BGE 120 II 243 C.3e.
221. BGE 123 III 391 C.3c; BGE 121 III 64 C.3b; BGE 116 II 300.

exclude his or her liability.[222] Article 337c Swiss Code of Obligations is not exhaustive; the employee may claim further damages, for example in cases of damage to his or her reputation (Article 49 Swiss Code of Obligations) or breach of secrecy obligations.[223]

§7. Sportspersons' Salaries

278. Employed sportspersons regularly receive salaries for their work (Article 322 Swiss Code of Obligations). If in doubt, the agreed salaries will be gross wages. Contributions to social security schemes and taxes have to be deducted from the agreed salary. If the employer does not apply for a work permit or does not prepare the documents the sportsperson requires to enter Switzerland, the employer is still obliged to pay the agreed salary (Article 324 Swiss Code of Obligations). The same is true if the employee is not able to work because of personal reasons such as sickness or accident (Article 324a Swiss Code of Obligations).

279. In addition to the salary, the sportsperson has a mandatory right to claim expenses (Article 327a Swiss Code of Obligations). It is possible to agree that expenses shall be compensated as part of the salary. However, expenses have to be declared for income tax purposes and contributions to social security schemes have to be deducted.

280. Sportspersons regularly receive bonuses for participating in competitions, winning competitions, gaining points or achieving certain ranks. Such bonuses are entirely dependent on achievement. Bonuses are defined either in the employment contract or in regulations forming an integral part of the contract.

281. Signing fees (special payments for signing a contract) and shares in future transfer payments are frequently agreed. Signing fees regularly qualify as part of the salary.[224] Shares in future transfer payments, however, are a special form of bonus (Article 322b Swiss Code of Obligations).[225]

---

222. Article 362 Swiss Code of Obligations.
223. Valloni, in *Sport und Recht*, ed. Arter & Baddeley, Berne 2007, 233.
224. In a decision of the High Court of the Canton of Zurich of 12 Jan. 2007 it was held that the promise of a substantial sum to a footballer in a dispute regarding the period of limitation of a claim had the character of a wage. The claim was qualified by the court as a claim of an employee arising out of an employment contract, so that the court affirmed a limitation period of five years pursuant to Art. 128 para. 3 Swiss Code of Obligations.
225. Balmelli, in *Sport und Recht*, ed. Arter & Baddeley, Berne 2007, 150.

§8. Personality Rights of the Employees

282. According to Swiss scholars and courts, employees have a right to be kept occupied as part of their personality rights (Article 328 Swiss Code of Obligations).[226] According to Article 328 Swiss Code of Obligations, the employer has to further the economic development of the employee. Not keeping busy a professional sportsperson may result in a breach of personality rights.[227] Being actually kept busy, for example, taking part in training with a professional squad is elementary to further develop and maintain professional skills.[228]

283. A sportsperson is entitled to at least train with the squad for which he or she has been hired. This is the only way for the employer to maintain the sportsperson's market value if he or she ceases to be used in competitions. Excluding a sportsperson from training therefore results in a breach of his or her personality rights (Articles 28 et seq. Swiss Civil Code), provided there are no disciplinary offences for which the sportsperson is responsible and which justify exclusion from training.

284. It further results from the personality rights of sportspersons that it must be possible for them to terminate the contract without having to pay an exit fee if the employer has no intention to use the sportsperson any longer.[229] For the same reason, the Swiss Federal Tribunal had considered transfer payments already before the *Bosman* case came to be illegal.[230]

§9. Termination of Employment Contracts

285. Swiss law distinguishes between temporary contracts and unlimited contracts of employment:

- Temporary contracts of employment end without notice of termination at the end of the agreed contract period (Article 334 Swiss Code of Obligations).
- Unlimited contracts of employment may be terminated by each contractual party by observing the statutory termination period. The terminating party needs to state the reason if the other party requests so (Article 335 Swiss Code of Obligations).

286. In accordance with the principle of parity of termination periods (Article 335a Swiss Code of Obligations), the termination periods for both the employer and employee must be the same. Furthermore, it is not possible to tie the termination to economic disadvantages that the other party would not suffer when terminating the

226. BGE 87 II 143; BGE 99 Ib 133.
227. Article 28 Swiss Civil Code.
228. Cf. BGE 102 II 220.
229. Geiser, in *Sport und Recht*, ed. Arter & Baddeley, Berne 2007, 26.
230. BGE 102 II 212 et seq.

contract. It is therefore illegal to provide for a contractual penalty for only one party.[231] According to the Qualification Commission of the SFL, temporary contracts giving the employer an option to extend the contract contradict the mandatory provisions of Article 335a Swiss Code of Obligations. It follows that the contract will not be extended, if the employer exercises the option and any contract entered into in the meantime with a new club will be valid.[232]

287. Both the employer and the employee may terminate the employment contract for valid reasons, that is, reasons which, according to the principle of good faith, make it impossible to continue the contract. Any termination for valid reasons has to be motivated in writing if the other party so requests (*see* Article 337 Swiss Code of Obligations). In the *Eddy Barea* case, a football player was suspended from the first team because he did not follow the coach's instructions. Thereupon, Barea terminated the employment contract without previous notice. The Swiss Federal Supreme Court upheld Barea's behaviour. The club's reaction was considered as disproportional and violated the legitimate interests of Baera as Barea's market value would have been substantially influenced without regular games and training. Therefore, Barea was able to terminate his contract without previous notice and ask for a compensation for personal suffering based on Article 49 in connection with Article 328 paragraph 1 of the Swiss Code of Obligations.[233]

288. If one party terminates the employment contract abusively in the sense of Article 336 Code of Obligations (i.e., due to personal qualities of the other party, for revenge, to frustrate claims or to prevent the other party from exercising constitutional rights), the other party can claim compensation (Article 336a Swiss Code of Obligations). The judge determines the amount, taking into account all circumstances; however, the compensation may not exceed an amount equal to six months of salary. The claimant may also have claims based on other grounds.

289. It is necessary to distinguish abusive termination from untimely termination, which is a termination during the so-called blocking period.[234] Terminations that are pronounced during such a protected period (e.g., pregnancy, military service, illness or accident) are null and void.

290. Article 337c Swiss Code of Obligations contains provisions regarding unjustified termination by the employer. In case of termination without valid reasons, the employee can claim an amount equal to what he or she would have earned if the employment contract had been terminated with notice or expired as provided in the contract. However, the employer may deduct a sum equal to the amount the employee saved or earned, or should have saved or should have earned, as a consequence of the termination of the contract. The judge may order the employer to

231. BSK-Portmann, N 4 to Art. 335a Swiss Code of Obligations; JAR 1990, 230.
232. Resolution of the Qualification Commission of the SFL of 10 Jul. 2008, published in: CAS 2008, 356.
233. Decision of the Swiss Federal Supreme Court 4_A 53/2011 of 28 Apr. 2011.
234. Articles 336 et seq. Swiss Code of Obligations.

pay the employee a compensation, which may not exceed an amount equal to six months of salary (Article 337c Swiss Code of Obligations). However, the employee cannot claim to be reinstated.

291. Article 337d Swiss Code of Obligations contains rules for the case that the employee unjustifiably does not come to or leaves work. The employer is entitled to a compensation equalling one quARTER of one month's salary. There is a statutory presumption that the financial loss of the employer equals one quARTER of one month's salary.[235] However, the employee can submit evidence that the employer has suffered no financial loss or a financial loss that is lower than the equivalent of one quARTER of one month's salary.[236] The respective statutory provision is mandatory; it is not possible to provide for contractual penalties if the employee terminates the contract early.[237] The employer can also claim compensation for further financial loss; however, the employer has to prove such loss. It is important to bear in mind that the legislature wanted to enable employees to be able to change their employer without having to face drastic financial sanctions.[238]

§10. Players' Unions

292. In Swiss sports, only a few players' unions exist.

293. The most important Swiss players' unions are the Swiss Association of Football Players (SAFP)[239] and the Swiss Association of Icehockey Players (SAIP).[240] SAFP is a member of Fédération Internationale des Associations de Footballeurs Professionnels (FIFPRO) and SAIP is a member of the World Association of Ice hockey Player Unions (WAIPU).[241] FIFPRO and WAIPU represent the interests of the players, vis-à-vis international sports organizations as well as in the EU Sectoral Social Dialogue Committees and also vis-à-vis the state administrations in legislative projects as for example when FIFPRO, SAFP, WAIPU and SAIP filed its comments to Swiss Federal Councillor the planned revision of the PILA regulating arbitration proceedings in Switzerland on 31 May 2017.[242] SAFP is the most developed union in the sport sector in Switzerland and is recognized by the SFL as well as by the Swiss Football Federation (SFV) as the official representative of players and SFL/SFV entered into a framework agreement with SAFP regulating the grounds for cooperation.[243] The players union SAFP and SFL/SFV do cooperate on

235. Article 337d para. 1 Swiss Code of Obligations.
236. Article 337d para. 2 Swiss Code of Obligations.
237. Zürcher Kommentar, N 17 to Art. 337d Swiss Code of Obligations; Berner Kommentar, N 6 to Art. 337d Swiss Code of Obligations.
238. Geiser, in *Sport und Recht*, ed. Arter & Baddeley, Berne 2007, 108.
239. *See* http://www.safp.ch.
240. *See* http://www.saip.ch.
241. *See* http://www.waipu.org.
242. See https://www.admin.ch/ch/d/gg/pc/documents/2829/Internationale-Schiedsgerichtsbarkeit_Stellungnahmen-Organisationen.pdf, pages 166 - 179.
243. More hereto under http://www.sfl.ch/news/news/artikel/neue-vereinbarung-mit-safp/.

various grounds. SFL/SFV and SAFP have for example introduced the Red Button App together to combat match-fixing.[244] But also negotiations concerning the content of the standard football player contract are conducted between SAFP and SFL/SFV.

294. From a legal point of view, unions are generally recognized in Switzerland. According to Article 28 of the Swiss Constitution, employees are allowed to join forces to protect their interests and to establish, join and abstain from associations. According to Article 28 paragraph 3 of the Swiss Constitution, strikes and lockouts are legal if they concern employment relationships and if there is no obligation to maintain industrial peace or to mediate disputes. However, sportspersons have not taken such legal steps until today.

§11. Jurisprudence of CAS Regarding the Termination of Employment Contracts of Football Players

I. From the *Bosman* Case to the FIFA Regulations on the Status and Transfer of the Players

295. In its landmark case *Bosman,* the European Court of Justice(ECJ) decided that the duty to pay a transfer sum after the expiry of the contract placed a restriction on the free movement of workers, and was prohibited by the European Community (EC) Treaty.[245] Abolishing the transfer system would have meant that football clubs would have tried to tie football players as early as possible by making them sign extremely long-term contracts. However, such extremely long-term contracts would again have been in breach of European competition law because football players would have been prohibited from rendering their services in the market. This issue sparked proceedings *IV/36 583-SETCA-FGTB v. FIFA* (European Commission). Supervised by the European Commission, FIFA developed the Regulations on the Status and Transfer of the Players to avoid that the old transfer system would be re-introduced, and acceptable legal standards were set up. FIFA's Regulations on the Status and Transfer of the Players, therefore aimed at finding a balance between the duration of the contracts, ensuring the contractual stability and the freedom of movement of the football players.

296. The clubs shall only receive training compensation for players who are transferred before the end of the season of their twenty-third birthday (Article 20 FIFA Regulations on the Status and Transfer of the Players). All players may change clubs upon expiration of their contract without any transfer sum.

297. Article 18(2) of the FIFA Regulations on the Status and Transfer of the Players, therefore provides for a maximum length of contract of three years for players under the age of 18 and five years for players older than 18. Upon expiry of this

---

244. *See* http://www.sfl.ch/news/news/artikel/red-button-meldesystem-fuer-spielmanipulationen/.
245. Decision of the ECJ C-415/93, Bosman, [1995] ECR I-4921.

contractual term, at the latest, the services of each football player are available without any obligation to pay any compensation whatsoever to the old club.

298. Furthermore, the Regulations of the Status and Transfer of the Players provide that contracts may be terminated (Article 17 [1] FIFA Regulations on the Status and Transfer of the Players *e contrario*) without hindering the footballer from working. Sanctions such as bans may only be imposed during the protected period (three years for players who were less than 28 years old when signing the contract/ two years for players who were under 20 years old when signing the contract, Article 17(4) FIFA Regulations on the Status and Transfer of the Players).

299. It follows that, apart from terminating the contract with just cause (Article 14 FIFA Regulations on the Status and Transfer of the Players) or with sporting just cause (Article 15 FIFA Regulations on the Status and Transfer of the Players), there is also a possibility to terminate the contract against a payment at any time after the protected period without having to refer to a just cause (Article 17 FIFA Regulations on the Status and Transfer of the Players *e contrario).* This allows football players to act like any other employee once the protected period is over and to react to changed circumstances (*clausula rebus sic stantibus*). The market around football players can therefore not be cemented by long contracts. There is only a restriction on terminating a contract during the course of a season because this would lead to imbalances in sporting competition (Article 16 FIFA Regulations on the Status and Transfer of the Players).

II. Determination of the Compensation According to the Jurisdiction of the CAS

300. If the football player terminates the contract early without reason, he or she has to pay compensation (Article 17 [1] FIFA Regulations on the Status and Transfer of the Players). CAS has repeatedly dealt with the calculation of such compensations when reviewing decisions by the FIFA Dispute Resolution Chamber:

- In *Webster,*[246] CAS decided that a football player has a right under Article 17(1) FIFA Regulations on the Status and Transfer of Players to terminate the contract without reasons prior to its expiry. In such cases, the footballer has to pay the remaining value of the employment contract, that is, the salary he or she would have received until the end of the contract.
- In *Matuzalem,*[247] CAS assumed that a football player may not terminate a contract early based on Article 17(1) FIFA Regulations on the Status and Transfer of Players. It decided that the football player had to pay compensation to cover the loss suffered by his former club comprising of: (i) the future salary, taking into

246. Arbitral Award of CAS in the matter of Wigan Athletic FC c/ Heart of Midlothian et al. (CAS 2007/A/1298–1230).
247. Arbitral Award of CAS in the matter of Shaktar Donetsk FC c/ Matuzalem and Real Zaragoza (CAS 2008/A/1519–1520).

account the prior salary, and (ii) a future transfer sum defined in the contract but never paid and (iii) a penalty to the amount of six months of salary.

301. The Swiss Federal Supreme Court was not able to correct any of the decisions of the CAS.[248] It can only review CAS decisions if the compensation for damages would have been considered a breach of the *ordre public*. In the following the correct calculation of the compensation based on Article 17 (1) FIFA Regulations on the Status and Transfer of Players under Swiss law will be shown.

III. Positive Interest in the Performance of the Contract as Compensation According to the Swiss Employment Law

302. One of the main issues the European Commission raised when introducing the new transfer system in 2002 was to ensure that compensation according to FIFA Regulations should not be in breach of the applicable national law. Article 17(1) therefore provides for an obligation to consider the law of the country concerned when determining compensation.

303. Basically, an employer does not suffer any damage from an unjustified termination of the employment contract by the employee. The employer saves the salary, which corresponds to the performance of the employee. Thus, the employer can just claim damages for the additional costs to find a new employee. The same is true in the world of football. It must be assumed that the salary corresponds to the performance of the player. Therewith, the club does in general not have any damages if a player leaves the club.

304. An exception to this principle is only possible if a player becomes a lot better during his employment. In this case the club just needs to pay the agreed salary, but profits from the improved performance of the player. Therefore, the club benefits financially, because the player is in fact worth more. Only if such a player leaves the club before the end of the contractual period the club suffers a damage.

305. Contrary to these basic principles, in the *Matuzalem* case, the CAS added different elements to calculate the alleged 'damage', whereby a substantial bigger economic loss than the loss effectively incurred had to be compensated. This is contradictory to the general concept of the Swiss law regarding the compensation of damages (but not against an international order public which would have had to be violated to allow the Federal Tribunal to annul the CAS award).

248. Decision of the Swiss Federal Supreme Court 4A_320/2009 of 2 Jun. 2010.

IV. 'Sport Specificity' of the Compensation

306. In the *Matuzalem* case, the CAS considered an additional compensation of EUR 600,000, what nearly corresponded to six monthly salaries, based on the criteria of the 'Sport Specificity'. Thereby the CAS referred to Article 337c paragraph 3 of the Swiss Code of Obligations.

307. The interpretation by the CAS is clearly in conflict with the mentioned article. This article just offers a legal basis for a payment of the employer to the employee. Such a clear wording of the law cannot be interpreted *contra legem* in favour of the employer, even if a sport-specific peculiarity would really exist, like an unusual disposition of the position of power during the contract negotiations.

308. Only Article 337d of the Swiss Code of Obligations would be applicable in this case, whereupon the employer can obtain a compensation for an unjustified termination without previous notice by the employee, in the amount of a quARTER of a monthly salary.

V. Violation of the Termination Parity

309. There is a basic principle of termination parity between employer and employee in Swiss employment law. This means that the same notice periods have to apply for the employer and the employee.[249] The termination of the contract cannot be made more difficult to one party than the other party (e.g., if economic disadvantages are connected to the termination of one party). Therefore, a contractual penalty in the case of a termination of the employment contract cannot be imposed only on one party.

310. The compensation that was granted in the *Matuzalem* case is definitely comparable to a contractual penalty. Therewith the contractual balance is significantly moved to the disadvantage of the employee in the case of an early termination. The compensation that was granted by the CAS leads to an unequal treatment of the employee and the employer and therefore violates the legal principle of the termination parity.

311. To ensure the termination parity, the same principle has to be applied for the employer and the employee to calculate the owed compensation.

249. Cf. Art. 335a of the Swiss Code of Obligations.

Chapter 3. Personality Rights

§1. Legal Basis

312. According to the theory of natural law, each human being has personality rights independent of state law, merely due to being a human being. Personality rights are personal and absolute rights, which must be protected.

313. The legal basis for personality rights are Articles 27 and 28 Swiss Civil Code. Article 27 Swiss Civil Code protects the personality from excessive contractual duties and Article 28 Swiss Civil Code from illegal infringements. Every human being is thus granted freedom to develop his or her personality.

§2. Extent

314. Article 28 Swiss Civil Code protects the values, which are the essence of the personal sphere of each person. It protects self-determination and dignity, as well as, rights such as physical and psychological integrity and the right to economic development. Article 27 Swiss Civil Code protects the individual from contractual engagements, which are excessive in terms of their subject matter, intensity or duration.

315. When interpreting Articles 27 and 28 Swiss Civil Code the basic constitutional rights have to be taken into consideration. These may be referred to when interpreting private law concepts (Article 35 paragraph 3 Swiss Constitution). When determining whether personality rights may be limited by a powerful sports organization, the purpose of the organization must be balanced against the personality rights of its members.[250]

§3. Limitations to Personality Rights

316. Individuals may only enter into less extensive contracts than legal persons may. Legal persons may be restricted to a very large extent by provisions in the articles of association in order to further the interests of the association.[251] Subordinated sports organizations' freedom may be limited due to the pyramid organization of sport and the principle of specificity of sport. However, the subordinated organization cannot fully give up its autonomy and it is not possible to give the

250. BGE 86 II 365 et seq. 376; BGE 111 II 245 et seq., 250 et seq.; Fuchs, Rechtsfragen der Vereinsstrafe, 117 et seq.

251. According to BGE 55 II 7 it is even possible to link legal persons that are members of an association inextricably with the existence of an association. In this case, the members are only free with respect to activities that are indifferent and secondary to the purpose of the association.

superior association veto rights regarding all decisions of the subordinated association.[252] This would be contrary to democratic principles.

317. It is questionable how far a sportsperson may be limited in his or her personality rights by consenting. Such consent would have to be voluntary, revocable and sufficiently concrete with regard to the infringement of personality rights.[253] However, these prerequisites are often not fulfilled in sports because young athletes only have limited knowledge of the rules of the associations and the consequences of their entry into the world of sports due to their young age.[254] The consent is not really revocable due to the monopolistic structure of sport under which the sportsperson would be excluded after revoking his or her consent. It follows that the personality rights may be limited only to a small extent. This has to be taken into account when interpreting the rules of sports organizations.

§4. Right to Participate

318. Due to the monopolistic organization, the stakeholders, that is, sportspersons, clubs and other groups, are very dependent on sports organizations. The stakeholders need the sports organization to exercise their sport.

319. The Swiss Federal Supreme Court has developed a right to be admitted to monopolistic organizations such as sports associations based on the personality right to economic progress.[255] Personality rights of the stakeholders may therefore only be limited if this is justified by the purpose of the sports organization and if there is no other less infringing way. It follows that sports organizations have to refer to a specific reason when limiting the right to participate. The sports organization's autonomy is therefore smaller, the weaker the link between the measure and the purpose the more severe the infringement of the stakeholder's personality rights.[256]

320. These principles were, for example, applied in the saga around the acceptance of Gibraltar as a member of the UEFA and the FIFA. The CAS came to the conclusion that based on the UEFA provisions nations like Gibraltar need to be accepted as members of the UEFA due to their personality rights. Thereafter, Gibraltar also successfully fought for its right to become a member of the FIFA.

---

252. BGE 97 II 114.
253. Baddeley, Le sportif, sujet ou objet? – La protection de la personnalité du sportif, 205 et seq.; Hausheer & Aebi-Müller, Das Personenrecht des Schweizerischen Zivilgesetzbuches, N 12.16 et seq.
254. Baddeley, Le sportif, sujet ou objet? – La protection de la personnalité du sportif, 209 et seq.
255. BGE 123 III 193 et seq.; BGE 131 III 97 et seq.; Basler Kommentar-Heini & Scherrer, N 12 to Art. 72 Swiss Civil Code.
256. Haas & Prokop, Die Athletenvereinbarung – Der Athlet als stilles Mitglied des Verbandes, 103 et seq.

Part III. Doping and Sport

Chapter 1. Legal Basis

321. Switzerland, like other European states, has ratified the Anti-doping Convention of the Council of Europe (SC 0.812.122.1). This Convention is a model for the Code enacted by the WADA (WADA Code). Furthermore, Switzerland signed of course also the UNESCO Convention against doping in sports (SC 0.812.122.1).[257]

322. The doping legislation of Switzerland, in principle, is stipulated in Articles 19 et seq. FAS. In addition to the FAS, the Act on Therapeutic Products (SC 812.21) and the Act on Narcotics (SC 812. 121) may also apply.[258]

323. The Swiss legislation on doping in the FAS prohibits the production, import, procuring, marketing, prescribing and distribution of drugs for doping purposes, and applying of methods for doping purposes to third parties (Article 22 paragraph 1 FAS). Unlike other states,[259] the doping by the athletes themselves is not outlawed (Article 22 paragraph 4 FAS). The sportsperson's self-endangering is not officially sanctioned in liberal Switzerland, but the punishment is left to the sports organizations. The sports organizations consistently follow the WADA Code and the Anti-doping Regulations of Swiss Olympic and require the sportspersons to subject themselves to these regulations.[260] These two sets of rules govern violations of the anti-doping regulations by the sportspersons.

257. For more details *see* above.
258. The Act on Therapeutic Products ensures the protection of human beings and animals to the extent that only high quality drugs that are safe and effective will be introduced and that these drugs are utilized accordingly (Art. 1 para. 2 lit. b ATP). The Act on Narcotics regulates substances that are addictive and preparations that contain morphine, cocaine and cannabis. Addictive psychotropic substances will be treated in the same way (Art. 1 FAN).
259. For example: Austria, Belgium or Italy.
260. To the Doping Statute 2009 of the Swiss Olympic *see* http://www.dopinginfo.ch/dmdocuments/statut_2009_def_unterschrieben.pdf.

Chapter 2. Anti-doping Foundation Switzerland

324. Responsible for the private fight against doping is the Anti-doping Foundation Switzerland. Since 1 July 2008 it has been the independent competence centre of the fight against doping in Switzerland. The mission of Anti-doping Foundation Switzerland is the conduct of doping controls, information and prevention, applied research and development, national and international cooperation with other doping organizations and taking all other measures that target clean and fair sport.

325. Anti-doping Foundation Switzerland is funded one half each by the Federal Government and Swiss Olympic. The appointment of services is made through performance-related mandates purchased by Anti-Doping Switzerland and Swiss Olympic respectively the Federal Office of Sports. They form the basis for financing and determine the goals of the Anti-doping Foundation Switzerland. The Foundation has no commercial purposes and does not aim for profit.

326. In the Articles 21–25 FAS the collaboration of Anti-doping Foundation Switzerland with the criminal authorities is regulated. The Anti-doping Foundation Switzerland needs to inform the authorities about the abuse of doping and is in return granted special information rights regarding investigations against doping. During the last years the Anti-doping Foundation Switzerland has made frequent use of such possibility and initiated several criminal proceedings. Furthermore, the Anti-doping Foundation Switzerland has the right to exchange data with foreign anti-doping agencies.

Chapter 3. Criminal Prosecution of the Abuse of Doping

327. For the prosecution of drug abuse, the crimes of being an accessory to doping under the FAS (Articles 22 et seq.), the Act on Therapeutic Products (Articles 86 et seq.) and the Act on Narcotics (Articles 19 et seq.) are crucial. Furthermore, there are the general provisions of the Swiss Penal Code.

328. In principle, it needs to be distinguished between so-called self-doping and so-called external doping.

329. With *self-doping* the sportsperson takes or administers drugs or applies the doping method to himself. The sportsperson has control over the act in each case. He should therefore be able to roughly estimate the risks of his actions. This case has to be distinguished from apparent self-doping where the sportsperson has taken the doping substances or applied the doping method to himself or herself but has no control over the act.[261]

330. *External doping*, however, arises if another person such as a doctor administers drugs, doping substances or pharmaceuticals or applies doping methods to the sportsperson. The sportsperson has no or only limited control over the act. Although it is forbidden to doctors to prescribe or handover doping in the competitive sport according to their professional code, external doping is common as well even though doctors are obligated to avoid the drug abuse of the athletes as far as possible.

331. In the case of self-doping, the sportsperson is not criminally punishable. However, theoretically, persons who participate in self-doping may be penalized under certain circumstances. In case of suicide, Article 115 of the Swiss Penal Code provides that only the person who for selfish motives incites or assists another to commit or attempt to commit suicide, if that other person thereafter commits or attempts to commit suicide, is punishable. The suicide itself is in general not subject to a criminal sanction in Switzerland. However, it is virtually impossible to imagine in what circumstances this requirement might be fulfilled. A sportsperson's participation in all other forms of self-endangering is in any case not punishable (Article 115 of the Swiss Penal Code, *a maiore minus*).

332. Of greater importance are the penal provisions in case of external doping. Here it is not the sportsperson that has control over the act, but a third party. With the administration of doping or the application of banned substances, the third party may kill the sportsperson or at least hurt or threaten the sportsperson's life. All of these offences are liable to prosecution, but the emphasis is on Articles 22 et seq. FAS, whereby external doping may be prosecuted with a custodial sentence of up to three years or a fine.

---

261. For example, False declaration of doping substances as vitamins or medicine by the doctor.

333. Self-doping or *external doping* in an improper sense is assumed if an athlete is tricked into or even forced to dope without being made aware of the risks and consequences. This was the case, for example, with the East German sportspersons who took steroids in the belief that the drugs in question were vitamins. In such cases, the athlete lacks the necessary control over the act and external doping with all its consequences must be assumed.[262]

262. Cf. FLACHSMANN, Doping im Strafrecht, 231 et seq.

Chapter 4. Reinforcement of State Law?

334. The reinforcement of legal standards to fight doping has been discussed in Switzerland for a long time. However, for the time being it is unlikely that new regulations will be introduced in this area. It is debatable whether special provisions in the Swiss Penal Code or penal law provisions in other statutes are necessary at all, especially since there are already instruments to inhibit the business of doping. Moreover, to some extent it is argued by legal writers that doping can be subsumed under the crime of fraud pursuant to Article 146 of the Penal Code or under the criminal provisions of the Law against Unfair Competition (UCL). Finally, the question arises whether additional intervention by the government in this area is desirable and appropriate or if athletes taking prohibited substances should only be called to account by the associations to which they belong.[263] The creation of a special criminal sanction against doping of athletes would discriminate the athletes in comparison with the rest of the population. Furthermore, it is questionable if the state should carry the task and the costs of the fight against doping. With the newly introduced FAS there are at least enough criminal sanctions to eliminate the athletes' entourage with criminal sanctions. The latest version of the WADA Code 2015 goes even further and prohibits athletes to work with persons that were found to do anything which would be sanctioned under the WADA Code (Article 10.2.1).

263. TEITLER, Rechtsnatur und Anwendung des WADA-Codes, 395 et seq.

Chapter 5. The Doping Procedure: Between Civil and Criminal Law

335. The Swiss Federal Supreme Court has held that the doping problem is a civil law matter. Therefore, private law cases cannot simply be determined on the basis of criminal law cases.[264]

336. It is undisputed that sports arbitration has its origin and its legitimacy in the civil law. Nevertheless, doping procedures have far greater similarities to criminal cases than to civil proceedings. For this reason, legal writers affirm the application of criminal law principles to the disciplinary law of the associations. This applies all the more so when it comes to monopolistic associations, and when the sanctions become stricter.[265]

337. Decisions to suspend a sportsperson from training and competition undoubtedly have a punitive character. The consequences associated with this are sometimes more serious than in criminal proceedings. The standard suspension from training and competition for four years (Article 10.2.1. WADA Code 2021) results in an occupational ban during this time with the consequence that the sportsperson has no income during the period of the ban and has to finish his or her sporting career. Furthermore, the affected sportsperson is discredited before a global public and stigmatized as a fraud.

338. The purpose of the doping ban does not differ from the purpose of state punishment. When imposing a doping ban, the focus is on the deterrent effect on the sports community and the affected sportsperson. The sports organization makes use of its monopoly, based on the one-place-principle in sports. The sportsperson cannot escape the sports jurisdiction, indeed is forced to be subject to this jurisdiction if he wishes to practice sports. The sportsperson will be – as in a state criminal proceeding – accused and finally convicted.

339. Although it is clear that the civil and criminal procedural principles cannot be directly applied to the doping proceedings of a sports association, it is still recognized that many civil and criminal judicial process principles will be applied by analogy to the proceedings of the sports organizations. This follows from the similarity of the proceedings of associations and state criminal proceedings.[266] This is also true for the principles of the ECHR, which must be considered in sports court

---

264. Decision of the Swiss Federal Supreme Court 5P.83/1999 of 31 Mar. 1999, C. 3.d.
265. FUCHS, Rechtsfragen der Verbandsstrafe, 109; Basler Kommentar-HEINI/SCHERRER, N 21 to Art. 70 Swiss Civil Code. Regarding the review of failings in the proceedings when excluding a member of an association, which is similar to a doping proceeding, *see* BGE 123 III 196; BGE 114 II 193 et seq.; BGE 90 II 346 et seq.
266. Cf. hereto as an example: Decision of the CAS 2004/A/777 ARecycling AG v/UCI, of 31 Jan. 2005, in which the CAS speaks out against the application of 'Gesinnungsstrafrecht' that is, penal law only by attitude.

proceedings.[267] Despite the private autonomy applicable to private law, the anti-doping organizations – like those involved in criminal and civil proceedings – are bound to take into account a certain minimum standard of procedural process principles.

340. It is widely acknowledged that the sportsperson has a right to a fair trial in doping proceedings. As early as 1914, the Swiss Federal Supreme Court recognized the right to a fair hearing as an non-waivable right with respect to exclusion from a cooperative, a society whose nature is similar to that of a sports association.[268, 269] This right is now undisputed regarding penalties for an association.[270]

341. The basis for all interventions in the legal position of a sportsperson is the principle of legality. Thus, all penalties require a sufficiently specific legal basis. The penalties must be foreseeable for the sportspersons. In doping proceedings, therefore, the principle of non-retroactivity and the principle of *lex mitior* as well as the prohibition of double jeopardy apply.[271]

342. Appeals against a doping ban at the CAS do not always lead to a confirmation or a reduction of the ban. The appealed decision can also be tightened by the CAS (so-called *reformatio in peius*). So did the FEI ban a horse jumper of Germany for 120 days (around four months) after two adverse analytical findings of his horse. The jumper appealed against this decision at the CAS and asked for a reduction of the ban to three months. However, the CAS increased the pronounced ban on the request of the national association of equitation to a period of eight months with its arbitral award of 30 April 2009. The appeal against this arbitral award in front of the Swiss Federal Supreme Court was unsuccessful.[272]

---

267. Particularly in proceedings relating to arbitration, state courts are required to ensure the arbitration panels meet at least the standards of the ECHR regarding the *ordre public*; HAAS, 73 et seq.
268. PACHMANN, Corporate Governance, 172 et seq.
269. BGE 40 II 374 et seq.
270. FUCHS, Rechtsfragen der Vereinsstrafe, 107 et seq.
271. Rule no. 25.2 WADA Code: '*Non-Retroactive Unless Principle of Lex Mitior Applies*'.
272. Decision of the Swiss Federal Supreme Court 4A_284/2009 of 24 Nov. 2009.

Chapter 6. Proving Doping According to the WADA Code

343. In contrast to the state law enforcement authorities, there are few coercive measures available to the anti-doping organizations in the fight against doping. The principal means of coercion is the direct sanction of sportspersons, even without a positive drug test if they appear too late for a doping control or cannot be found at the pre-announced location.[273]

344. It seems justifiable, given the vital significance of anti-doping for sports organizations, that anti-doping organizations reserve the right to ease the burden of proof under certain provisions.[274] Even if the anti-doping organizations manage to prove illicit substances in the body of a sportsperson, if the presumption of innocence is strictly applied, this fact alone would not suffice to suspend a sportsperson for violation of anti-doping regulations. The anti-doping organization would also have to demonstrate the sequence of events leading to this finding and the intent to violate the anti-doping regulations or the breach of the duty of care to the sportsperson.[275]

345. Any presumption that eases the burden of proof is to the detriment of the athlete, but it can only affect the subjective facts or rather the ability to obtain a reduction of the penalty because of the absence of liability.[276]

346. The most important easing of the burden of proof in the WADA Code is the so-called *strict liability* pursuant to rule no. 2.1.1 WADA Code. According to this rule, each sportsperson can directly be held responsible if a banned substance is found in his or her test results. The breach of the anti-doping rules is assumed regardless of whether the banned substance came into the sportsperson's body on purpose, negligently or accidentally.

347. Due to the special relationship between sports organizations and sportspersons, the *strict liability* of the WADA Code is in accordance with the Swiss legal system, provided that the anti-doping organizations are able to prove that the sportsperson has used illicit substances. The Swiss Federal Supreme Court has held on several occasions that the rule whereby doping is assumed in case the test is positive for an illicit substance is not against the *ordre public*.[277]

348. The special relationship between sportspersons and sports organizations deriving from *strict liability* at the same time includes a strong sense of loyalty to the sports organizations. The rules of the sports organizations must ensure that no

273. Rule no. 2.3 and no. 2.4 WADA Code.
274. Cf. Eufe, Die Unschuldsvermutung im Dopingverfahren, 56 et seq.
275. The requirements for behaviour to be criminally sanctionable under the criminal law are that the objective and subjective elements of an offence are fulfilled.
276. Adolphsen, Dopingverfahren, 254.
277. Decisions of the Swiss Federal Supreme Court 5P.83/1999 of 31 Mar. 1999 C. 3d and 4P.105/2006 of 4 Aug. 2006 C. 8.

innocent sportsperson is convicted as a result of *strict liability* and that sportspersons have the opportunity to defend themselves against the consequences of *strict liability*. Otherwise, the concept based on the special relationship between sportspersons and sports organizations would be incomplete. The reason for this is that the sanctioning of a member is in effect an ethical condemnation of the conduct alleged. Therefore, members of an association can only be punished in case they are at fault and, thus, by ensuring the principle of fault. However, it is permissible to shift the burden of proof, and thus to provide for a presumption of fault to the athlete's detriment, provided that the athlete has the possibility and it is practically possible for him to prove that he is not at fault.[278] Unfortunately, the past has shown that it is extremely difficult for athletes to show their innocence forcing athletes to find questionable explanations for the substances in their urine or blood.

349. The athlete's burden of proof must further be reduced the more time has passed. In case of the re-analysis of eight or ten year old blood samples of athletes the requirement for a logical explanation of the athletes on how the prohibited substance came into their urine or blood must, hence, be much lower than with recent samples. The same is true if very low amounts of a substance are found which could have come into an athlete's body by chance.

350. In addition to *strict liability,* the WADA Code provides for aNOTHer significant alleviation of the burden of proof. Pursuant to rule no. 3.2.1 WADA Code, there is a presumption that all WADA accredited laboratories will have complied with the 'International Standard for Laboratories' when examining an assay.[279] In this case, it is for the sportsperson to prove that: (i) there has been a departure from the International Standard for Laboratories and (ii) that this may have led to the positive doping test. Only in such cases is the anti-doping organization then required to prove that the doping test was not positive due to a deviation from the International Standard for Laboratories.

351. According to rule no. 10.5.1 WADA Code the athlete can prove his innocence. The athlete needs to show that the violation of the anti-doping regulations was caused without his default (so-called *no fault* or *no negligence*). If the evidence of any forbidden substance in his body proven, the athlete has to prove how the forbidden substance entered into his organism to lift the ban.

---

278. NOTH, Comeback oder Stayback? Gedanken zur Durchsetzbarkeit der Comeback-Regelung im Doping-Statut der Swiss Olympic Association, 444 et seq.

279. Due to the alleviation of the burden of proof, the determination of a doping offence according to the WADA Code will be substantially and procedurally simplified. Substantially, the existence of an illegal substance is sufficient. Procedurally the test result will be protected based on the assumption that the laboratory standard is met; ADOLPHSEN, Dopingverfahren, 246.

352. Possible ways to prove no fault or no negligence are, for example, cases of medical emergencies,[280] unforeseeable results of actions that are considered harmless[281] or sabotage.[282] In the jurisprudence of the CAS the standard of proof is, however, extremely high.

353. In the last case a female wrestler of Azerbaijan was banned for two years, although a former rival confessed that she had secretly put the forbidden substance in a bottle of mineral water of the affected athlete. In spite of the saboteur's confession the proof of no fault or no negligence could not be provided in the eyes of the CAS, which is not really comprehensible. The Swiss Federal Supreme Court could not revise this decision, because it is bound to the determination of the facts of the case by the CAS.[283]

280. Cf. Decision of the CAS 2005/A/990 of 24 Aug. 2006.
281. Cf. Decisions of the CAS 2009/A/1926 and 2009/A/1930 of 17 Dec. 2009, where a tennis player kissed an unknown cocaine consumer during a party.
282. Cf. Decision of the CAS 2007/A/1399 of 17 Jul. 2008.
283. Cf. Decision of the Swiss Federal Supreme Court 4A_416/2008 of 17 Mar. 2009.

Chapter 7. Indirect Proof of Doping via Biological Passport and Alternative Methods

354. Doping methods are becoming more and more elaborate. With skilful timing and continuously new performance-enhancing substances, sportspersons are often a small but significant step ahead of the doping control bodies and can thereby prevent the direct detection of doping. This has been impressively proven by Lance Armstrong who has been tested negative hundreds of times. For this reason,[284] various international sports organizations and the WADA have developed a biological passport, by which an individual long-term blood profile of each sportsperson can be established through regular measurement of various blood parameters. In case the blood parameters of a sportsperson differ from his long-term blood profile, this can be seen as an indication that the sportsperson has made use of an illicit substance (the 'Haemotological Module' or 'blood module'). After seven years of development the WADA approved and brought into force the first version of the Athlete Biological Passport Operation Guidelines (hereinafter: 'WADA ABP') in 2009. The 2014 implemented version of the WADA ABP Guidelines introduced a second module, the 'Steroidal Module' which monitors selected urinary steroid concentrations over time in order to detect steroid doping.[285]

355. Apart from the WADA ABP there are also other recent doping tests that are based on indirect detection methods.[286] These indirect doping tests try to prove the use of forbidden (exogenous) substances by testing endogenous substances and establishing that these endogenous substances could – beyond any doubt – not have been produced naturally. Such doping tests are, however, extremely difficult to build as there could be many unknown reasons how these endogenous substances are produced. The athletes could, for example, have a very special genetic background, or the endogenous substances could be produced due to the very extreme training conditions of the athletes.

356. Of course, direct evidence – in the doping procedure this would be the discovery of forbidden substances in the body – is always the most reliable form of proof. Interestingly, the past has shown that it is not always sure whether a forbidden substance is in fact of exogenous origin. Many steroids have been proven to originate endogenously such as boldenone and norandrosterone after several athletes had been sanctioned. Such a previously wrong state of science puts innocent athletes in extremely difficult situations. Due to the principle of strict liability it

284. In order for the blood test results to be comparable, the blood must be taken in a highly standardized procedure. It requires medically trained personnel and transport, especially the temperature of the transport must be ensured. In addition, a laboratory accredited by the WADA is necessary for the analysis.

285. The WADA ABP is accessible under https://www.wada-ama.org/en/resources/athlete-biological-passport/athlete-biological-passport-abp-operating-guidelines, last visited 1 Dec. 2016.

286. For example, the human growth hormone test which was the subject of the discussions in connection with the famous *Andrus Veerpalu* case; TAS 2011/A/2566 Andrus Veerpalu c. International Ski Federation (FIS).

would be up to the athletes to scientifically show what the current state of science has not been able to show which is almost impossible.

357. Even in criminal law, the authorities are not always able to prove all elements of an offence directly. This is particularly true for the subjective elements of the facts, such as the knowledge and the intention of the offender. In general, the subjective state of mind of an offender cannot be directly proven and so has to be inferred from the evidenced external facts. Indirect reasoning – in the doping procedure this would be variations in the long-term blood count – is therefore generally recognized as being on par with direct reasoning.[287]

358. However, indications may be misleading and so have to be assessed very carefully and critically.[288] The requirements for proof through scientific evidence of disputed facts were developed by the Swiss Federal Supreme Court particularly in connection with paternity determination processes. According to the Swiss Federal Supreme Court, for a probability level using the biostatistical method (the Essen-Moeller Method), which was applied before DNA (Deoxyribonucleic acid) tests came into use, there must be a probability of paternity of at least 99.8%.[289] From this case law, it is clear that indirect reasoning is admissible only if the probabilities of the elements of the facts in question that need to be proven are scientifically as close as possible to the direct reasoning.

359. This principle is also acknowledged in sports law. The CAS requires a necessary degree of probability of more than 99.9% for the reliability of the recent Epo-tests as evidence.[290] The same is demanded by writers on sports law. With reference to the scientific works regarding the development of the organic blood passport, EMANUEL requires a degree of probability within the framework of indirect reasoning that is extremely high.[291] This extremely high probability of guilt has just been confirmed in the *Veerpalu* case in which WADA had not been able to show that its human growth hormone test would lead beyond any reasonable doubt – i.e., a probability of 99.99% – to reliable results.[292]

360. The WADA ABP, in its mandatory part in Annex L, provides for a sophisticated multistage process for coming to a result through indirect reasoning. The WADA, in setting up the WADA ABP, was well aware of how difficult it is to base a breach of the anti-doping rules solely on blood or urine parameters. These various steps shall ensure that the indirect reasoning is as close to the direct reasoning as is currently scientifically possible. The process is the basis for allowing a general indirect reasoning under the WADA Code to be considered at all.

287. HAUSER, SCHWERI & HARTMANN, §59 N 14.
288. HAUSER, SCHWERI & HARTMANN, §59 N 14.
289. BGE 101 II 16, C. 2.b; cf. also BGE 104 II 299 et seq.; BGE 112 II 14 et seq.
290. Decision of the CAS 2003/A/452 in the matter of *IAAF v. Fédération Royale Marocaine d'Athlétisme and Boulami*; Decision of the CAS 2001/A/343 in the matter of *UCI v. Hamburger*.
291. EMANUEL, 198, in particular FN 45.
292. TAS 2011/A/2566 Andrus Veerpalu c. International Ski Federation (FIS).

361. By this indirect reasoning process the aim is to exclude any doubt of existence of a doping offence. Since this absolute avoidance of doubt is not possible and therefore the indirect proof is always somewhat weaker than the direct, the required degree of proof must be set at the upper end of the WADA Code or above in order to respect the principle of proportionality.

362. For these legal reasons the scientific standards to establish the reliability of an indirect doping test are very high and it is up to the anti-doping authority to prove the reliability of the indirect doping test and the decision limits.[293] However, the athlete must be given the possibility to review the way the indirect doping test was established. Otherwise, the athlete's right to be heard would be violated.[294] Unfortunately, in the past the WADA had even started to establish the reliability of the indirect doping test and its decision limits the active athletes. The *Andrus Veerpalu* case had shown that by using an indirect doping test which had not fulfilled the necessary standard of proof many potentially innocent athletes were convicted.[295] Such practice is – from an ethical and legal point of view – not acceptable. For the protection of the athletes it is necessary that the reliability of the doping tests is sufficiently established before the test is used.

293. *See* Art. 3.1 WADA Code.

294. TAS 2011/A/2566 Andrus Veerpalu c. International Ski Federation (FIS); *see also* PACHMANN, CAS etabliert neue Standards für indirekten Dopingnachweis, CaS 2013/2.

295. *See* Art. 3.1 WADA Code.

Part IV. Sport and Commerce

Chapter 1. Sport and Competition Law

§1. Introduction

363. The monopolistic structure of sports and increasing commercialization of sport has led to an increase in application of competition law to sports organizations. It has become common ground that limitations to competition must be justified by the principle of specificity of sport. However, limitations to competition, which are not justified by specificity of sport are illegal.

§2. Application of Competition Law to Sports Organizations

364. Due to the one-place principle and the monopoly of sports organizations, competition law applies to sports organizations, also because their rules and acts may have an impact on the economic competition between participants. Due to the association of clubs in sports organizations, it is possible that collective market dominance may occur in markets different from those in which the sports organizations originally act, for example, due to regulations regarding dress code and placing of players.[296]

365. Other than in the US, where the sports leagues together with all participants are regarded as legal entities between whose participants there is no economic competition, sports organizations are regarded as combinations of independent enterprises in the sense of cartel law in Switzerland.[297]

296. *See,* for example, the decision of the CFI of 26 Jan. 2005 in the matter of *Piau v. European Commission and FIFA*, T-193/02, N 76 et seq.
297. Hannamann, Kartellverbot und Verhaltenskoordination im Sport, 351 et seq.; Decision of the CFI of 26 Jan. 2005 in the matter of *Piau v. European Commission and FIFA*, T-193/02, N 112 et seq.; Decision of the ECJ of 18 Jul. 2006 in the matter of *Medina und Majcen v. Commission*, C-519/04 P, N 38. According to these decisions sport organizations are regarded as an association of enterprises because their direct and indirect members are performing economic activities.

366. All rules issued by sports organizations therefore fall within the application of the EC Treaty.[298] This also applies to sport-specific rules such as doping rules. According to the ECJ, such rules are subject to review as to whether they comply with EU competition laws.[299]

367. For Switzerland, Philipp is of the opinion that in principle competition law always applies to acts of sports organizations.[300] The Cantonal Court of the Canton of Valais confirmed in a decision regarding interim measures that cartel laws apply. The SFL was considered having a dominant position.[301] About a year later, the commercial court of the Canton of Aargau ordered SFL in ex parte proceedings to qualify a player outside the transfer period for a football club.[302] In addition, international sports organizations domiciled in Switzerland cannot escape the impact of EU competition law on Switzerland because the case law of the ECJ has to be complied with in Switzerland in certain areas due to the sectoral treaties.[303] Moreover, the rules of the international sports organizations domiciled in Switzerland also have an impact on the European Market, which leads to the fact that the international sports organizations have to comply with EU competition law.

368. From the point of view of the members and stakeholders of sports organizations, the services offered are often essential facilities in the sense of competition law. For athletes and clubs access to the services of sports organizations is a prerequisite for exercising a sport at a certain level and for earning money. Athletes therefore may have a claim to be admitted or at least to be allowed to participate based on the duty of the dominating enterprise/monopoly to treat all business partners equally. It is illegal to abusively refuse business contacts.[304]

369. Such an admittance to the sporting events of a sport organizer was granted by the Cantonal Court of the Canton of Vaud on 24 June 2011. After the French middle-distance runner Hind Dehiba was banned by the IAAF between 2007 and 2009 because of a doping offence, the Diamond League Meeting Lausanne denied her participation, although the doping ban was already over. The reason thereof was an agreement between the big European athletics meetings, whereupon former doping offenders, who were punished with a ban of two years or longer, were neither allowed to participate at their meetings anymore, nor invited to participate, even if the ban was already over. In the eyes of the Cantonal Court of the Canton of Vaud this agreement was an illegitimate competition agreement that made it impossible

298. Decision of the ECJ of 18 Jul. 2006 in the matter of *Medina und Majcen v. Commission*, C-519/04 P, N 23 et seq., 27.
299. Decision of the ECJ of 18 Jul. 2006 in the matter of *Medina und Majcen v. Commission,* C-519/04 P, N 42. According to this decision there is no exemption for sports.
300. Philipp, Rechtliche Schranken der Vereinsautonomie und der Vertragsfreiheit im Einzelsport, 18.
301. Decision of the Cantonal Court of the Canton of Vaud of 20 Oct. 2003, in: CAS 2004, 37 et seq.
302. Decision of the Commercial Court of the Canton Aargau of 19 Oct. 2004, in: CAS 2005, 242 et seq.
303. *See,* for example, Art. 2 in connection with Art. 16 of the Agreement between Switzerland and the EU on the Free Movement of Persons.
304. Article 7 para. 2 lit. a CartA.

for the athletes to compete at a proper level. Therefore, it is certain that the athletes are entitled to get access to sporting events, if they fulfil the sporting criteria. Otherwise a doping ban would be equal to a lifelong ban at the discretion of the monopoly sports organizations.

§3. Specificity of Sport

370. The principle of specificity of sport may constitute a legitimate business reason for limiting competition. Reasons such as the need to limit the number of participants or the balance of sport may require, under certain circumstances, limitation to competition. However, the need for uniform regulation of sport by sports organizations only goes as far as there is a sport-specific need for that. There was no such need for the FIFA Players Agent Regulation; it was therefore subject to an inquiry as to its compliance with EU competition law.[305]

371. The hierarchic monopolistic structure of sport is only legitimate as far as it is absolutely necessary for enacting and enforcing uniform sports rules. This sports-specific necessity has been concretized in a couple of cases in the last two decades:

- In *Bosman,* the ECJ decided that the rules of football associations regarding limitations for foreign players and the limitations to the free movement of workers after expiration of the contractual term by imposing the duty to pay a transfer sum was illegal.[306]
- In *Lehtonen,* the need for certain transfer periods was confirmed because transfer during championships could change the equilibrium of sport, meaning that the results of other teams could no longer be compared.[307]
- Finally, in *Deliège,* it was decided that international sports organizations may determine the number of participants per nation, even if a different sportsperson was better compared to everybody else.[308]
- The ECJ judgment in *Medina and Majcen* confirmed sports-specific rules limiting EU law (doping limits for Nandrolon), as long as such rules comply with the current state of science.[309]

---

305. Decision of the CFI of 26 Jan. 2005 in the matter of *Piau v. European Commission and FIFA*, T-193/02, N 73, 105.
306. Decision of the ECJ of 15 Dec. 1995 in the matter of *Union royal belge des sociétés de football association ASBL v. Bosman*, coll. 1995, I-4921, N 106 et seq.
307. Decision of the ECJ of 13 Apr. 2000 in the matter of *Lehtonen v. Fédération royale belge des sociétés de basket-ball ASBL*, C-51/96 and C-191/97.
308. Decision of the ECJ of 11 Apr. 2000 in the matter of *Deliège v. Ligue belge de judo ASBL and EJU*, C-51/96 and C-191/97.
309. Decision of the ECJ of 17 Jul. 2006 in the matter of *Medina und Majcen v. Commission*, C-519/04 P, N 54.

- In the recent judgment by the ECJ *Oliver Bernard,* it was decided that a sport-specific compensation payment (compensation for training in football) may not exceed what is absolutely necessary for reaching the sport-specific purpose.[310]

372. In summary, sport-specific limitations of competition law are legal, as long as they do not exceed what is absolutely necessary for organizing competitions and ensuring their orderly course. All other limitations to competition are illegal.

373. In view of this case law and a threatened action to the ECJ, the international football organizations settled with G-14, the association of the most important European football clubs, when they claimed compensation for sending their national players to the national football teams. However, in the meantime, some other interesting rules of the sports federations such as Rule 40 of the Olympic ChARTER which prohibits athletes to carry out sponsorship activities and social media activities during the Olympic Games has become the focus of the competition authorities. The IOC has been forced to reduce the reach of Rule 40 and to give more rights to the athletes during the Olympic Games. In fact, it is highly questionable whether the IOC should have any right to limit the athletes sponsorship rights and social media activities during the Olympic Games. Other major sports events such as the FIFA World Cup do not have such excessive restrictions.

§4. Influence of the Antitrust Law on the Game

374. The antitrust law especially guarantees the right to participate in a sporting event if the sporting event is the only adequate way to exercise the sport. Based on Article 7 of the Federal Act on Cartels and other Restraints of Competition (CartA) the denial of business connections, i.e., the exclusion of clubs or athletes, which fulfil the athletic criteria for participation, is illegitimate. Based on this provision it is even possible to step into the game with preventive measures.

375. Such preventive measures were requested by the FC Sion, a football club from the Canton of Vaud, which was excluded from participation in the European League by UEFA, because some non-licensed players had played in the qualification games for the European League. The claim for preventive measures at the Cantonal Court of the Canton of Vaud to obtain permission to participate in the European League was based on arguments under the antitrust law. According to Article 5 paragraph 1 lit. b of the Swiss Civil Procedure Code the Cantonal Court of the Canton of Vaud declared itself competent. With the decision of 13 September 2011 the Court ordered UEFA with an ex parte preventive measure to authorize the participation of the FC Sion in the European League 2011/2012. However, UEFA did not act according to the decision, and even put up with the possible penalization

310. Decision of the ECJ of 16 Mar. 2010 in the matter of *Olympique Lyonnais SASP v. Oliver Bernard/ Newcastle United*, C-325/08.

of its organs by not reversing the exclusion of the FC Sion. In the following decision the Cantonal Court of the Canton of Vaud prohibited UEFA explicitly to validate the corresponding results on 16 September 2011.

376. Therewith the Cantonal Court has irrevocably affected the sporting competition based on the antitrust law. The interests of the other clubs were seen as less important in the face of the main issue prediction. Therefore the Cantonal Court affirmed that the rules of play cannot be in breach with the mandatory Swiss law.

Chapter 2. Free Movement in Swiss Sports

377. With the Agreement on the Free Movement of Persons between Switzerland and the EU of 21 June 1999, in force as of 1 June 2002,[311] the basic principle that the free movement of labour shall be applicable within the EU has been extended to Switzerland. Swiss nationals and EU nationals received the right to freely choose their place of work and residence in Switzerland and in all Member States of the EU. There is thus a non-discrimination rule regarding nationality. Even though Switzerland decided in February 2014 to limit the free movement of EU nationals to take residency in Switzerland there are no real effects on sports expected.

378. The Agreement on the Free Movement of Persons also had a significant impact on professional sport. All persons performing sports as an economic activity may rely on the non-discrimination rule of the Agreement on the Free Movement of Persons. The coaches may, for example, take up employment in all EU countries and Switzerland and their education will be recognized as equivalent. In principle, the same is true for sportspersons.

379. When designing sporting contests, often the criterion of nationality plays an important role (so-called foreigner clause). The question of how this can be compatible with the freedom of movement then arises. In the *Bosman* ruling, the ECJ held that the foreigner clause in the team sports in question was not compatible with the EU law.[312] The restrictions regarding the participation in sporting competitions based on nationality (national team) were, by contrast, regarded permissible due to a sports-specific exigency. To what extent the FIFA's aim for a 6 + 5 rule, for which the FIFA regards the requirement of a sport-specific exigency to be fulfilled because of the promotion of young talents for national teams, will endure in light of this jurisprudence is not yet clear. Its legitimacy is at least questionable.

380. In Switzerland, the jurisprudence has also confirmed the application of the Agreement on the Free Movement of Persons. In the case of Basel Magic, it was held that the rule of a sports organization (i.e., of the Swiss Floorball Association) that had limited the number of foreign players from the EU, was inadmissible.[313] A violation of the Agreement on the Free Movement of Persons was as well assumed in a decision of the district court VIII Bern-Laupen of 13 June 2008 when Swiss Athletics introduced a 'foreigner clause' (the limitation of the foreigners that are maximal allowed in a competition) into its regulations. The mandatory Swiss law, that is, the treaty with the EU, limits the activities of sports organizations.

---

311. SC 0.142.112.681.
312. Decision of the ECJ of 15 Dec. 1995 in the matter of Bosman, C-415/93.
313. Decision of the Court of Appeal of the Canton of Berne of 15 Nov. 2003 (S-0395/II/2003).

Chapter 3. The Role of Switzerland as a Host

§1. Background

381. A survey by the International Academy of Sports Science and Technology (AISTS) showed that the forty-five main international sporting associations headquARTERed in Switzerland contributed an average of CHF 1.07 billion (some USD 1.16 billion) annually to the Swiss economy between 2008 and 2013.[314, 315]

382. These numbers show that sport and sporting associations have experienced significant professionalization and commercialization in recent years. In line with this growth, correspondingly numerous measures are either in the process of being implemented or at the planning stage to combat the increased scope for corruption and betting manipulation in sport at the national and international levels. It is therefore incumbent on Switzerland, as a hub of international sporting associations, to rise to the challenge with a range of measures of its own. This article highlights the most important changes in Switzerland regarding the investigation and prosecution of corruption in sport.

§2. The Current Situation

383. Although Switzerland is perceived to be one of the countries least affected by corruption,[316] regular amendments to the criminal law on corruption are necessary as it applies to international sport organizations.[317] The seven-member Swiss Federal Council – which serves as the Swiss head of state – approves such amendments.

I. Bribery under Swiss Criminal law

384. Article 322*ter* of the Swiss Criminal Code punishes the active and passive bribery of Swiss or foreign public officials. These rules are special torts, which means that bribery is punishable under criminal law only if the individual bribed is a public official. A public official must be either a member of an authority or a court, an official, an officially appointed expert, a translator, an interpreter, a referee or a member of the army.[318]

385. In the year 2016 new provisions on the bribery of private individuals came into force. Before, sports organizations were not subject to the provisions of the

314. This section bases on the published article Valloni & Neuenschwander, p.321.

315. Bousigue & Stricker.

316. *See* Transparency International, 'Corruption by Country/Territory: Switzerland', http://*www.transparency.org/country#CHE* .

317. *See* the press release of the Federal Council from 30 Apr. 2014 about the amendments to the Swiss Criminal Code (criminal law on corruption).

318. *See* Arts 322*ter* and 322*quater* of the Swiss Criminal Code.

swiss anti-bribery and corruption law. Private corruption merely was a criminal offence if it led to a distortion of competition within the meaning of the Federal Act against Unfair Competition (UCA). The applicability of the Federal Act against Unfair Competition presupposed a competitive relationship between the participating parties in such an act, however.[319] Hence, it had been unclear whether the act was applicable in the field of sport or not. In a ruling given in 2004, the Federal Council had expressed the opinion that the act did merely apply to non-governmental organizations (NGOs) – and therefore sports organizations – if they are in a competitive relationship.[320]

386. This has been repeatedly criticized both at an international level and in parliament (e.g., the lack of convictions was criticized).[321] In its message on the revision of the anti-corruption law the Federal Council stated that – due to the controversy that arose regarding the suspicion of corruption in connection with the awarding of the 2018 and 2022 FIFA World Cups – the criminal offence of private bribery must be detached from the concept of unfair competition and included in the Criminal Code as a separate criminal offence.[322] The Federal Council further highlighted that only with this amendment the position of international sports federations could be clarified.[323]

387. Finally, the new Articles 322^{octies} and 322^{novies} were included in the Criminal Code. Private bribery is now considered a criminal offence under the Swiss Criminal Code and is generally prosecuted ex officio (i.e. that such crime has to be prosecuted by the State prosecutor in case of any knowledge of such crime and without any intervention of any third party). The provisions on bribery of individuals entail both the act of bribing (Art. 322^{octies} CC) and the reception of a bribe (Art. 322^{novies} CC). The act of bribing is defined as the offer, the promise or the giving of an undue advantage to a person in order that the person carries out or fails to carry out an act in connection with his official activities which is contrary to his duties or dependent on his discretion (Art. 322^{octies} CC). The reception of a bribe is considered the demand, the securitization of the promise or the acceptance of an undue advantage in order that the receiving person carries out or fails to carry out an act in connection with his official activities which is contrary to his duties or dependent on his discretion. The application of Articles 322^{octies} and 322^{novies} CC is limited to cases where there is a triangular relationship, i.e., the scope of the provision is limited to business and officials activities.[324] The person who bribed [*extraneus*] or can be bribed (employee, shareholder, agent or other auxiliary person of a

319. Message of the Federal Council concerning the Approval and Implementation of the Criminal Law Convention and the Additional Protocol of the Council of Europe on Corruption (Amendment of the Swiss Criminal Code and the Federal Law against Unfair Competition), BBl 2004 6983.
320. *Ibid.*, p. 7007.
321. GRECO evaluation report of 21.10.2011, § 87.
322. Message of the Federal Council concerning the amendment of the Criminal Code (anti-corruption law), BBI 2014 3591.
323. BBI 2014 3593.
324. BBI 2014 3600, 3609; see also *inter alia* Basler Kommentar-Pieth, N 3 to Art. 322octies CC; Praxiskommentar-Betz, N 10 to Art. 322octies CC.

third party; [*intraneus*]) is in a trust relationship with a third party who is the victim of the bribe (employer, corporate entity, principal, principal of the auxiliary person; [*principal*]).[325]

388. Indeed, with this amendment of the Criminal Code on private bribery the basis to clarify the legal situation regarding the corruption in sports organizations could be built. As a consequence, it would de lege lata be considered an act of private bribery if members of an association received financial benefits in preferring the bid of a city that was aiming to host a major sporting event. Besides, if an attempt was being made, with bribery payments to or from private companies, to influence a competitive relationship, such as the conclusion of sponsorship agreements, then such an act could be qualified as bribery under Article 322^{octies} CC, Article 322^{novies} CC respectively. It remains to be seen what influence the amendment will have from a practical point of view.

II. Anti-Money-Laundering Rules

389. One of the major changes in Swiss law regarding the fight against corruption in sport associations has concerned the amendments to the anti-money-laundering rules. In recent years the Organization for Economic Co-operation and Development (OECD), through its Financial Action Task Force (FATF) on anti-money-laundering (also known as the Groupe d'Action Financière: GAFI), has urged its member countries – including Switzerland – to tighten their anti-money-laundering regulations.[326] On 12 December 2014, the Act on the Implementation of the Revised Recommendations of FATF was adopted by the Swiss Parliament.[327] In these amended recommendations the FATF has extended the definition of a politically exposed person (PEP) to include senior politicians and officials of international sports organizations based in Switzerland.[328]

390. The most important amendments, which now also affect officials of sports organizations, are that cash transactions may not exceed CHF 100,000 (some USD

325. Handkommentar-Wohlers, N 2 to Art. 322^{octies} CC.

326. Swissinfo.ch, 'Switzerland tightens its money-laundering rules', 13 Dec. 2014, http://*www.swissinfo.ch/eng/business/coming-clean_switzerland-tightens-its-money-laundering-rules/41168000.*

327. The Federal Council decided on 29 Apr. 2015 to set the federal law in two steps into force. Firstly, the forthcoming autumn 2015 Peer Review of the Global Forum on transparency and exchange of information for tax purposes requires as soon as possible the enactment of the provisions on transparency of legal entities and bearer shares, which is why these provisions are set in force on 1 Jul. 2015. On the contrary the remaining legislative amendments require either the drafting of implementing regulations at an ordinance level or certain implementation work by the affected norm addressees. With enactment on 1 Jan. 2016, the necessary time should be given in particular to financial intermediaries and self-regulatory organizations according to the Money Laundering Act in order to take the necessary time to arrange the implementation. *See*: https://www.sif.admin.ch/sif/de/home/themen/bekaempfung-der-finanzkriminalitaet.html.

328. Message of the Federal Council concerning the Implementation of the Recommendations of the Financial Action Task Force, Revised in 2012, SR 13.106', BBI 2014 585, p. 620.

108,000) and that serious tax offences are considered as a predicate offence to money laundering.[329] This means that a seller has to identify and register any person who wants to pay more than CHF 100,000 in cash, or the money has to be transferred.

§3. CONCLUSION

391. As the most important hub for the world's most important sports organizations, it is crucial that Switzerland lead by example in the fight against corruption in sport. It seems that the country's legislature is now starting to see this; this may be why Switzerland is the first signatory of the Convention on the Manipulation of Sports Competitions.[330]

392. Protecting the integrity and credibility of sport requires enhanced governmental regulation. The indictment by US authorities and arrest of fourteen current and former FIFA officials in Zurich on 27 May 2015 [331] shows that sport organizations' Corporate Governance rules were clearly not sufficient. The fight against corruption in sport is primarily the task of the private sports organizations, yet states' legal systems and their governments must provide these organizations with the necessary legal framework. In the past sport organizations in Switzerland always asserted their autonomy, and until now the state has granted this autonomy. With autonomy comes responsibility, however, and whether this responsibility has been lived up to or not in the past remains an open question. Given that an organization of the stature of FIFA was apparently unable to do so, it seems the only logical consequence that the state now intervened in a regulatory way which is likely to happen in other areas as well.

393. Corruption in sport must be combated by all stakeholders joining forces, working together with the state authorities. Legal reforms are a first and important step in the right direction. It is clear that, in Switzerland at least, the force of criminal authority was required, to make use of compulsory measures, as the civil law was inadequate to deal with illegal activities carried out by the most powerful organizations, such as the FIFA and the IOC.

---

329. Swissinfo.ch (13 Dec. 2014).

330. *See* Council of Europe, 'Convention on the Manipulation of Sports Competitions', *http://conventions.coe.int/Treaty/EN/Treaties/Html/215.htm*. This treaty, pledging better prevention and prosecution of match-fixing and corruption in sports, was discussed and signed by thirty European sports ministers in Magglingen/Macolin, Switzerland, in 2014, and according to the Swiss Federal Office of Sport (Bundesamt für Sport: BASPO) the Swiss sports minister, Ueli Maurer, led the meeting: http://*www.baspo.admin.ch/internet/baspo/de/home/aktuell/sportminister_unterzeichnen_konvention_gegen_wettkampfmanipulation.html*.

331. This is the scandal surrounding FIFA regarding the arrests in Zurich on 27 May 2015 as well as the start of criminal proceedings in the United States against several FIFA officials: *see*, for example, SCHWEIZER Radio und Fernsehen, 'Zum Nachlesen: Protokoll der Ereignisse um den Fifa-Skandal', 27 May 2015, http://*www.srf.ch/news/international/zum-nachlesen-protokoll-der-ereignisse-um-den-fifa-skandal*.

Chapter 4. Bidding for Sporting Events

§1. Set of Problems

394. The awarding of sporting events, in particular of the international sport federations, has become very lucrative in the course of the commercialization of sports. Therefore, the organizers try to convince the deciding body – in general the (board) members of the sport federation – of their advantages with all possible means.

395. After the Salt Lake City Affair the bidding process of the IOC was revised because of corruption, and in particular the visits of the IOC members to the potential host cities were stopped. Despite these measures the bidding process of the IOC is still not immune against improper and even illegal influence of the organizers.

396. There was also constant criticism of FIFA about the way the FIFA Executive Committee selects the host country for the FIFA World Cup. After members of the FIFA Executive Committee were bribed, allegedly with a sum of USD 1,000,000, during the bidding process for the FIFA World Cups 2018 and 2022, the FIFA launched an Ethic Commission and the accused members of the Executive Committee were excluded from the selection process. At the FIFA Congress in 2015 the selection process was finally amended (*see* Article 69 paragraph 2 FIFA Statutes). The General Secretariat evaluates the candidate countries and the FIFA Council proposes in an open ballot a maximum number of three to the Congress which chooses the host country for the FIFA World Cup. Unfortunately, the vote of the FIFA Congress is not open. Just the result is made public.

§2. Legal Actions Against the Choice of the Host City

397. As all other decisions of an association the decision concerning the awarding of sporting competitions can be appealed according to Article 75 of the Swiss Civil Code and/or declared null and void (for more information *see* below).

398. Additionally, the other routes could also be pursued. As the bribery of sports federations' officials has become illegal one could argue that this made the entire decision null and void. Further, it would be thinkable to file a report to the competition commission complaining about the sport federation which is illegally making use of its dominant position according to Article 7 CartA. These legal means have so far not been explored.

§3. Possible Claims Against the Sport Federation

399. Civil Claims of unsuccessful bidders are basically possible based on Articles 41 and 8 of the Swiss Code of Obligations, or *culpa in contrahendo*.

400. According to Article 41 of the Swiss Code of Obligations anybody who unlawfully causes loss or damage to another party, whether intentionally or negligently, is obliged to provide compensation. As the damage is usually only a financial damage, it will further be necessary to base the claim on a special clause, which has the purpose to avoid such damages.

401. According to Article 8 of the Swiss Code of Obligations a person who publicly promises remuneration or a reward in exchange for the performance of an act must pay in accordance with his promise. If he withdraws his promise before performance has been made, he must reimburse any person incurring expenditure in good faith on account of the promise up to the maximum amount promised unless he can prove that such person could not have provided the performance in question.

402. Based on *culpa in contrahendo* someone invited by an organizer to bid and afterwards does not adhere to the procurement directives is liable too.

403. In any case, it has to be evaluated on a case-by-case basis if a liability of the sports association really exists. However, no candidate has so far tried to legally pursue these routes.

§4. Criminal Liability of the Persons in Charge of the Decision

404. The Swiss Criminal Code only sanctions office holders and not officials of private organizations. The Articles 322*ter* et seq. of the Swiss Criminal Code are only applicable if a civil servant in the sense of Article 110 paragraph 3 of the Swiss Criminal Code is bribed. As outlined above (see above *Bribery under Swiss Criminal law*) in more detail this gap has been closed with the Articles 322^{octies} and 322^{novies} of the Criminal Code. Officials of sports associations are now also subject to the anti-bribery regulations.

Chapter 5. Selection Criteria and Selection Decisions

405. For organizational reasons national and international sports organizations often establish access restrictions for sporting events. Participants must meet certain athletic requirements. Thereby, sportspersons are, in principle, restricted in their rights to free professional development. However, such restriction is in fact necessary due to the specificity of sports. The question is according to what principles this restriction should be given effect. This question is in particular important in the case several athletes fulfil the sporting selection criteria.

406. At the selections, two different interests collide: the sports organization cannot allow all sportspersons to participate for logistical reasons and therefore has to make a choice. While the sports organization wishes a wide discretion when making a selection decision, the sportspersons have an interest in their selection being as foreseeable and fair as possible. These interests must be balanced against each other.

407. A prerequisite for establishing the selection criteria and for making a selection decision is that the body that makes those decisions: (i) either acts free from any conflicts of interest or that (ii) the interests of all participants are adequately represented in the decision-making process. Otherwise the decision may possibly be challengeable due to the presumption of a procedural error.[332]

408. From the jurisprudence of the CAS has emerged that the sports organizations will be protected in their decisions if they had reserved discretion in their selection criteria. The reason for such jurisprudence is the fact that the CAS simply applies the regulations of the sports federations without reviewing whether any mandatory law requires more strict selection criteria.[333] In contrast, the principle of legality of the association and especially the antitrust law requires that 'hard' and performance-based selection criteria need to be established so, that the performance power in the target competition can be assessed as well as possible. Also in the light of this background, there is no complete freedom of choice for the sports organizations. At least any decision based on a reserved discretion has to be justifiable on material (sporting) grounds. Otherwise the inappropriate exertion of the discretion may be challenged.

332. To the application of the so-called Business-Judgment-Rule *see* PACHMANN, Corporate Governance, 191.

333. *See* CAS High Court 06/2002, *Andrea Schuler v. Swiss Olympic and Swiss-Ski*, Decision of 12 Feb. 2006; CAS High Court 06/2008, *Isabella Dal Balcon v. Comitato Olimpico Nazionale Italiano and Federazione Italiana Sport Invernali*, Decision of 18 Feb. 2006; *see* as well BGE 121 III 350, where a sport association acts illegal, if an additional elimination contest is required after the communication of the selection criteria.

Chapter 6. Sponsorship

§1. Definition and Demarcation

409. Basically sponsors and patrons or benefactors have to be differentiated from each other.

410. The *sponsor* always receives a consideration by the sportsperson or the sports organization for his services. The sponsor provides the sportsperson or the sports organization with funds, equipment or other services, for which the sponsor will typically have the right to advertise. These mutual benefits are in balance with each other.

411. In contrast to the sponsors, the *patrons* and the *benefactors* do not expect a direct return for their support. These contracts are therefore more likely to qualify as gifts within the meaning of Articles 239 et seq. Swiss Code of Obligations.

412. In many cases, the patrons and the benefactors will be officially called and thanked in public. Of course this also provides all patrons and benefactors with a certain contribution – their 'selfless' reputation will be ameliorated. The distinction between sponsors and patrons or benefactors will therefore always be somewhat unclear.

§2. Legal Qualification of the Sponsorship Agreement

413. In the Swiss doctrine, the sponsorship agreement is referred to as a synallagmatic permanent contract sui generis.[334] The services of the contracting parties are reciprocal over a long period of time. However, often the contracts with *patrons* and *benefactors* are called sponsorship contracts which makes their legal qualification more difficult.

414. As a contract of no specific type, the sponsorship agreement may embody elements of an employment agreement (Articles 319 et seq. Swiss Code of Obligations), of a purchase contract (Articles 184 et seq. Swiss Code of Obligations), of a contract for a simple partnership (Articles 530 et seq. Swiss Code of Obligations), of a mandate (Articles 396 et seq. Swiss Code of Obligations), of an agency agreement (Articles 418a et seq. Swiss Code of Obligations) and of a licence agreement (compare Articles 275 et seq. Swiss Code of Obligations). Which provisions will apply depend on what provisions will fit best regarding the nature of the specific contractual services. Because of the variety of sponsorship agreements, it may not be clearly determined in advance which provisions of mandatory and non-mandatory law apply.

334. Netzle, Sponsoring von Sportverbänden, Zurich 1988, 11 et seq.

415. The content of the sponsorship agreement is limited by mandatory law. It is, for example, inadmissible to require the sponsored party to conduct any particularly dangerous acts or to bind himself for life (*see* Article 27 paragraph 2 Swiss Civil Code). Contracts with impossible contents are (partially) void (Article 20 Swiss Code of Obligations).

§3. Legal Barriers: Alcohol and Tobacco Advertising

416. Sponsorship for alcohol and tobacco are legally restricted. Since 1964, the advertising of tobacco on radio and television is prohibited in Switzerland. Also, since 1995 the advertising of tobacco that is targeted at teenagers and children under 18 is prohibited. This includes the supply of free promotional items to teenagers and advertising in places where mainly teenagers hang out.[335] This ban also applies to domestic and foreign broadcasters, provided that the programmes broadcast in Switzerland, nationwide or in the regions are specifically addressed to the Swiss public.

417. In the agreement with the (EC) concerning the participation of Switzerland in the EU film supporting programme media, it was agreed, that with respect to the advertising of alcohol on television the law of the country of origin shall apply. According to this agreement, any advertising that is lawful in the country of origin shall be admissible in Switzerland.[336]

418. In contrast to the EU, where tobacco advertising in newspapers and magazines has been banned since 2005, in Switzerland no absolute ban on advertising of tobacco has been adopted at the federal level. The legislative body has spoken out against a parliamentary motion to that effect, because this massive restriction was deemed as economically harmful. Thus, in general, public space is available for billboard advertising of tobacco companies and they can be sponsors of major sporting events.[337]

419. At the cantonal level, however, many Cantons have begun to ban tobacco advertising that is visible from public ground. The Swiss Federal Supreme Court has considered these cantonal advertising bans admissible. These advertising bans are compatible with the freedom of expression, the economic freedom, the principle of guarantee of ownership and the law on the internal market.[338]

§4. Legal Disputes in Sponsoring Relationships

420. Where Swiss law is to be applied, Articles 97 et seq. of the Swiss Code of Obligations are applicable in cases of non-performance or poor performance of

335. Article 10 RTVG.
336. SC 07.074.
337. The most famous example is the Davidoff Swiss Indoors, an ATP 500 tournament in Basle.
338. BGE 128 I 295 et seq.

sponsorship contracts. Such remedies allow the creditors to insist on the fulfilment of the contract, to require the payment of damages or rescind the contract. There is not much case law on sponsorship deals because the parties usually conclude confidentiality agreements and prefer to settle disputes through mediation and/or arbitration. The gain of reputation as a characteristic of a sponsorship agreement contract usually survives the contract period. Therefore, neither the sponsor nor the sponsored party wants to fight out their disputes legally afterwards.

Chapter 7. Broadcasting

§1. Holder of Television Rights

421. The question of the holder of broadcasting rights is governed by national law. Under Swiss law, it will first be checked as to whether and, if so, what rights at a sporting event can exist at all and who is entitled to these rights.

422. Direct property rights in terms of Articles 641 et seq. Swiss Civil Code in the product of a 'sport event' are generally disregarded because of the lack of possibility of actual exercisable ruling power. Thus, it is necessary to check whether legal protection from intellectual property rights can be derived for sports events as works or services. In this context, the Copyright Act is potentially of relevance. However, its application in connection with sports events in Switzerland was negated. The same is true according to the jurisprudence of the ECJ, which held recently that 'the English Premier League cannot claim any copyrights regarding its football games, as these sporting events are not intellectual creations of a creator and therewith no creations in the sense of the copyright act'.[339]

423. The ownership and possession rights (so-called home-right) of a stadium gives the holder the right and opportunity to concede the broadcasting right namely the right, to broadcast the sports event through a live broadcast signal and commercial audiovisual records via a transmission rights agreement to a third party. The spectator may be contractually prohibited to broadcast through a spectator's contract. If the broadcasting right is transferred to a third party by means of a contractual relationship, the latter receives de facto control over the signal as a result of his or her 'own production' of the live transmission signal and he or she is able – within the applicable legal order – to shape this control in his or her own discretion through agreements with host broadcasters and the respective broadcasting company. The question of whether the live television signal of a football game is a proprietary work in the sense of an 'other audiovisual work' under the Copyright Law is debated in the Swiss legal doctrine and it seems, judicially not decided yet.

§2. How Are These Rights Being Marketed?

424. In addition to broadcasting on television, there are other forms of media exploitation. We distinguish three forms of exploitation rights: (a) the primary exploitation rights, which are limited to the direct transfer of a sports event, (b) the secondary exploitation rights, which are the rights to record sport events in order to replicate them either partially or completely for broadcast and (c) the third exploitation rights, which include the sale of recordings on video and other media as well as the use of photographs (e.g., for the internet).

339. 3.Decision of the ECJ of 4 Oct. 2011 in the matters C-403/08 and C-429/08.

425. All commercial rights are used in different ways. Thus, for example, the television signal is also broadcasted via DSL (Digital Subscriber Line) or mobile broadcasting technologies. With a television broadcasting at the same time, new marketing opportunities are offered, particularly with the possibility of downloadable clips on mobile devices such as smartphones or tablets. Such broadcastings are almost feasible in television quality; nevertheless, the potential exclusivity of a holder of television rights is not always affected. Thus, key competitive scenes, all goals or summaries of the entire event can be made available for viewing at any time, so-called on-demand-recall, or can be forwarded in near-live to interested individuals. A parallel playback to television broadcasting on the internet, so-called streaming is not independently exploitable. It is widely acknowledged that streaming on the internet – in comparison to television – is not an independently exploitable right, but only a broadcast on a different platform. However, new media opened up new ways to consume media and with recent concerns of competition authorities on the joint selling of sport media rights, broadcast rights are nowadays often split up into separate rights packages that are sold separately (and in proper tender procedures). A broadcast on the internet can be commercially interesting if the event cannot be fully placed on television, which presently concerns less media-oriented events. In this case, especially for minority sports, a broadcast on the internet opens a chance to make the sporting competition accessible to a wider audience, possibly upon the payment of a fee.

§3. Influence of Competition Law?

426. The autonomy of sports organizations is restricted from the standpoint of competition law if a dominant position or a special relationship of dependency exists. As to whether the ownership of the rights to a sports event in fact constitutes a dominant position can only be assessed in each individual case, after an exact market demarcation of the factual, geographic and temporal aspects. A potential central marketing of broadcasting rights can further accentuate any monopoly position, especially in the downstream media markets. The European Commission accepts the joint selling of broadcasting rights, provided certain conditions were fulfilled.[340] These include, *inter alia*, the sale of the rights through open and transparent procurement procedures, the limitation of the rights' duration (usually not exceeding three years) and the breaking down of the rights into different packages to allow several competitors to acquire rights.

427. From the perspective of competition law, the central marketing of sports media rights seems to be extremely problematic under both Swiss law and the competition laws of other European countries. By jointly selling their media rights (as

340. The European Commission has set forth the main principles in the UEFA Champions League (COMP/37.398), the FA Premier League (COMP/38.173) and Bundesliga (COMP/37.214) decisions.

opposed to the sale by the individual clubs themselves), the clubs hinder competition between each other regarding the price and terms and the design of these rights (including the use of the rights for free television, pay-television and new media).

428. In principle, the applicability of competition law to the actions of the sports organizations in Switzerland is affirmed. In addition, the international sports organizations with residency in Switzerland cannot escape the impact of EU competition law on Switzerland, particularly since the jurisprudence of the ECJ must be observed as a consequence of sectoral agreements in certain fields.

Chapter 8. Ambush Marketing

§1. Term

429. Ambush Marketing is a term of the advertising industry and not a legal concept. In general, the term has a negative connotation, since it is a generic term for various promotional measures that aim to associate a product or a service positively with an event, without the existence of an approval of the organizer for this relationship. However, the term 'Ambush Marketing' provides no indication as to the legality or the illegality of an activity.

430. The term Ambush Marketing is known and popular since the Football World Cup 2006 in Germany at the latest. Before and during the UEFA EURO 2008 it became a much-discussed topic in Switzerland, particularly because the UEFA requested a change in legislation in this regard (which was not accepted in the end).[341] Such changes in legislation are often requested by the international sports federations which led the Olympic Games in London to the London Olympic Games and Paralympics Games Act 2012 prohibiting any resale of tickets and the use of any words that had anything to do with the 2012 London Olympic Games.

§2. Remedy

431. Organizers of major events will find protection against unwelcome Ambush Marketing primarily in intellectual property rights. Trademark law may be intensively used as protection against the misuse of 'event brands'. Special importance is attached to so-called famous brands. They grant a general right of protection for all goods and services without any requirement for similarity which is otherwise required under Swiss trademark law, for example, the Olympic Rings. In contrast, some other 'event brands' of international sports federations can hardly be considered as famous brands.

432. Furthermore, copyright provides protection for intellectual creations. In this context, it needs to be considered that the copyright on photographs of sports events also includes the broadcasting rights.

433. Similar to trademark protection, design law can be considered for the protection of event symbols such as logos, mascots, and emblems and event and sports dresses.

434. From a civil law perspective, the so-called corporate and brand name right also offers protection against Ambush Marketing, in addition to the trademark law. Furthermore, protection rights can be derived from the 'home rules', personal rights and contract law.

---

341. Cf. Thaler, Ambush Marketing mit der UEFA EURO 2008, 160–179.

435. From a fair trade law perspective, Article 2 of the UCL provides protection from unwanted publicity. However, the remedy to be effected hereby is not clear and requires further definition by the courts. This led to the fact that, in the run-up to the UEFA EURO 2008, the introduction of a privileged legal protection regarding sports events under the competition law was discussed by the sports organizers. But, the bill containing a new Article 3e*bis* of the competition law was rejected. Accordingly, no direct prohibition on referring to sporting events exists as such in Switzerland. Therefore, the general rules of competition law, and thus, the general clause of the fair trade law and the codified special provisions in Article 3, still apply, but they do not provide for fundamental protection of a sporting event.[342]

342. Cf. THALER, Ambush Marketing mit der UEFA EURO 2008, 179–180.

Chapter 9. Betting in Sports

436. In Switzerland, the market for gambling is not liberalized. The Federal Lotteries and Commercial Betting Act (LBA)[343] bars private providers from offering and brokering commercial betting (Articles 1 and 33 LBA). Only the non-commercial offering of betting, in which the entire pool will be distributed back to the players, is allowed in Switzerland.

437. In Switzerland, only Swisslos and Lottery of Romande are allowed to offer sports betting. They are obliged to return a portion of their profits to the sport. This profit is distributed by the Sport Toto Society and the cantonal sports-toto funds.

438. As it is difficult for organizers of sporting events in Switzerland to finance their events, the betting ban is under political pressure. At present however, foreign football teams, sponsored by a betting provider, that play in Switzerland in an international competition have to remove the logo of their sponsor.

439. Nevertheless, private betting companies from other countries offer their services to Switzerland by internet. Swiss law is factually undermined, although the offering of such betting is illegal in Switzerland. Participants from Switzerland will, however, not be sanctioned.

440. Pursuant to Article 513 Swiss Code of Obligations, claims on (sports) bets are not legally enforceable in Switzerland.

441. Although sports betting is valued by many fans and became a major economic sector in other countries, the impact is not always appreciated by the sports organizations. The *Hoyzer* case and the *Fenerbace Istanbul* case have shown that there is a risk that referees may be bribed. To this end, FIFA has created a warning system (so-called Early Warning System), which should identify potential frauds in cooperation with bookmakers and betting providers. SFL/SFV and SAFP have, for example, introduced the Red Button App together to combat match-fixing.[344] This is a system that allows the players and staff to anonymously report a match-fixing incident.

442. On 1 January 2019, new provisions on the measures to combat competition rigging came into force. Direct as well as indirect competition rigging is now considered a statutory offence under the Sport Promotion Act.[345] Persons committing direct or indirect competition rigging will be held liable to a custodial sentence not exceeding three years or to a monetary penalty.

---

343. SC 935.51.
344. *See* http://www.sfl.ch/news/news/artikel/red-button-meldesystem-fuer-spielmanipulationen/.
345. Articles 25a and 25b Federal Act on the Promotion of Sport and Exercise (Sport Promotion Act, SpoPA).

443. Besides, on 1 September 2019 Council of Europe Convention on the Manipulation of Sports Competitions came into force in Switzerland. The convention aims to prevent and detect manipulation and to promote coordination and cooperation among nations, especially since manipulation of sports competitions is considered a problem that cannot be solved at the national level alone. Furthermore, the manipulation of sports competitions shall be combatted in order to protect the integrity of sport and sports ethics in accordance with the principle of the autonomy of sport.[346]

346. Article 1 Council of Europe Convention on the Manipulation of Sports Competitions (Magglingen Convention).

Chapter 10. Regulation of the Player-Agent Business

444. Switzerland has no specific laws for player-agent agreements in sports. Moreover, the agents of players have formed unions or established their own rules (self-regulation), as known from other sectors.

445. Of the sports organizations it is the FIFA that has replaced the former FIFA regulations on agents with the new regulations on working with intermediaries.[347] The new FIFA regulations contain minimum requirements which have been implemented in various ways at national level worldwide. However, the new FIFA regulations failed to address serious concerns in relation to the activities of intermediaries. This is also the view of the EU Sectoral Social Dialogue Committee for Professional Football. UEFA, FIFPRO Division Europe, the ECA and the EPFL have agreed on 17 November 2017 in Brussels on a joint resolution in this regard. It is a fact that the transparency in financial transactions involving intermediaries had not improved as a consequence of the new FIFA regulations. Furthermore, the number of individuals or companies acting as intermediaries had increased substantially, which may have had the effect of pushing demand for even younger players. The quality of the services provided to clubs and players by intermediaries had generally decreased. Important to note is also that the new FIFA regulations had had little impact on slowing down the inflation of fees paid to intermediaries but actually contributed to further disproportionate growth of such payments. Apart from that it is important to note also that a lack of consistency in the implementation of the rules from one territory to aNOTHer had made some national 'markets' more attractive than others for intermediaries. Clear is also that the administrative burden on all parties (i.e., national associations, national leagues, clubs and players) had increased unnecessarily and to no positive effect. Hence, it is clear that more effective and sustainable regulatory framework is required to address the many challenges associated with the activities of intermediaries.

446. The SFV[348] has regulated the player-agent business as requested by the FIFA regulations but kept it at the minimum standard and did not introduce stronger rules. Apparently, there are no similar rules of other sports organizations.

447. According to the Swiss Federal Supreme Court the player-agent agreement – despite the elements of an agency or brokerage agreement, which is qualified as a mixed contract – is subject to the provisions of the mandate pursuant to Articles 394 et seq Code of Obligations. The application of the provisions of the mandate means primarily that a player and an agent may basically terminate their professional relationship at any time. It is not possible to deviate from this right.

---

347. FIFA Players' Agent Regulations (2015) (accessible via http://www.fifa.com).
348. SFV Regulations for Intermediaries (2017) (accessible via http://org.football.ch/portaldata/28/Resources/dokumente/de/04_nichtamateure_und_vermittler/4.4_SFV-Reglement_Arbeit_mit_Vermittlern.pdf).

448. Furthermore, the Employment Services Act (ESA)[349] may be applied if work is placed for a consideration. The aforementioned Act contains a number of provisions for the protection of job seekers. The ESA is, in particular, of major importance with respect to team sports such as hockey and football. However, the ESA must be observed by anyone who regularly places work for a consideration in Switzerland. These placement officers need an operating permit of the cantonal employment office if work is placed in Switzerland (even in case they already have a permit from a foreign country) and, for placements abroad an authorization of the State Secretariat for Economic Affairs (SECO) is required.[350] This permit is also required from every intermediary acting on Swiss territory. A permit is only granted to companies registered in the Swiss Commercial Register with appropriate business premises and conducting no other business, which could jeopardize the interests of job seekers or employees.[351] The managing persons must be a Swiss national or a foreigner with a residence permit, having a good record and must guarantee to offer a professional placement.[352] It is essential that the placement contract, which is provided for a consideration, is in writing and provides for all services and the compensation payable.[353] Agreements that prevent job seekers to turn to aNOTHer agent are void (prohibition of exclusivity clauses).[354] Contract provisions that oblige job seekers to pay the agency fee again if they enter into further employment agreements with the same employer but without the help of the agent are also void.[355] In addition to a registration fee of maximum CHF 40, the agent can require from the job seeker a commission for the successful placement, the amount of which is determined by the Federal Council ('*Bundesrat*') and currently limited to 5% of the initial gross annual salary.[356] For persons who intentionally place work without the required permit the ESA provides in its criminal law provision for penalties of up to CHF 100,000.[357] An employer who intentionally calls for services of an agent not in possession of the required permit will be penalized with forfeiture to the amount of up to CHF 40,000.[358] The agent who intentionally violates the provisions regarding the commission will be penalized with forfeiture to the amount of up to CHF 40,000.[359] Hence, intermediaries from foreign countries mandatorily need such a state licence or they have to work together with someone who has such a licence in Switzerland.

---

349. SC 823.11.
350. Article 2 para. 2 and para. 3 ESA.
351. Article 3 para. 1 ESA.
352. Article 3 para. 2 ESA.
353. Article 8 para. 1 ESA.
354. Article 8 para. 2 lit. a ESA.
355. Article 8 para. 2 lit. b ESA.
356. Article 3 para. 1 of the Ordinance on fees, commissions and deposits related to the ESA (SC 823.113). It may well be that quite a number of football players might be able to reclaim some of the fees paid to the agents based on this provision. However, to our knowledge there were no such cases so far.
357. Article 39 para. 1 lit. a ESA.
358. Article 39 para. 2 lit. a ESA.
359. Article 39 para. 2 lit. d ESA.

Chapter 11. Optimization of the Athletes' Taxation in Switzerland

449. The optimization of the tax burden of athletes is not unknown in the sports industry.[360] Due to their very particular situation, there are various possibilities to consider and special challenges to face. An athlete often faces cross-border situations and is, therefore, subject to taxation in several countries.

450. Income from sport (prize money, starting fee, salary) is usually taxed at the place of the competition or the work place.[361] In contrast, royalty income is usually taxed at the beneficiary's domicile. Hence, a common way for athletes to reduce their tax burden is to use an interposed company in a jurisdiction with beneficial tax rates.[362] The athlete transfers his intellectual property rights (mostly image rights and trademarks)[363] to this company. The interposed company exploits the transferred IP rights by licensing the IP rights of the athlete to sponsors or the athlete's employer. The employer then splits the athlete's remuneration into direct salary payments to the athlete, including social security charges, and royalty payments free of social security charges payable to the interposed company. The athlete and the employer, therefore, will not pay social security charges on the royalties.

451. The company can capitalize some of the income and only reimburse a fixed compensation to the athlete in order to control the athlete's personal income and tax situation. The company and the athlete will be taxed on their profit and income in the applicable jurisdiction and the athlete can control the movement of money inflow from the interposed company. Logically, these interposed companies are set up in jurisdictions such as Switzerland which offer favourable tax rates.

452. Such structures sometimes face resistance from tax authorities, if the athlete is only employed by one employer and the interposed company only licenses image rights to this employer. The tax authorities might classify the total remuneration as salary and basis for social security charges. To foster the acceptance, it is recommended that: (i) the interposed company is not completely owned by the athlete; (ii) the interposed company licenses image rights to more than one counterparty; (iii) the interposed company exploits image rights of more than one athlete; and (iv) the company has substance[364] at the companies' domicile.[365]

---

360. For further reference *see* PACHMANN/Wehrli, Where to go with Athletes' tax optimisation after the crack down on the Licence Box Model? Possibilities of structuring Athletes' tax in Switzerland, Global Sports and Taxation Review, September 2015, 34 et seq.
361. As outlined in the OECD double taxation treaty model convention, Art. 17.
362. *See also* Morreau, 'France: The use of a foreign interposed company by sports persons' in: June 2014 *Global Sports Law and Taxation Reports* 36 et seq- Morreau describes the form generally observed in France but the logic can be applied internationally.
363. For example, 'ROGER FEDERER' is a registered trademark.
364. For example, the company should be managed locally and should have employees in the country of residence.
365. Morreau (2014) 38.

453. In the last years the OECD has increased the pressure to abolish such special tax regimes. Athletes owning interposed companies being taxed at a preferential IP rate are re-analysing the potential tax burden after the abolition and are comparing it to other options. In international comparison, Switzerland already offers very competitive tax rates for ordinarily taxed Swiss companies and could be one of the next domiciles for athletes' IP companies.[366] However, to avoid adverse tax consequences, the transfer of IP rights should be carefully planned and executed. Additionally, athletes who are not yet Swiss residents and who do not compete in Switzerland, should consider the advantages from the Swiss lump-sum tax regime.[367] Even athletes, who perform business and are fully taxed in Switzerland, find an attractive tax situation in Switzerland.

366. PACHMANN/Wehrli (2015), 35.
367. PACHMANN/Wehrli (2015), 36 et seq.

Part V. Legal Measures in Sports Cases

Chapter 1. Proceedings at the Court of Arbitration for Sport

§1. Legal Basis for the CAS

454. The CAS is a non-governmental organization resolving legal disputes of sports disputes. Mandatory provisions characterize the arbitration procedure of the CAS. For example, there is the fixed seat provision of S1 CAS Code. Consequently, Swiss law applies to questions regarding CAS' arbitration legitimacy. In accordance with Article 176 PILA, an arbitration is international, when at least one party neither is seated nor has its habitual residence in Switzerland. The so-called *lex arbitri*, hence, the law governing the arbitral proceedings, is in international cases Articles 176–194 PILA respectively for national cases Articles 353–399 CPC.[368]

455. Because of the New York Convention, CAS arbitral awards are enforceable in all its Member States. However, in sports the arbitral awards do usually not need to be recognized and declared enforceable in the other countries as the international sports federations enforce the CAS awards with their monopoly power immediately. This system increases the power of the CAS tremendously and eliminates any state interference. The arbitral awards of the CAS are usually not reviewed by foreign courts in the enforcement proceedings.

456. There are two main prerequisites for the validity of an arbitration, first, the existence of an arbitration agreement and second, that the disputed subject matter is arbitrable. For its validity, an arbitration agreement has to meet the requirements of Article 178 PILA respectively Articles 357 et seq. CPC. Since January, 1 2021 Article 178 paragraph 4 PILA explicitly stipulates that the provisions on international arbitration apply by analogy to an arbitration clause in a unilateral transaction or in articles of association, which obviously often occurs in sports matters. Sports law disputes are usually of pecuniary nature. Such disputes are considered arbitrable, in accordance with Article 176 PILA respectively Article 354 CPC.

457. Sports organizations regularly include in their contracts with athletes an arbitration clause. ANOTHer possibility is that such contract refers to articles of association or other regulations, which provide an arbitration clause.

368. Born, p. 490; Redfern & Hunter, paras 1.09 et seq.

458. Swiss jurisprudence considers arbitration clauses in sports disputes as admissible. It is sufficient if the articles of association or other regulations of the sports organization contain an arbitration clause. There are no higher demands for compliance with the procedural requirements. The Swiss Federal Supreme Court considered an arbitration clause to be valid regarding a dispute of a player and his old club when a player asked a sports organization to issue a permit to play for the new club but the employment contract with the old club on which the dispute was based did not contain any arbitration clause or any reference to any arbitration clause at all.[369]

459. The arbitrability of a dispute is a jurisdictional issue. The arbitrability of employment disputes is controversially discussed, as the parties cannot dispose independently all their claims, in accordance with Article 354 CPC, in the context of employment law. Namely, the employees cannot resign their claims according to Articles 341 and 361 et seq. of the Swiss Code of Obligations beforehand. Therefore, at least these claims are not arbitrable if the arbitration agreement is concluded before the dispute started.[370] However, the legal situation is not completely clear.

§2. Exclusive Jurisdiction, Impartiality and Independence of the CAS

460. The exclusivity of the jurisdiction of CAS depends on the arbitration clause. The statutes of the international sports organizations always foresee an exclusive jurisdiction of CAS. This means that the athletes do not have the possibility to appeal a decision of an international sports organization to the state courts in Switzerland.

461. In an antitrust procedure against the International Skating Union the European Commission criticized the exclusive jurisdiction of the CAS by stating that in case of anti-competitive ineligibility decisions of the International Skating Union, the Appeals Arbitration rules reinforce the restriction of their commercial freedom and the foreclosure of potential competitors.[371]

462. Recently, the Federal Supreme Court dismissed an appeal to set aside a CAS award by finding the CAS is an independent and impartial tribunal that has jurisdiction irrespective of the fact that Appellant did not voluntarily consent to the arbitration agreement. The Swiss Supreme Court reinforced the jurisdiction of the CAS and confirmed the decision of the European Court of Human Rights in the case *Mutu & Pechstein v. Switzerland.*

369. *See* Decision of the Federal Supreme Court 4A_548/2009 of 20 Jan. 2010.
370. Cf. Decision of the Swiss Federal Supreme Court 4A_71/2010 of 28 Jun. 2010.
371. Decision of the European Commission AT.40208 of 8 Dec. 2017.

I. *Mutu & Pechstein v. Switzerland*

463. Indeed, in the case *Mutu & Pechstein v. Switzerland*, the independence and impartiality of the CAS as well as the exclusivity of the jurisdiction of the CAS was disputed.

464. The famous German ice skater, Claudia Pechstein, was tested positive due to too high reticulocyte levels during the world speed skating championships in 2009. After the decision of the CAS, which confirmed the two-year ban issued by the International Skating Union,[372] Ms Pechstein appealed to the Federal Supreme Court seeking to have the award set aside. She *inter alia* argued that the members of the CAS were not independent and impartial due to the way CAS arbitrators are appointed. The Federal Supreme Court rejected the appeal.[373]

465. At the same time, Ms Pechstein also applied to German courts. The Higher Regional Court of Munich considered the arbitration agreement as invalid since Ms Pechstein's consent to the arbitration agreement was involuntary due to the monopoly position of the Skating Union and the factual forced signing of the agreement in order to be able to compete and earn a living.[374] Ultimately, this decision from the previous instance was overturned by the German Supreme Court.[375]

466. Furthermore, Ms Pechstein appealed to the European Court of Human Rights (ECHR). The ECHR found that the right of a fair trial under Article 6 paragraph 1 ECHR was violated as Ms Pechstein was not granted a public hearing. All other claims – including the allegation on the impartiality and independence of the CAS tribunal – were rejected. Regarding the validity of the arbitration agreement the ECHR emphasized that it should be differentiated between voluntary arbitration and mandatory arbitration. In a mandatory arbitration the athletes are compelled to resort to arbitration because otherwise they could not execute their sport on a professional level. The ECHR thus held that in such cases the guarantees of the Convention must be granted. In a voluntary arbitration however, parties may voluntarily waive certain rights guaranteed by the Convention.[376]

467. There are three main takeaways from the Pechstein decision of the ECHR. First, States can indeed be held liable in arbitration proceedings. Switzerland could be sued since it upheld the decision of the CAS. Second, the ECHR generally confirms the independence and impartiality of the CAS. Third, the rights granted by the ECHR must be guaranteed in compulsory arbitrations.

468. With regard to public hearings, the CAS already reacted to the Pechstein decision and included the right to public hearings in Article R58 of the CAS Code.

---

372. CAS 2009/A/1912 and CAS 2009/A/1913 of 25 Nov. 2009.
373. Cf. Decision of the Swiss Federal Supreme Court 4A_612/2009 of 10 Feb. 2010.
374. Decision of the Higher Regional Court of Munich U 1110/14 of 15 Jan. 2015, reason 2./A./II./3.
375. Decision of the German Supreme Court KZR 6/15 of 7 Jun. 2016, para. 69.
376. See Decision of the ECHR 40575/10, 67474/10 of 2 Oct. 2018, *Mutu and Pechstein v. Switzerland*.

469. Concerning the impartiality and independence of the arbitrators, the ECHR indicated that among others the manner of appointment of the arbitral tribunal's members and their term of office, the existence of guarantees against outside pressure and the question whether the body presents an appearance of independence determine whether a tribunal can be regarded as independent. The ECHR did not find that there was a structural problem in the CAS appointment system that would result in a lack of independence and impartiality. The ECHR did also not consider the CAS to lack independence and impartiality solely on accounts of its financial arrangements.[377]

470. It is important to note that two judges – including Switzerland's judge – expressed a joint dissenting opinion concerning the appointment system of arbitrators in CAS proceedings. In the view of the two judges, the CAS does not appear independent. They considered that 'the structural problems of the CAS as an arbitration institution should have led the ECHR to find a violation of Article 6 § 1 in its section on the independence and impartiality of the courts'.[378]

II. *Ali Riza and others v. Turkey*

471. As opposed in the case *Pechstein v. Switzerland* – where the ECHR did not find a violation of Article 6 paragraph 1 ECHR since under the CAS rule arbitrators have the duty to disclose their independence and impartiality and are subject to challenges for violation of these duties – in *Ali Riza and others v. Turkey* the ECHR held that there had been a violation of Article 6 paragraph 1 ECHR on account of the lack of independence and impartiality of the body, the Arbitration Committee of the Turkish Football Federation ('the TFF'), which had decided on disputes concerning Ömer Riza, a professional football player and Serkan Akal, a referee.[379] In particular, the Court found that the influence of the executive body of the TFF, the Board of Directors, which had always largely consisted of members of football clubs, over the organisation and functioning of the Arbitration Committee, was excessive. According to the ECHR, the TFF law did also not provide appropriate safeguards to protect members of the Arbitration Committee from any outside pressure.

472. This decision is paramount for all sportspersons because it sets forth that Arbitration Committees of Sport Federations must be independent and impartial. This will lead to a lot of structural changes all over the sport sector. The decision furthermore clarifies that players must have an equal representation in these arbitration bodies of Federations. It strengthens the composition of the FIFA Disputes

377. Decision of the ECHR 40575/10, 67474/10 of 2 Oct. 2018, *Mutu and Pechstein v. Switzerland*, para. 151.
378. Decision of the ECHR 40575/10, 67474/10 of 2 Oct. 2018, *Mutu and Pechstein v. Switzerland*, para. 28.
379. See Decision of the ECHR 30226/10 and 4 others of 28 Jan. 2020, *Ali Riza and others v. Turkey*.

Resolution Chamber that also includes judges selected by the players union FIFPRO, which is the right way and an example in terms of dealing with disputes in the sports sector.

III. *Ezequiel Matias Schelotto v. His Former Agent*

473. At the core of the case was a forum selection clause vesting the competence in the commercial court of Buenos Aires in Argentina. The clause, however, contained a further reference to national (Dispute Settlement Body of the Argentine Football Association (AFA)) and international bodies of associations (Players' Status Committee of the FIFA).

474. The Court of Arbitration for Sport (CAS) held that it was competent to decide the case and awarded the agent an amount of more than EUR 672,000. The appeal filed against the CAS award was upheld by the Swiss Federal Supreme Court. In essence, the Swiss Federal Supreme Court ruled that the disputed clause did not show the required degree of certainty to establish consent to arbitrate.[380] The Supreme Court thus held that the CAS award is to be annulled and that CAS did not have competence to decide the case.

475. The ruling reflects the practice of the Supreme Court applying a two-step approach with respect to the substantive validity of an arbitration agreement in commercial arbitration. The Supreme Court – except in sports-related arbitration cases – initially applies a rather strict approach concerning the consent to arbitrate. Once the parties' consent to arbitrate is established, the Court adopts a more liberal approach. This is however one of the very rare cases where the Court applied a strict approach concerning the consent to arbitrate in the area of sports arbitration.

476. Since CAS was established in 1984, only very few awards have been set aside by the Supreme Court. Accordingly, it appears to be difficult to overturn sports-related arbitration cases. Against this background various players unions such as the FIFPRO, WAIPU and SAFP on behalf of more than 72,000 athletes worldwide filed a proposal to the Swiss Federal Council suggesting necessary changes to the Swiss Private International Law Act ensuring adequate protection of athletes' rights (from page 166 onwards). The proposal *inter alia* suggests widening the grounds for refusal in sports-related arbitration cases, allowing an appeal against arbitrary awards as it is already the existing law for domestic arbitration in Switzerland. In doing so, for example, violations of mandatory employment law provisions by CAS could be appealed to the Supreme Court. In order to adequately protect athletes' rights on an international level in international sport arbitration cases, the Swiss legislator should act accordingly and provide the possibility to appeal against arbitrary awards in sports-related arbitration cases.

---

380. Decision of the Swiss Federal Supreme Court 4A_432/2017 of 22 Jan. 2018.

§3. Appeal Procedure, Ordinary Procedure and Anti-Doping Procedure

477. As per 1 January 2019, the CAS Code was amended. Before, the CAS had two chambers. The revised rules provide for a new chamber for all dispute concerning doping matters. The doping division was previously only an ad hoc arbitration tribunal at international sporting events such as the Olympic Games. The CAS now consists of three chambers. One chamber decides as an ordinary arbitral tribunal (Ordinary Arbitration Division) in disputes submitted to it, the second chamber functions as an appellate court (Appeal Arbitration Division) against final decisions of sports organizations and the third chamber resolves disputes related to anti-doping matters as a first-instance authority or as a sole instance (Anti-doping Division) (S20 CAS Code). In addition, it is possible to submit to the CAS legal questions for consultative assessment. Dispute mediation may also be conducted through the CAS. Most decisions of the CAS are issued by the Appeal Division.

478. For proceedings of the Ordinary Arbitration Division and the Appeal Arbitration Division, the general provisions of the CAS Code (R27–R37 CAS Code) are applicable. For ordinary arbitration procedures R38–R46 of the CAS Code are relevant. For appeal arbitration procedures R47–R59 of the CAS Code are applicable. Proceedings before the Anti-doping Division are governed by the CAS ADD Rules.

§4. Applicable Law

479. According to Article 187 PILA respectively Article 381 CPC, the arbitral tribunal shall decide the dispute in accordance with the law chosen by the parties or, in the absence of a choice of law, according to the law to which the case has the closest connection. The parties may even authorize the arbitral tribunal to decide on the basis of equity.

480. Even though the CAS Code foresees rules regarding the choice of law, such choice of law is always subsidiary to the choice of law made by the parties. Before turning to the CAS Code it needs to be reviewed whether an explicit choice of law of the parties exists. Only if such choice of law does not exist, the choice of law in the CAS Code applies.

481. For the ordinary procedure, R45 of the CAS Code states that the panel decides the dispute according to the law chosen by the parties. In the absence of such choice of law, Swiss law applies. The parties may authorize the panel to decide *ex aequo et bono*.

482. In appeal procedures the CAS decides the dispute according to R58 of the CAS Code based on the applicable regulations and the rules of law chosen by the parties. In the absence of such a choice, the CAS decides according to the law of the country in which the federation, association or sports-related body – which has issued the challenged decision is domiciled, – or according to the rules of law that the tribunal deems as appropriate to apply. If the tribunal considers an appropriate law, it shall give reasons for its decision.

483. In considering the applicable law in appeal procedures, the CAS is primarily bound to apply the rules established by the sports organizations. However, it is worth mentioning that these rules are based on and limited by the law under which they were adopted. Therefore, Swiss law is regularly applicable, since most international sports organizations have their registered seat in Switzerland. Due to the extremely liberal Swiss law and the strong autonomy for associations, sports organizations in Switzerland try to bind the CAS to its rules and help to develop these rules. It is crucial, however, that the CAS has to apply the law ex officio. It has, in particular, to observe the hierarchy of Swiss law if the decision is to be made in connection with an association or an organization based in Switzerland. The hierarchy is as follows: First, the mandatory law must be observed (Article 63 paragraph 2 Swiss Civil Code), thereafter the articles of association and then the non-mandatory statutory law (Article 63 paragraph 1 Swiss Civil Code) and finally, regulations and other decrees by an association. Only if the articles of association allow the regulations to deviate from the non-mandatory statutory law the regulations will supersede the non-mandatory statutory law.[381]

484. An arbitral tribunal seated in Switzerland must of course apply all provisions of the applicable law ex officio. Furthermore, there are provisions that are part of the public policy of a legal order that are not expressly agreed upon by the parties but need to be applied to the case because they demand effect in any case. Such overriding mandatory rules are collected under the term 'positive *ordre public*'. These overriding mandatory rules include, in particular, the substantive competition law provisions. According to the Swiss Federal Supreme Court, EU competition law, including the competition law of the Member States, is part of the positive *ordre public*.[382] For this reason, it is clear that also the CAS, as an arbitral tribunal seated in Switzerland, has to apply the provisions of relevant competition laws.

485. The very arbitration friendly Swiss law provides, in Article 187 paragraph 2 PILA for international arbitration and in Article 381 paragraph 1 lit. b of the CPC for national arbitration that the parties may also authorize the arbitral tribunal to decide equitably (ex aequo et bono). In such case, the parties agree on an equity clause instead of a choice of law clause, which means that the arbitral tribunal is not obliged to apply certain statutory provision but to find a solution that in the specific case and under consideration of all circumstances represents a fair solution.[383] However, it is also clear that the parties, in agreeing on an equity clause, cannot exclude the applicability of provisions belonging to the positive *ordre public*, such

381. HEINI, PORTMANN & SEEMANN, Grundriss des Vereinsrechts, 21.
382. BGE 120 II 155 C. 6.a.
383. Basler Kommentar-WEBER-STECHER, N 93 pursuant to Arts 12–17 CartA (with further references).

as the mandatory provisions of competition law.[384] This is because a decision on equity may not contradict the negative or the positive *ordre public*. Hence, the arbitral tribunal has to apply the mandatory provisions of competition law even if an equity clause had been agreed upon. Since the mandatory provisions of competition law must be applied even if an equity clause had been agreed upon, the same applies, of course, if a sports organization refers to all provisions of the law of the organization in terms of a choice of law clause. By doing so, the sports organization cannot circumvent the provisions that the organizational rules of the sports organization are based on (so, for example, mandatory competition law) as well as the rules that belong to the positive *ordre public*. The CAS has in any case to consider and apply mandatory competition laws.

§5. Appeal Procedure

486. An appeal against the decision of a sports organization can, indeed must, be submitted to CAS if that is stipulated by the articles of association or the regulations of the sports organizations. An appeal must be filed within twenty-one days after the Appellant has received the decision of the sports organization (R49 CAS Code) if the provisions of the sports association do not provide for a longer deadline.[385] Thereafter, the Appellant has a further ten days in order to file the appeal brief (R51 CAS Code). Such deadline may be extended. In this appeal brief, the Appellant has to put forward the facts and legal arguments and submit its evidence.

487. Pursuant to R56 of the CAS Code, after the filing of the appeal and the answer the parties are no longer allowed to supplement their arguments or present new evidence unless it is ordered by the President of the panel or there exist extraordinary circumstances.

488. After the appeal and answer there is often a hearing, unless the panel, after having consulted the parties, is of the opinion that such hearing is not necessary (R57 CAS Code). At a hearing, the witnesses are cross-examined and other evidence will be taken. Parties will generally be given the right to comment on the legal documents and the results of evidence. The hearing itself is usually conducted *in camera*.[386] As previously mentioned, due to the critics of the European Court of

---

384. Basler Kommentar-Weber-Stecher, N 94 purusant to Arts 12–17 CartA (with further references).

385. In front of the CAS the deadline for challenging resolutions of an association is thirty days after the resolution of the association has been taken note of, pursuant to Art. 75 of the Swiss Civil Code. The legality of shortening the time period of a challenge is therefore untenable and must be rejected, although there are some scholars who consider a shortening to be admissible; *see* Bernasconi & Huber, 268 et seq.

386. The lack of publicity for the proceeding was already contested before the Swiss Federal Supreme Court. But the court held that it has not the power to review violations of the Human Rights Conventions if they are not considered as violations of the order public; *see* Decision of the Swiss Federal Supreme Court 4A_612/2009 of 10 Feb. 2010, C. 4. Whether such jurisprudence is legal in the light of Art. 6 para. 1 ECHR is subject to Claudia Pechstein's appeal to the ECHR.

Human Rights in the matter of *Mutu & Pechstein*, hearings can now be held publicly at the request of a physical person who is party to the proceeding (R57 CAS)

489. In principle, the appeal has no suspensive effect. The suspensive effect must be requested by either party. Otherwise, it is possible that the decision of the association is already enforceable although the appeal is still pending before the CAS.

§6. Object of the Appeal

490. The object of the appeal based on association law is according to Article 75 of the Swiss Civil Code, a decision of an association. However, before a legal action can be taken, the internal legal means within the association have to be exhausted.

491. The right to appeal a decision is in particular questionable, if an individual or a subsidiary organ of the association simply states the intention of the association. Only if it derives from the statement of the individual that the intention of the association is clearly stated a final decision of the association can be assumed. In all other cases the letters are only considered as informal non-appealable statements.

492. The District Court of Zurich had to decide in a case of a Turkish football club whether a letter from the head of the secretariat of the FIFA Player's Status Department had to be considered as an appealable decision or not. The head of the secretariat explained in the mentioned letter, that FIFA does not deal with the dispute, because the Turkish Football Association had already decided the case. In the eyes of the District Court of Zurich this letter was just an informal letter, whereas no appealable decision was given.[387]

493. Also CAS considered in its decision dated 16 December 2008 a letter of FIFA's Head of Legal Affairs and the Head of Player's Status Committee not as an appealable decision, but rather as an informal letter. The Swiss Federal Supreme Court indirectly confirmed these findings, even though it was not able to fully review the case under Article 190 paragraph 2 lit. c PILA.[388]

§7. The CAS Decision

494. The CAS panel makes its decision by a majority vote. The decision will be reasoned. Before the decision is signed and sent to the parties by fax, it will be submitted to the Secretary General of the CAS, who may make formal corrections and

387. Decision of the 1st Division of the District Court of Zurich CG030235 of 7 Feb. 2005.
388. Decision of the Swiss Federal Supreme Court 4A_62/2009 of 23 Jun. 2009.

may alert the panel to fundamental principles (R59 CAS Code).[389] Such interference of the Secretary General of the CAS is in certain constellations quite questionable as the Secretary General of the CAS directly reports to the ICAS which is dominated by the sports federations.

495. The CAS can decide freely on the content of the decision. According to R57 CAS Code, the panel has full power to reassess the facts and the law. The CAS may issue a new decision that replaces the previous decision of the sports organization or it may rescind the decision and return it to the lower court.

496. The rule in R57 CAS Code, according to which the CAS may replace the decisions of the sports organization with its own decision, contradicts the principles of the Swiss law on associations and the autonomy of associations. The action to appeal a decision of an association pursuant to Article 75 Swiss Civil Code, which is essentially what the appeal to the CAS is about, is required because the autonomy of associations is mandatory and of cassation nature.[390] Consequently, the courts are not allowed to replace the decisions of associations with their own decisions. The courts may only reassess whether the decision of the association is justifiable. However, it is possible that a decision may be partly rescinded.

497. The problem goes even further. In case the CAS replaces the decision of the sports organization with its own new decision, it not only interferes in the autonomy of the associations, but also in turn creates a new decision, which can be reviewed only by the Swiss Federal Supreme Court with its limited cognition. It is therefore impossible to have the legality of a substantially wrong (new) decision of the CAS reviewed.

§8. CAS Anti-Doping Division

498. As previously stated, the CAS established a new Anti-doping Division. The purpose of the CAS ADD is to provide international sports federations in particular with a 'court of first instance for doping-related disputes'. The CAS ADD hears anti-doping cases pursuant to a delegation from the World Anti-Doping Code signatories, such as the International Olympic Committee (IOC), the International Federations of sports on the Olympic programme (Olympic IFs) and decides whether or not there has been a violation of their anti-doping rules, as well as orders any sanction, if applicable, in accordance with the WADC (A1 ADD Rules). The proceedings before this new chamber are governed by a separate set of procedural rules, the ADD Rules. These rules have been established in conjunction with the applicable anti-doping rules of the WADC (A1 ADD Rules).

---

389. Therefore, the question arises, whether this does not violate the independence of the arbitration panel. Apparently, this question has not been reviewed by the Swiss Federal Supreme Court because, so far, evidence for such influence on the decision was missing.

390. Pachmann, Corporate Governance und Sportverbände, 336 with further references.

499. Pursuant to the ADD Rules, the CAS ADD shall be the first-instance authority to conduct proceedings and issue decisions when an alleged anti-doping rule violation has been filed with it and for imposition of any sanctions resulting from a finding that an anti-doping rule violation has occurred (A2 ADD Rules). The rules set forth a closed list of ADD-arbitrators (A8 ADD Rules). An appeal can be filed to the CAS Appeals Division which decides under the provisions applicable to the appeal arbitration procedure of the CAS Code.

500. Highly problematic is the choice of the Panel. In case the sports association does not agree the sole arbitrator is chosen from a very small list of persons available to decide the dispute. As the rules stand at the moment it does not make any sense for the sports associations to agree on a three-person panel.

501. The introduction of the CAS ADD make it in the end much more expensive for the athletes to object to any anti-doping violations as they face two CAS instances which are in general dominated by the sports associations.

§9. The CAS Ad Hoc Division

502. For the Olympic Games the CAS forms one specific ad hoc division. All disputes arising in connection with the Olympic Games are decided by this division. The ad hoc division starts working ten days before the Olympic Games begins and ends its work with the Closing Ceremony.

503. This ad hoc division, like the CAS Panels, is an arbitral tribunal that is based on Articles 176–194 PILA. Although the ad hoc division has an office on the site of the Olympic Games, its registered office is nevertheless in Lausanne, Switzerland. For the CAS ad hoc division at the Olympic Games only very few arbitrators are selected from the closed list of arbitrators which makes it in certain constellations quite difficult to get a completely independent and impartial Panel.

504. At the Olympic Games the athletes are offered to choose their legal representation from local lawyers who deal with their case pro bono. Even though this sounds at first quite promising it is quite questionable whether such system gives the athletes equal arms against the highly specialized and well-paid lawyers from the sports federations.

505. Appeals according to Articles 190 et seq. PILA are also admissible against the decisions of the CAS ad hoc division.

Chapter 2. Legal Measures Against CAS Decisions

§1. Introduction

506. With decisions of the CAS, the first question to ask is whether domestic facts or international facts are concerned. Whereas for domestic facts the Swiss Civil Procedure Code of 19 December 2008, that was implemented on 1 January 2011, is applicable, with international facts the PILA is applicable. In both cases a complaint to the Swiss Federal Supreme Court is possible. However, the reasons for an appeal are wider under the Swiss Civil Procedure Code than under the PILA.

507. For example, in a proceeding of the WADA – a foundation having its registered seat in Switzerland but with an office in Canada – against a sportsperson residing in Switzerland, the appeal procedure according to the Swiss Civil Procedure Code is applicable. Only if there is an international element the appeal procedure pursuant to the PILA applies. This clarification must be made in advance, especially as the CAS regularly refrains from attaching a detailed statement of appeal to its decisions.

508. The possibility to overcome a judgment is of major importance. This may be relevant if, for example, new medical knowledge can explain a particular blood count. Sportspersons are not hindered in their search for the material truth. In the following section, the available remedies will be briefly described.

§2. Remedies According to the Pila

I. Expedited Provisional Measures

509. In its jurisprudence the Swiss Federal Supreme Court repeatedly confirmed that, with doping affairs, it is possible to decide for a suspensory effect pursuant to Article 103 paragraph 2 (CFSC) Code on the Federal Supreme Court or positive orders pursuant to Article 104 CFSC, if time is urgent, there exists an irrevocable detriment and there is a positive forecast regarding the merits of the prima facie case.

510. In the *Pechstein* case, the Swiss Federal Supreme Court ordered a positive expedited provisional measure for the first time in a doping case and obliged the sports organization to allow the sportsperson to participate in a qualifying race for the Olympic Games.[391] Unfortunately, the Swiss Federal Supreme Court's latest decisions on Provisional Measures show clearly a reluctance to grant them if there are not very good chances to successfully overturn the arbitral award (which is virtually never the case).

---

391. Order of the Swiss Federal Supreme Court of 7 Dec. 2009 in the matter of 4A_612/2009.

511. The proceedings before the Swiss Federal Supreme Court provide the sportspersons only theoretically with sufficient legal protection in urgent cases, so that their right to continue their professional activities is ensured until the final decision of the Swiss Federal Supreme Court is made.

II. Appeal to the Swiss Federal Supreme Court

A. *Peculiarities of Sports Law*

512. In matters of international arbitration, the Swiss Private International Law Act provides that the referral of a decision to the Swiss Federal Supreme Court may be excluded. But, in the *Cañas* decision in the year 2007, the Swiss Federal Supreme Court stated that this exclusion is not permissible because of the monopoly position of the sports organizations and the unilateral imposition of the arbitration clause.[392] This decision made it clear that an appeal to the Swiss Federal Court against the decisions of the CAS is always permissible. After such decision more and more appeals were successfully made to the Swiss Federal Supreme Court.

Figure 3a Successful Appeals per Year (1989–2016)

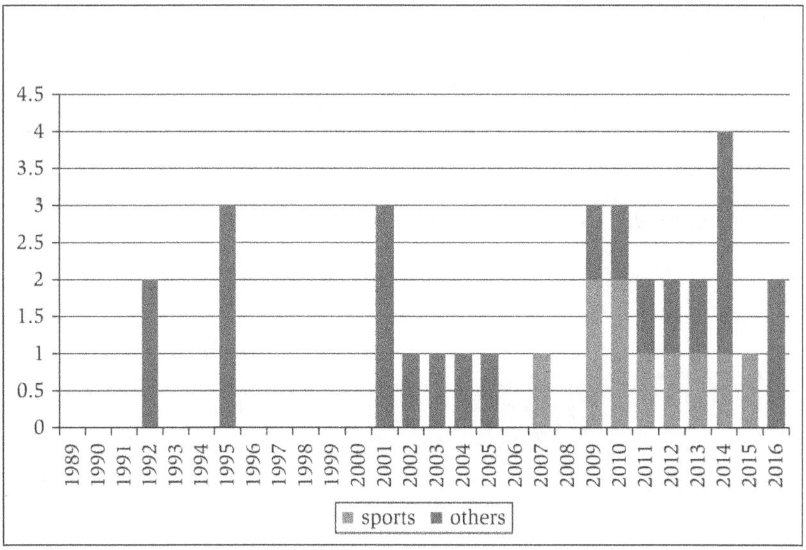

392. BGE 133 III 235.

Figure 3b Successful Appeals per Year in Sports Law Cases (2017–2020)

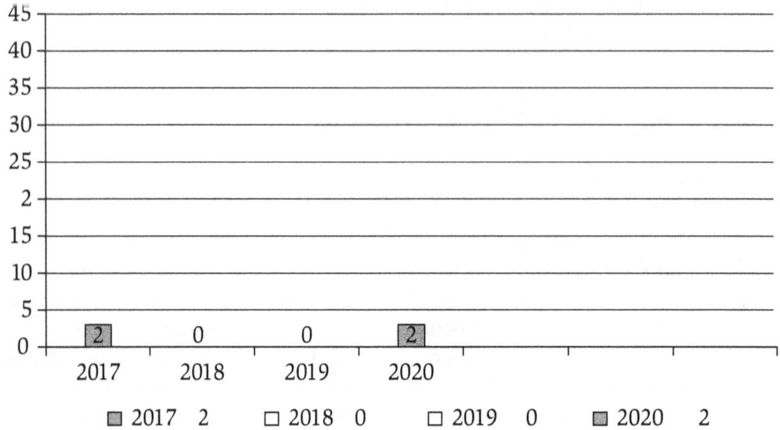

513. Nevertheless, it must be pointed out that appeals to the Swiss Federal Supreme Court regarding sport arbitration cases pursuant to Article 77 CFSC were generally unsuccessful. A lot of appeals were dismissed.[393] The extremely restricted cognition of the Swiss Federal Supreme Court under Article 190 paragraph 2 PILA almost always proved to be insurmountable. Only in matters of jurisdiction, where the Federal Supreme Court has no limits on its cognition, were decisions rescinded more often. It thus appears that the CAS still has a very wide discretion due to the conception of international arbitration in Switzerland. The decisions of the CAS are virtually non-challengeable by means of an appeal to the Swiss Federal Supreme Court.

Figure 4a Decision on the Merits 1989–2016: Sports 111

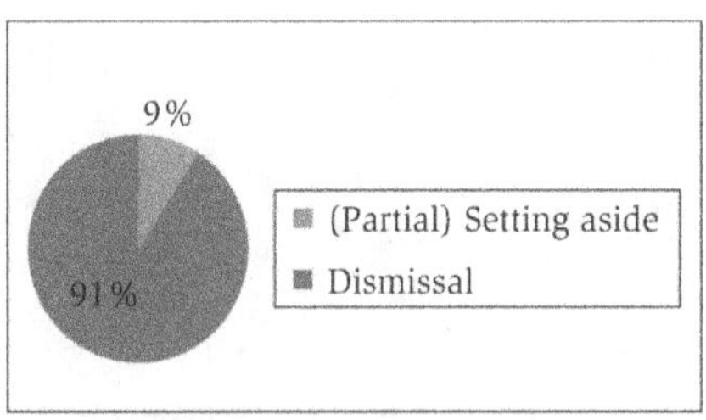

393. The appeals were only successful in the *Cañas* Decision and the Decision of the Swiss Federal Supreme Court 4A_400/2008 of 9 Feb., 4A_358/2009 of 6 Nov. 2009, 4A_490/2009 of 13 Apr. 2010 and 4A_456/2009 of 3 May 2010.

Figure 4b Decision on the Merits 2017–2020: Sports 83

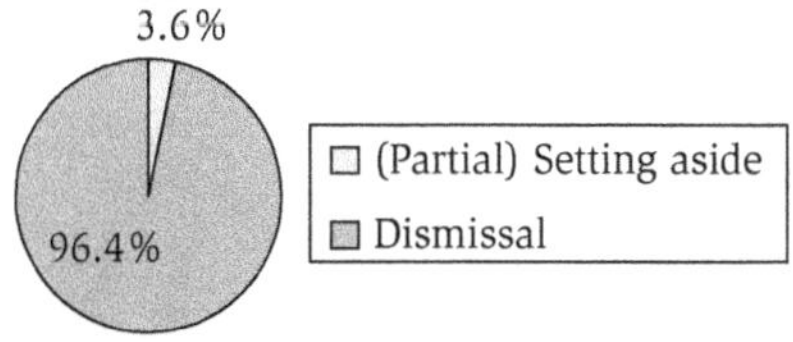

514. The reason for this is that the grounds of an appeal are extremely limited. One of the essential characteristics that the legislative body pursued when regulating Chapter 12 of the PILA was to reduce the possibilities to challenge arbitration awards to a minimum, especially in comparison to domestic arbitration. However, the legislative body did this in consideration of commercial arbitration, and not sports arbitration. The last few years have demonstrated that these restrictive statutory provisions are inappropriate for sports arbitration. In particular, it must be noted that sportspersons in sports arbitration, in contrast to ordinary commercial arbitration, do not voluntarily put themselves under the control of an arbitral tribunal; rather the sportsperson who refuses to submit to sports arbitration cannot perform his or her occupation. The equality between the parties that is a characteristic of arbitration does not apply in sports.

B. Appeal Reasons in General

515. Despite this difference in nature, so far – pursuant to Article 190 PILA – only the following issues may be appealed. The list is, under the jurisdiction of the Swiss Federal Supreme Court, also exhaustive for sports law.[394]

394. *See* BGE 128 II 50 C. 1a, 53; BGE 127 III 279 C. 1a, 282.

Figure 5a Success of Appeal under Article 190 PILS (If Admitted) 1989–2016

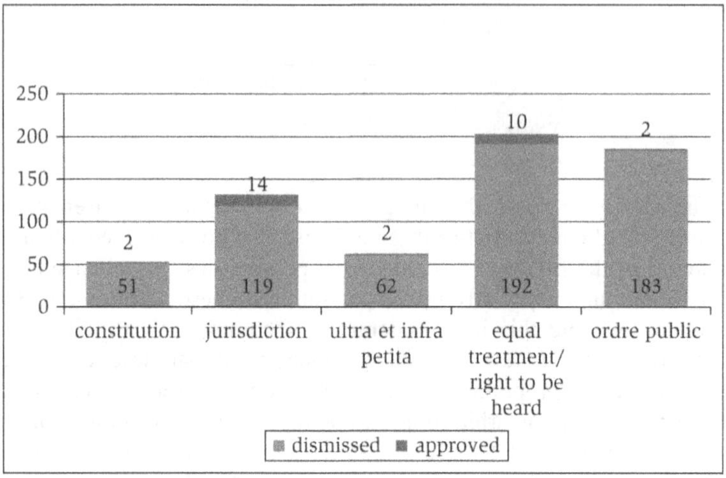

Figure 5b Success of Appeal under Article 190 PILS (If Admitted) 2017–2020

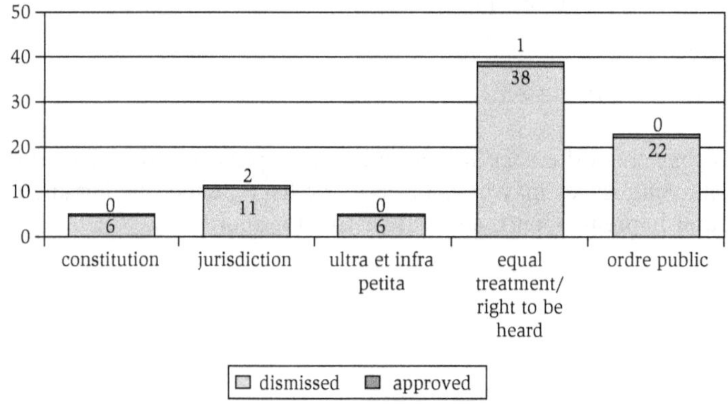

Note: Plus one additional revision case that was successful.

C. *Wrong Appointment of the Arbitral Tribunal (Article 190 Paragraph 2 lit. a PILA)*

516. This provision aims to guarantee that the stature of a judge according to Article 30 paragraph 1 Federal Constitution of the Swiss Confederation (CSC) and Article 6 paragraph 1 ECHR is protected.[395] It shall be ensured that the ruling body provides for a sufficient guarantee that its jurisprudence is independent. The condition for invoking this appeal ground is that the respective breach of the regulation

395. BGE 118 II 361 C. 3c.

(lack of independence or impartiality) could not have been addressed earlier in the proceedings. In general the parties have to challenge an arbitrator as soon as they have notice of such grounds.

517. The jurisdiction of the Swiss Federal Supreme Court is quite generous and has always stated that the CAS is an independent and impartial arbitral tribunal.[396] In BGE 129 III 445, the Swiss Federal Supreme Court came to the conclusion that even if the Appellant is facing the IOC as respondent, the CAS is qualified as an independent arbitral tribunal. This is surprising due to the fact that the ICAS, which appoints the arbitrators and in particular the President of the panel, is dominated by the IOC respectively the sport federations. In any case, a party and its counsel need to exert elementary research regarding the CAS arbitrators' independence, and need to challenge the arbitrators according to the CAS Code within seven days if there are any doubts about their impartiality or independence. At least the Swiss Federal Supreme Court held that CAS arbitrators do not have to disclose information, which a party or its counsel can exert with reasonable effort.[397]

518. Regarding the number of arbitrators, the Swiss Federal Supreme Court held that parties' arbitration agreement has primacy.[398] Hence, only if the parties did not agree on a number of arbitrators, the Division President can decide in accordance with R40 paragraph 2 CAS Code. However, a party which disagrees with the decision of the Division President has to raise its concerns immediately. Otherwise, a party would waive its right to appeal and implicitly accept the tribunal's composition.[399]

D. *Missing Jurisdiction of the Arbitral Tribunal (Article 190 Paragraph 2 lit. b PILA)*

519. With this objection, the arbitrability pursuant to Article 177 PILA and also the involvement in establishing a jurisdiction under Article 186 paragraph 2 PILA may be censured.[400] The formal validity of the arbitration agreement pursuant to Article 178 paragraph 1 PILA and the substantive validity of the arbitration agreement in the sense of Article 178 paragraph 1 PILA may also be censured.

520. The Swiss Federal Supreme Court stated lately that the arbitration agreement between two parties in sports disputes is being considered in its jurisprudence with a 'certain goodwill' in favour of the arbitration agreement's validity.[401] The

396. Decision of the Federal Supreme Court 4P_105/2006 (arbitrator of Appellant selected by CAS and lawyer of defendant, who is also a CAS arbitrator, are sitting together during the same period of time on aNOTHer CAS panel); BGE 4A_506/2007 of 20 Mar. 2008 (2 arbitrators members of the same association as one party).
397. Decision 4A_110/2012 of the Swiss Federal Supreme Court.
398. Decision 4A_282/2013 5.2 et seq of the Swiss Federal Supreme Court.
399. BGE 136 III 605 at 3.2.2.
400. Decision 4A_654/2011 of the Swiss Federal Supreme Court; BGE133 III 139 cons. 5.
401. Decision of the Swiss Federal Supreme Court A_640/2010 of 18 Apr. 2011.

generosity of the Swiss Federal Supreme Court is in particular given in cases of arbitration clauses by reference.[402] The fast disputes resolution by a specialized court is of course of utmost importance in sports disputes. However, political reasons are most likely the real reasoning behind this jurisdiction. Switzerland furthers the domiciliation of sports organizations. In comparison to normal (commercial) arbitrations there are in sports arbitrations not two parties that have agreed voluntarily on the arbitration clause but the athletes are factually forced to agree on the arbitration clause. Such a factual compulsion should lead to a stricter control of the arbitration agreement or at least the Swiss Federal Supreme Court should exercise a stricter control of the decisions of CAS.

521. The Swiss Federal Supreme Court considered the CAS only in a few cases as incompetent. In the *Gert Thys* case the CAS simply based its competence on a fax of the anti-doping administrator to the legal representative of the athlete, wherein it assumed the competence of the CAS.[403] In the eyes of the CAS this fax was the offer for the conclusion of an arbitration agreement, which the athlete accepted implicitly. Fortunately, the Swiss Federal Supreme Court held that the CAS was not allowed to assume such an implicit arbitration agreement. The fax just expressed the wrong opinion of the CAS regarding its jurisdiction.

522. In the case of the ice hockey player *Florian Busch* the CAS based his competence on an application form that was signed by every player for the Ice Hockey World Championships, which the participants had to sign every year. The Swiss Federal Supreme Court held therefore that the arbitration clause is only valid for disputes in connection with the respective World Championship; the arbitration clause could not be considered as a general arbitration agreement.[404]

523. Finally, the question of the objective and subjective scope of the arbitration agreement may be censured.[405] Also, the fact that the arbitral tribunal, in its decision on jurisdiction, has not made the necessary findings of fact may be challenged.[406] Even the mere summary examination of arbitral jurisdiction may be challenged.[407] Moreover, within Article 190 paragraph 2 lit. b PILA, the violation of the *lis pendens* provision stated in Article 9 PILA may be censured.[408] According to the Swiss Federal Supreme Court's jurisprudence, an arbitral tribunal violates Article 190 paragraph 2 lit. b PILA if it does not apply the competition law of the

402. *See,* for example, the decision of the Swiss Federal Supreme Court 4A_460/2008 of 9 Jan. 2009, where the Swiss Federal Supreme Court affirmed the opinion of the CAS, that a professional football player is bound to the articles of association of the FIFA by accepting the articles of association of his national association. He therewith accepts the CAS as arbitral tribunal.
403. Decision of the Swiss Federal Supreme Court 4A_456/2009 of 3 May 2010.
404. Decision of the Swiss Federal Supreme Court 4A_358/2009 of 6 Nov. 2009.
405. BGE 117 II 94 C. 5b.
406. *See* BGE 4P_226/2004 of 9 Mar. 2005 C. 4.3.3.
407. BGE 128 III 50 C. 2b; BGE 121 III 495 C. 6d.
408. BGE 127 III 279 C. 2a.

state on whose market the anti-competitive agreement has its impact, even though this has been brought forward by a party.[409]

524. However, any objections to jurisdiction of the CAS have to be addressed already during the CAS proceedings. A jurisdiction appeal pursuant to Article 190 paragraph 2 lit. b PILA must be taken against the first, correctly inaugurated, challengeable decision, otherwise it will be forfeited.[410] An appeal is not only possible against partial arbitral decisions and final arbitral decisions but also against preliminary and intermediate decisions (Article 190 paragraph 3 PILA).

525. When assessing the question of jurisdiction and substantive preliminary questions, the Swiss Federal Supreme Court has full cognition.[411] Nevertheless, the Swiss Federal Supreme Court is bound by the facts established by the CAS.[412] An exemption may only be made if exceptional new facts and evidence within the meaning of Article 55 CFSC are admitted[413] or the CAS had determined the established facts by violating procedural guarantees. For example, if the CAS determines the meaning of the arbitration agreement by an objective interpretation according to the principle of good faith, then this is a legal question that can be reassessed with full cognition.[414] In contrast, if the CAS determines the actual will of the parties, this is a determination of facts that, in principle, cannot be reassessed, unless the CAS violated process principles when determining the parties' will. Since the Swiss Federal Supreme Court has full cognition with respect to the objection against jurisdiction, less stringent standards are applied regarding the requirements for explanatory statements. Even simple legal criticism on the legal opinion of the arbitral tribunal should be sufficient. All multiple explanatory statements must be challenged in connection with an appeal against jurisdiction, provided that the individual explanatory statements are sufficient to establish the jurisdiction. If the decision is only partly challenged, the Swiss Federal Supreme Court will not approve the appeal.

526. With an appeal to the Swiss Federal Supreme Court, a request may be made that the decision of CAS shall be rescinded and, in case the arbitral tribunal has wrongly denied competence, that the Swiss Federal Supreme Court finds the CAS is competent.[415] Compared to other appeal reasons the Swiss Federal Supreme Court is in cases of the questionable competence entitled to issue a reformatory judgment (and not just to annul the decision of CAS). However, the Swiss Federal Supreme Court can find the CAS not to be competent.[416]

409. *See* BGE 118 II 193 C. 5.
410. *See* BGE 120 II 155.C. 3b bb.
411. *See* BGE 129 III 727 C. 5.2.2.; BGE 128 III 50 C. 2a; BGE 117 II 94.
412. *See* Decision of the Federal Supreme Court 4A_42/2007 in the matter of Besiktas/Del Bosque.
413. *See* BGE 129 III 727 C. 5.2.2; BGE 128 III 50 C. 2a; BGE 119 II 380 C. 3c.
414. *See* BGE 4P_284/1994 of 17 Aug. 1995 C. 3a.
415. *See* BGE 117 II 94 C. 4.
416. *See* BGE 128 III 50.

527. The Swiss Federal Supreme Court held that party's objection of a sole arbitrator and its request to submit the dispute to an arbitral tribunal of three arbitrators is a ground to challenge an award, in accordance with Article 190 paragraph 2 lit b PILA.[417] However, parties have to distinguish the challenge of jurisdiction and the challenge of an arbitrator in accordance with Article R34 CAS Code. Regarding the latter, the ICAS and not the Swiss Federal Supreme Court shall decide. A party needs to challenge a tribunal's jurisdiction timely.[418] By implication, without challenging, parties waive the right to challenge an award.

E. Decisions Disregarding the Petita (Article 190 Paragraph 2 lit. c PILA)

528. There are basically three alternatives under this provision:

(1) the arbitral tribunal awards more than the parties have requested (ultra petita);
(2) the arbitral tribunal awards something different from what the parties have requested (extra petita);
(3) the arbitral tribunal does not decide on one of the parties' requests.

529. The objection grounds pursuant to Article 190 paragraph 2 lit c PILA represent a particular aspect of the parties' right to be heard and prohibit the arbitral tribunal from including claims in its arbitral award, to which the parties could not take a position either in fact or in law.[419]

530. The decision of the arbitral tribunal about issues not covered by the arbitration agreement falls under lit. b, but not under lit. c of Article 190 PILA.

F. Breach of the Principle of Equal Treatment of the Parties or the Right to Be Heard (Article 190 Paragraph 2 lit. d PILA)

531. The parties are to be granted equal chances to point out their arguments in the sense of Article 182 paragraph 3 PILA. The arbitral tribunal shall ensure the equality of arms and non-discrimination.[420] The Swiss Federal Supreme Court considers the right to be heard protected under Article 183 paragraph 3 and Article 190 paragraph 2 lit. d PILA to correspond to the right protected under Article 29 paragraph 2 CSC.[421] Each party has the right to comment on the facts and the legal arguments, to file motions to take evidence, to participate in the evidence taking or at

417. Decision 4A_476/2012 of the Swiss Federal Supreme Court.
418. Decisions A4_314/2012 and A4_550/2012 of the Swiss Federal Supreme Court.
419. BGE 120 II 172 C. 3a; BGE 116 II 80 C. 3a.
420. BGE 129 III 445 C. 5.1.
421. BGE 127 III 576; BGE 119 II 388; BGE 117 II 347; BGE 116 II 85.

least to comment on the result of the taking of evidence and to participate in hearings.[422] This right includes as a minimum standard, the right to have the arbitral tribunal consider the issues that are relevant to decide the case.[423] As a basic principle, a party which did not participate in the arbitration cannot invoke a lack of the right to be heard since such challenge would violate the principle of good faith.[424]

532. However, this appeal ground is very restrictively applied.[425] According to the Swiss Federal Supreme Court, the right to be heard does not contain a right for a materially correct decision (prohibition of the 'révision au fond').[426] According to the Swiss Federal Supreme Court, the right to make oral representation to the arbitral tribunal is also not covered by this objection ground.[427]

533. Due to many objections concerning the violation of the right to be heard, it is crucial that this assertion is already raised in the arbitration proceeding.[428] Since otherwise, if brought forward for the first time to the Swiss Federal Supreme Court, the assertion will be forfeited (ultimately, breach of good faith if not timely asserted).[429] Furthermore, the right to claim a violation of the right to be heard is also forfeited if the party declares during the CAS proceedings that their right to be heard was granted.

534. In the Decision 4A_400/2008 of 9 February 2009, the Swiss Federal Supreme Court had to judge a case, in which a player's agent pleaded a violation of the right to be heard, because the CAS based his decision on a legal argument that was unforeseeable for the parties. According to the considerations of the Swiss Federal Supreme Court the parties have to be heard regarding all legal questions and legal provisions, on which the arbitral tribunal intends to base his decision if their decisiveness was not foreseeable for the parties in aNOTHer way.

535. According to the Swiss Federal Supreme Court, the right to be heard is of a formal nature, so that the breach of that principle of law may lead to the rescission of the contested decision, regardless of whether or not this may lead to a different decision on the merits.[430] The Swiss Federal Supreme Court then held on

---

422. BGE 116 II 639 C. 4c.; BGE 117 II 346 C. 1a; BGE 130 III 35 C. 5.
423. *See* BGE 133 III 235.
424. Decisions 4A_682/2012 and 4A_620/2012 of the Swiss Federal Supreme Court.
425. There is no right to be heard on the arbitration panel's legal qualification of facts (introduced by the parties); *see* Besiktas/Del Bosque BGE 4A_42/2007. It does not include the right to receive a reasoned international arbitration decision; BGE 134 III 186 C. 6.1, 187; Decision of the Swiss Federal Supreme Court 4A_18/2008. The blatantly contradictory fact finding or the non-consideration of evidence does *not* per se constitute a breach of the right to be heard; if, however, the fact finding or the consideration of evidence constitutes a formal denial of justice, the right to be heard is breached; decision A4_522/2012 of the Swiss Federal Supreme Court.
426. BGE 127 III 576 C. 2b.
427. BGE 117 II 346 C. 1b aa.
428. BGE 119 II 388.
429. BGE 126 III 254; BGE 119 II 388; BGE 116 II 644 and Decision of the Swiss Federal Supreme Court 4P.103/1989 of 23 Oct. 1989 C. 2c.
430. BGE 121 III 331 C. 3c.

several occasions that apparently false findings or findings contrary to the file are not in themselves sufficient to rescind an international arbitration award.[431] This jurisprudence is not convincing because an apparent error or apparently false findings or findings contrary to the file, respectively, do constitute NOTHing but a clear breach of the right to be heard.

G. Breach of the 'Ordre Public' (Article 190 Paragraph 2 lit. e PILA)

536. A decision is incompatible with the *ordre public* if it misconceives the essential and largely accepted values that prevail in Switzerland and which need to be part of the foundations of every judicial ruling.[432] There are two possible categories of violation of *ordre public*:

(1) violations of the substantive law (substantive law *ordre public*); and
(2) violations of the procedural law (procedural law *ordre public*).

537. Examples for substantive law ordre public violations: pacta sunt servanda, prohibition of abuse of rights, principle of trust and good faith and the prohibition of discrimination as well as the personality rights and the prohibition of excessive binding. The breach of these fundamental legal rules has to be contradictory to the legal order and to the systems of values and the result (not the reasoning) of the arbitral decision has to breach ordre public.[433] The Swiss Federal Supreme Court is very restrictive in the application of this appeal ground. Even the incorrect application of mandatory laws or the violation of human rights does not per se constitute a breach of ordre public.[434] The contested decision has to breach ordre public and the Swiss Federal Supreme Court has ruled on several occasions that a decision cannot be rescinded if the reasoning alone appears contrary to the ordre public, but rather only if the breach of ordre public affects the dispositive part of the decision.[435]

538. In 2012, the Swiss Federal Supreme Court annulled for the very first time an arbitral award due to a violation of the material of *ordre public*.[436] This was the case when the FIFA prohibited the football player Matuzalem to play football worldwide for not having paid the compensation for the breach of his employment contract. The Swiss Federal Supreme Court found that such regulations were – contrary to the amount of the compensation awarded to the former club – excessively binding on the football players and annulled the award.

431. BGE 127 III 577. C. 2b; BGE 121 III 331; BGE 116 II 636.
432. BGE 132 III 389 C. 2.2.3.; BGE 120 II 155.
433. BGE 132 III 389 C. 2.2/2.2.3.
434. BGE 116 II 634 C. 4.
435. BGE 116 II 634 C. 4; BGE 120 II 155 C. 6a; BGE 128 III 191 C. 6b.
436. Decision of the Swiss Federal Supreme Court 4A_558/2011 dated 27 Mar. 2012.

539. Examples for procedural law *ordre public* violations: Right to an impartial and unbiased expert appointed by the arbitral tribunal[437] and the res judicata effect.[438] However, the lack of a justification of the decision does not constitute a breach of 'ordre public' and there is no autonomous right to rescind the arbitral award because of blatantly wrong establishment of the facts.[439]

H. Cognition of the Swiss Federal Supreme Court

540. There are even further limits on the Swiss Federal Supreme Court's authority to reassess arbitral awards. The Swiss Federal Supreme Court does not have the authorization to correct or complete the facts of the case ex officio (Article 77 paragraph 2 and Article 105 paragraph 2 CFSC); the Swiss Federal Supreme Court is bound by the facts established by the CAS. Further, the Swiss Federal Supreme Court does not apply the law ex officio (Article 77 paragraph 2 and Article 106 paragraph 1 CFSC); the parties have to argue which law applies and how the law is to be applied. Finally, the Swiss Federal Supreme Court is not authorized to decide the case instead of the CAS (Article 77 paragraph 2 and Article 107 paragraph 2 CFSC). It has only a function as a court of cassation. The Swiss Federal Supreme Court can only annul a CAS decision and send it back to the CAS for a new decision.

541. Also, with respect to sports arbitration, which in contrast to ordinary arbitration is affected by a serious imbalance between the parties, the Swiss Federal Supreme Court still strictly follows the statutory requirements. Even substantively false decisions, which clearly suffer from an inner conflict and are arbitrary, will not be annulled by the Swiss Federal Supreme Court.[440]

III. Revision

542. The PILA does not contain any provision for the revision of decisions of an arbitral tribunal within the meaning of Articles 176 et seq. PILA. In constant adjudication (before and after the CFSC came into force) the Swiss Federal Supreme Court has therefore filled this gap in the law and provided the parties an international arbitration proceeding with the extraordinary remedy of revision.[441]

543. Reasons for a revision based on Articles 121–123 CFSC is given in civil law cases in particular, if: (i) significant procedural rules were violated, (ii) the European Court of Human Rights convicted Switzerland pursuant to a violation of the ECHR, (iii) criminal proceedings came to the conclusion that a crime affected

437. BGE 128 III 191 C. 4a.
438. Decision of the Swiss Federal Supreme Court 4A_490/2009 of 13 Apr. 2010, according to which the non-observance of the res judicata is a violation of the 'ordre public'.
439. BGE 120 II 155 C. 6a; BGE 119 II 380 C. 3c.
440. *See* Decision of the Swiss Federal Supreme Court 4A_612/2009 of 10 Feb. 2010.
441. BGE 134 III 286 et seq; BGE 118 II 199, 200 et seq; cf. also BGE 129 III 727, 729.

the decision to the disadvantage of a party, or if (iv) a party later gets to know significant facts or discovers significant evidence, that could not be brought forward in the earlier proceedings, excluding the facts or evidence that came into existence after the decision was rendered.

544. Consequently, a sportsperson convicted of doping may request a revision of the decision of the CAS in front of the Swiss Federal Supreme Court pursuant to Article 123 CFSC, if he can, for example, based on new scientific findings prove that the substance that was found in his body was produced endogenous. Should such evidence have come only into existence after the decision that was rendered a revision is excluded and the athlete would need to turn to the sports federation for a completely new decision.

545. In case the Swiss Federal Supreme Court approves the appeal, it does not decide itself about the matter, but sends it back to the arbitral tribunal, which has decided in that matter, or a new, still to be formed arbitral tribunal (which will be necessary in the case of lack of independence of the original CAS panel).[442]

§3. Remedies According to the Swiss Civil Procedure Code

I. The Appeal to the Swiss Federal Supreme Court

546. A decision of an arbitral tribunal with respect to national facts can be appealed according to Article 389 CPC at the Swiss Federal Supreme Court.

547. An appeal to the higher civil court of the Canton (like it was possible under Article 36 Concordat on Arbitration of 27 March 1969 (CoA)) is only possible if the parties have agreed on such appeal procedure. For the CAS, this would be the Cantonal Court of the Canton of Vaud.

548. In principle, the appeal to the Swiss Federal Supreme Court has also no suspensive effect. According to Article 103 CFSC the suspensive effect must be requested, which in doping affairs is generally necessary and possible. In the case of *Danilo Hondo* (that was decided under the old CoA) the Cantonal Court initially granted suspensive effect, which was confirmed by the Swiss Federal Supreme Court, on the grounds that the interest of the sportsperson to participate in sporting competition prevails. The general interest to combat doping and the need to re-establish the ranking of participating sportspersons was considered less important.[443]

549. The grounds of appeals according to the CPC (respectively earlier under the CoA) are similar to the ones of the PILA, but differ in one fundamental point.

442. BGE 134 III 286; BGE 118 II 199.

443. Order of the Swiss Federal Supreme Court of 11 Sept. 2006 in the matter of 4P.148/2006 of 10 Jan. 2007.

Pursuant to Article 393 lit. e CPC, a decision of a national arbitral tribunal may be annulled if the decision arbitrary in the outcome, was clearly based on actual findings contrary to the files or there is an evident breach of law or equity. The decisions of arbitral tribunals in national matters are therefore significantly more open to challenge than decisions of arbitral tribunals in international matters.

550. In this context the question arises, to what extent the sport federations can declare the regulations of the PILA applicable for the national arbitration based on Article 353 paragraph 2 CPC. For such a limitation of the appeal grounds Article 353 paragraph 2 CPC requires an explicit statement of the parties in the arbitration agreement. Due to the jurisdiction of the Swiss Federal Supreme Court regarding the need for an explicit statement in connection with the waiver of the right to appeal based on Article 192 paragraph 1 PILA, it is not possible to exclude the appeal grounds of the CPC in the world of sports. The voluntariness of the declaration by the athlete is missing.[444]

II. Revision

551. In addition to the appeal procedure the Swiss Civil Procedure Code provides the possibility for the revision of arbitral awards (Articles 396 et seq. CPC). The request for a revision must be directed to the higher civil court of the Canton, based on Article 356 paragraph 1 CPC. The grounds for a revision are the same as those currently demanded for an international arbitral award.

§4. Remedies According to the ECHR

552. The decision *Mutu & Pechstein v. Switzerland* and *Ali Riza v. Turkey* of the ECHR indicates that in the case of compulsory arbitration the guarantees of the Convention will be granted by the ECHR. Thus, a country where arbitration proceedings are taking place may be sued if the rights provided for in the Convention are violated during these arbitration proceedings. An appeal to the ECHR may be available in compulsory arbitrations.

§5. Other Legal Procedures

553. In principle, due to the autonomy of the associations, each sports organization may render a new decision at any time. This means, for example, that a sportsperson who subsequently has substantial doubts as to his disciplinary conviction always has the opportunity to request the sports organization to reassess its decision. This decision could then be challenged again through all instances.

---

444. Cf. BGE 133 II 235 C. 4.3.2.2.

554. Should the sports federation refuse to render such new decision the refusal to issue a decision may be appealed to the CAS.

§6. SPORTS AND COVID-19

I. Introduction

555. Since the outbreak of the Covid-19-pandemic the world of sports has not been the same. The world's biggest sport events, such as the Olympic Games and the UEFA European Championship, had to be postponed due to the global pandemic. Moreover, empty stadiums, travel restrictions as well as training restrictions etc. have had and still have a detrimental impact on anyone involved in the world of sports, most notably on federations, associations, clubs and sportsmen and -women.

556. Without matches with spectator in the stadiums, sport clubs are missing the important spectator and catering revenues that normally cover a large part of the budget. Sponsorship income is also lost, as many sponsorships are tied to ongoing match operations. Individual athletes are often financed by prize money and sponsorships. At the moment, there are neither competitions nor will the sponsorship income amount to the regular sum. Thus, many athletes were or are currently without income. It is all the worse that due to the postponement of the Olympic Games planned sponsorship income was lost.

II. Measures by the Government

A. Financial Aid for Sports Organisations

557. In order to be able to maintain the structures in Swiss team sports in the Covid-19-pandemic, the Federal Council and the Parliament decided to support professional and semi-professional clubs with non-repayable (a-fonds-perdu) contributions. The parliament amended the corresponding legal basis on 19 March 2021. The Federal Council adopted the associated ordinance amendments on 31 March 2021.

558. As stipulated in the Swiss Covid-19 Act the Confederation provides support in the form of a-fund-perdu contributions amounting to a maximum of CHF 115 million. The contributions are granted to football and ice hockey clubs with a team playing in one of the two professional leagues as well as basketball, handball, floorball, volleyball, women's football and women's ice hockey clubs with a team playing in the highest league for their sport (Article 12b paragraph 1 Covid-19 Act). Pursuant to Article 12b paragraph 3 Covid-19 Act the contributions are paid in compensation for the reduction in revenues from matches in the national championship that have been played since 29 October 2020 without spectators or with a reduced number of spectators as a result of measures taken by the Confederation. The contributions however are bound to the conditions provided for in Article 12b paragraph 3 Covid-19 Act. These conditions *inter alia* set forth that a club must not distribute dividends or shares of profits and must not repay capital contributions for five years following receipt of the contributions.[445] Furthermore, the club must – in order to receive contributions – decrease the average salary to the maximum insured salary for the purposes of compulsory accident insurance (CHF 148,200) or reduce the average salary that exceeds this amount by at least 20%.

559. This means that for all employees of the club, i.e., players, coaches and other staff members, earning more than an average of CHF 148,200, clubs must deduct 20% of the salary. Since all players have employment contracts with set salaries, these contracts would have to be amended in order to meet the conditions. This presupposes that especially the players and coaches would have to voluntarily forego part of their salaries. For some clubs it might be difficult to meet this requirement, mainly if they granted salary increases the previous year. Furthermore, it seems that for clubs paying higher salaries, it is easier to meet the salary reduction condition.

560. The Confederation may further support clubs that are basically solvent, but which face cash flow problems even after being granted contributions under Article 12*b* with interest-free loans amounting to a maximum of CHF 235 million. These must be repaid within ten years at the latest. The borrower moreover shall provide collateral recognised by the Confederation amounting to at least 25% of the loan amount.[446]

B. Financial Aid for Individual Athletes

561. Individual athletes may apply for the payment of compensation for loss of earnings to persons who must suspend or significantly reduce their gainful economic activity as a result of measures in connection with controlling the Covid-19 pandemic. Pursuant to Article 15 paragraph 1 Covid-19 Act. Only persons with a loss of earnings or income that in their business represents a drop in turnover of at least 30% in comparison with the average turnover in the years 2015–2019 are deemed to have suffered a significant reduction in their gainful economic activity.

562. The compensation is 80% of the average earned income before entitlement to the allowance began. It shall not exceed CHF 196 per day.[447]

---

445. Article 12b Covid-19 Act.
446. Article 13 Covid-19 Act.
447. See Art. 5 Ordinance on measures in the event of loss of earnings in connection with the coronavirus (Covid-19).

III. Conclusion

563. The Covid-19 pandemic is damaging for people involved in sports. The Swiss Government provides financial aid for sports organisations and individuals. Albeit, there is room for certain criticism regarding the constitution of the financial aid, it can be essential for organisations and individuals to be able to apply for it.

Selected Bibliography

ADOLPHSEN, Jens. 'Aktuelle beweisrechtliche Fragen im Dopingverfahren'. In *Sport und Recht.* Edited by ARTER & BADDELEY. Bern 2007, 239 et seq.

AEBI-MÜLLER, Regina E. & RÜFENACHT, Michael. 'Die Arbeits- und Treuepflicht des Sportlers: Welche Pflichten treffen den angestellten Sportler?'. In *Sport und Recht.* Edited by ARTER & BADDELEY. Bern 2007, 113 et seq.

ARTER, Oliver & SCHWEIZER, Eva. 'Verantwortlichkeit des Veranstalters von Sportanlässen'. In *Sport und Recht.* Edited by ARTER. Bern 2004, 17 et seq.

ARTER, Oliver. 'Der Zuschauer im Sport'. In *Sport und Recht.* Edited by ARTER. Bern 2005, 31 et seq.

BADDELEY, Margareta. 'About the Proper Application of Rules of Sports Federations – Comments on the Phonak Case'. *Causa Sport* (2005): 28 et seq.

BADDELEY, Margareta. 'Gesellschaftsformen für Sportvereinigungen'. In *Sport und Recht* Edited by ARTER. Bern 2004, 103 et seq.

BADDELEY, Margareta. 'La décision Canas: Nouvelles règles du jeu pour l'arbitrage international du sport'. *Causa Sport* (2007): 155 et seq.

BADDELEY, Margareta. 'La relation entre médecin et sportif'. In *Droit et sport,* Coll. CIES, vol. 2, Bern 1997, 37 et seq.

BADDELEY, Margareta. L'association sportive face au droit: Les limites de son autonomie, thesis, Geneva: Basel and Frankfurt am Main, 1994.

BADDELEY, Margareta. Le sportif, sujet ou objet? – La protection de la personnalité du sportif, Rapports et communications de la Société suisse des juristes. 2/1996, in: RDS 1996 II 139 et seq.

BADDELEY, Margareta. 'Le statut personnel du sportif'. In Chapitres choisis du droit du sport, Etudes et Recherches du Groupe Interfacultaire des Sciences du Sport, Geneva 1993, 67 et seq.

Badertscher, Beat. Der Ausschluss aus dem Verein nach SCHWEIZERischem Zivilgesetzbuch. thesis, Zurich 1980.

Baeriswyl, Bruno. 'Datenschutzrecht und Sport'. In *Sport und Recht.* Edited by ARTER & BADDELEY. Bern 2006, 133 et seq.

BALMELLI, Marco. 'Entschädigung von Sportlern: Erscheinungsformen, rechtliche Qualifikation und Vertragsgestaltung'. In: *Sport und Recht.* Edited by ARTER & BADDELEY. Bern 2007, 143 et seq.

BALMELLI, Marco & Damian Heller. 'Gutachten Sportbetrug und Good Governance'. Basel: Basel Institute on Governance, 5 December 2012.

Baumann, Andreas, 'Die Klub-Lizenzierung durch die Swiss Football League (SFL)'. *Causa Sport* (2006): 464 et seq.

Selected Bibliography

Becker Stefan, Detlef. Sportregeln und allgemeine Rechtssätze im Normen- und Wertgefüge des Sports. Münster 1999.

Beloff, Michael, Tim Kerr & Marie Demetriou. *Sports Law*. Oxford 1999.

BERETTA, Piera. Wirtschaftliche Vereine in der Schweiz. thesis, Basel 2001.

BERETTA, Piera. 'Wirtschaftliche Vereine und Corporate Governance'. In *Aktuelle Fragen aus dem Vereinsrecht*. Edited by RIEMER. Zurich 2005, 1 et seq.

BERNASCONI, Michele & Michel Huber. 'Die Anfechtung von Vereinsbeschlüssen: Zur Frage der Gültigkeit statutarischer Fristbestimmungen'. *SpuRt* (2004): 268 et seq.

Berger Bernhard & Franz Kellerhals. Internationale und interne Schiedsgerichtsbarkeit in der Schweiz. Bern, Vienna 2006.

Berger, Chantal. Les aspects juridiques du dopage dans le sport professionnel. thesis, Neuchâtel 1997.

Betz, Katrin. 'SCHWEIZERisches Strafgesetzbuch'. in *Praxiskommentar*. 3rd edn. Zurich 2017.

Biojout, Pascal. Le sponsoring: analyse économique du comportement des entreprises en matière de parrainage sportif. Limoges 1985, 7 et seq.

Bizzini, Lucio. 'Equilibre et déséquilibre du sport chez l'enfant de 6 à 14 ans'. In Un champion à tout prix, Les droits de l'enfant et le sport. Sion 1999, 93 et seq.

Blackaby, Nigel, et al. 'REDFERN and HUNTER on international arbitration'. 6th ed. Oxford: Oxford University Press, 2015.

Bodmer, Hans. Vereinsstrafe und Verbandsgerichtsbarkeit (dargestellt am Beispiel des SCHWEIZERischen Fussballverbandes). thesis, St. Gallen 1989.

Bondallaz, Jacques. 'La responsabilité civile de l'organisateur d'une manifestation sportive en droit suisse'. In *Droit et sport*, Coll. CIES, vol. 2, Bern 1997, 63 et seq.

Bondallaz, Jacques. 'La responsabilité pour les préjudices causés dans les stades lors de compétitions sportives'. Coll. CIES, vol. 1, thesis, Bern 1996.

Bondallaz, Jacques. Toute la jurisprudence sportive en Suisse, Exposé systématique de plus de 600 arrêts. Coll. CIES vol. 3, Bern 2000.

Bondallaz, Jaques. 'La punissabilité des atteintes à l'intégrité corporelle dans les sports impliquant notamment des contacts physiques entre adversaires'. PJA (1999): 273 et seq.

Borchard, Michael, Die Wirksamkeit der im deutschen Lizenzfussball verwendeten Musterverträge. Bielefeld 1999.

BORN, Gary, 'International Commercial Arbitration – Second Edition'. Kluwer Law International: Alphen aan den Rijn 2014.

Bothor, Peter, 'Zur Rechtgültigkeit von TV-Exklusivverträgen der englischen Football Premier League'. *SpuRt* (2000): 181 et seq.

Bourg, Jean-François & Jean-Jacques Gouget. Analyse économique du sport. Paris 1998.

Bousigue, Amandine & Claude Stricker. 'The Economic Impact of International Sports Organisations in Switzerland 2008–2013'. Lausanne: International Academy of Sports Science and Technology, 2015.

Boutellier, Roman & David Müller. 'Doping: Zielkonflikt zwischen Chancengleichheit und Sicherheit'. *Causa Sport* (2007): 263 et seq.

Breitenmoser, Stephan & Remus Muresan. 'Spielräume für sportspezifische Regelungen nach der "Bosman"-Rechtsprechung'. *Causa Sport* (2004): 138 et seq.
Brüschweiler, PHILIPP. 'Neuerungen bei der FIFA – Spielervermittlerreglementierung'. *Causa Sport* (2008): 32 et seq.
Buchberger, Markus, Die Überprüfbarkeit sportverbandsrechtlicher Entscheidungen durch die ordentliche Gerichtsbarkeit. Berlin 1999.
Bucher, Andreas. Personnes physiques et protection de la personnalité. 4th edn. Basel 1999.
Bühler, Josef. 'Besteuerung der Spielerprämien anlässlich der UEFA EURO 2008^{TM}. Causa Sport (2007): 342.
Burgener, Louis. La Confédération suisse et l'éducation physique de la jeunesse. vol. 2, La Chaux-de-Fonds 1952.
Bussard, Jean-Claude. 'Les manuels fédéraux et l'institutionnalisation de l'éducation physique'. In *Sports et formes,* Lausanne (2001): 51 et seq.
Cadosch, Roger M. 'Besteuerung von Sportlern im internationalen Verhältnis'. In *Sport und Recht,* Bern 2007, 297 et seq.
CDDS, Le Conseil de l'Europe et le sport 1992–1993, Strasbourg 1993.
CDDS, Le Conseil de l'Europe et le sport 1967–1991, vol. I, Strasbourg 1992.
CDDS, Le Conseil de l'Europe et le sport 1967–1991, vol. II, Strasbourg 1992.
CDDS, Le Conseil de l'Europe et le sport 1994–1996, Les Conventions, Strasbourg 1996.
CDDS, Le Conseil de l'Europe et le sport 1994–1996, Strasbourg 1996.
Chablais, Alain & Jean-Louis DUC. In Droit et sport, Coll. CIES, vol. 2, Bern 1977, 313 and 327 et seq.
Chappelet, Jean-Loup, Le Système olympique. Grenoble 1991.
Chappuis, Christine & Bénedict Winiger. (eds). Journée de la responsabilité civile 2000. La responsabilité fondée sur la confiance, Publications du Centre d'études juridiques européennes, Zurich 2001.
Chappuis, Fernand. 'L'influence des règles de comportement sportif sur le droit pénal: l'exemple du ski et du snowboard'. Droit et Sport, Coll. CIES, vol. 2, Bern 1997, 291 et seq.
Ciocca, PHILIPPe. Les relations contractuelles entre un sportif professionnel et son représentant. Thesis, Lausanne 1995.
Commission Européenne. DG X, Le modèle sportif européen. Document de consultation de la DG X, Brusseles 1998.
Commission Européenne. DG X, L'impact des activités de l'Union européenne sur le sport. Edition 1995, Brusseles 1995.
Commission Européenne, DG X, l'Union européenne et le sport, Brusseles 1996.
Conseil de l'Europe pour le sport et Statut du Fonds pour le sport, amendment to the resolution (78) 75; CDDS, Le Conseil de l'Europe et le sport 1967–1991, vol. I, 41 et seq.
Conseil de l'Europe, Le sport et le droit, Actes du dix-huitième Colloque de droit européen, Maastricht, 12–14 Octobre 1988, Strasbourg 1989.
Corbat Claude, Les peines statutaires. Thesis, Fribourg 1974.
Dalleves, Louis. 'Problème juridiques de la lutte contre le dopage'. In *Rivista di diritto amministrativo e tributario ticinese.* vol. 1, Bellinzona 1994, 233 et seq.

Selected Bibliography

Dalleves, Louis. 'Questions juridiques relatives au dopage'. In *Chapitres choisis du droit du sport*. Etudes et Recherches du GISS 2/1993, Genève 1993, 115 et seq.

Dalleves, Louis. 'Responsabilité civile en matière d'accidents de sport'. In *Chapitres choisis de droit du sport*, Geneva 1993, 91 et seq.

Däppen, Robert. Rechtsprobleme des SCHWEIZERischen Tennissports und seiner Verbandsstrukturen.

Zurich 1992, 114 et seq.

De Mondenard, Jean-Pierre. Dictionnaire des substances et procédés dopants en pratique sportive. Paris 1991.

De Mondenard, Jean-Pierre. Le dopage aux Jeux Olympiques: la tricherie récomensée. Paris 1996.

De Mondenard, Jean-Pierre & Bernard Chevalier. Le dossier noir du dopage: les produits, les dangers, les responsable, Paris 1981.

Del Fabro, Marco. 'Der Trainervertrag'. In *Sport und Recht*, Edited by ARTER. Bern 2005, 101 et seq.

Donatsch, Andreas. 'Gedanken zum strafrechtlichen Schutz des Sportlers'. RPS 107 (1990).

Doyez, Louis-Frédéric. performed by Professor Colin, L'Union européenne et le sport: l'arrêt Bosman, Reims 1998/1999 http://reimsscd.ent.sirsidynix.net.uk/client/fr_FR/default/search/results/?ln=fr_FR&q=Doyez+Louis-Fr%C3%A9d%C3%A9ric&rw=0.

Dubey, Jean-PHILIPPe. La libre circulation des sportifs en Europe. Coll. CIES, vol 5, Fribourg, Bern and Bruxelles 2000.

Dubey, Jean-PHILIPPe. 'Le droit communautaire de la reconnaissance des diplômes et qualifications sportifs'. In *Droit et sport*, Coll. CIES, vol. 2, Bern 1997, 185 et seq.

Duc, Nicolas. La responsabilité civile des usagers des pistes de ski. Thesis, Lausanne 2000.

Eggenberger, Peter. 'Rechtliche Besonderheiten der Major League Soccer'. *Causa Sport* (2004): 80 et seq.

Eichenberger, Luz. Die Eidgenössische Sportkommission 1874–1997. Macolin 1998.

Eichenberger, Luz. Die Eidgenössische Sportschule Magglingen. Macolin 1994.

Eichenberger, Luz. 'Mise en place et développement des institutions du sport suisse (XIX et XXème siècles)'. In *Sports et formes*, Lausanne 2001, 79 et seq.

Eichenberger, Richard. Zivilrechtliche Haftung des Veranstalters sportlicher Wettkämpfe. thesis, Zurich 1973.

EMANUEL, Bernd. Dopingnachweis durch indirekte Beweis methoden 'Biologischer Pass'. *SpuRt* (2009): 195.

Emmerich, Volker. 'Sport und Medien aus kartellrechtlicher Sicht'. In *Sport und Medien, Recht und Sport*, Band 13, 1990, 57 et seq.

Engel Pierre. Contrats de droit suisse. Bern 2000.

Engel, Pierre. Le calcul des votes et des majorités en droit privé suisse. RSJ No. 81, Zurich 1985, 303 et seq.

Engler, Marc. 'Die strafrechtliche Verantwortlichkeit des Veranstalters von Sportanlässen'. In *Sport und Recht*, Edited by ARTER & BADDELEY. Bern 2008, 99 et seq.

EUFE, Tillmann. Die Unschuldsvermutung im Dopingverfahren. thesis, Berlin 2005.

Faber, Alexander. Doping als unlauterer Wettbewerb und Spielbetrug. Thesis, Weinfelden 1974.
Fähndrich, Franco. Der Persönlichkeitsschutz des Sportlers in seiner Beziehung zu den Massenmedien. thesis, Lucerne 1987.
FLACHSMANN, Stefan & Isenring Bernhard. 'Sanktion von Doping im Strafrecht'. *Causa Sport* (2004): 231 et seq.
Fritzweiler, Jochen, Bernhard Pfister & Thomas Summerer. Praxishandbuch Sportrecht. Munich 1998.
Fritzweiler, Jochen. Doping – Sanktionen, Beweise, Ansprüche, Bern 2000.
FUCHS, Christoph. Rechtsfragen der Vereinsstrafe. thesis, Zurich 1999.
Garrigues, Christian. Activités sportives et droit communautaire. Strasbourg 1982.
Gattiker, Monika. 'Die rechtliche Stellung des Arztes bei Doping und Heilmittelmissbrauch'. In *Sport und Recht*. Edited by ARTER. Bern 2004, 193 et seq.
GEISER, Thomas. 'Arbeitsverträge mit Sportlern'. In *Sport und Recht*. Edited by ARTER & BADDELEY. Bern 2007, 79 et seq.
Gerum, Oliver. 'Die gesellschaftliche Bedeutung des Sports von der Antike bis zur Gegenwart'. In *Sport und Recht*. Edited by ARTER. Bern 2005, 17 et seq.
Giger, Hans. 'Neue Wege der Konfliktbereinigung im Sportbereich (1. Teil)'. *Causa Sport* (2006): 478.
Giger, Hans. 'Neue Wege der Konfliktbereinigung im Sportbereich (2. Teil)'. *Causa Sport* (2006): 561.
Grothe, Helmut & Matthias Frohn. 'Rechtsstaatliche Verfahrensgarantien in der Sportgerichtsbarkeit: Wayne Rooney, Paul Stefford und Art. 6 EMRK'. *Causa Sport* (2008): 104 et seq.
Gschöpf, Marwin. Haftung bei Verstoss gegen Sportregeln. Vienna 2000.
Gschwend, Felix. Die Rechtsstellung der Dachverbände. thesis, Basel 1994.
Gurovits Kohli, Andràs A. 'Die zivilrechtliche Haftung bei Zuschauerausschreitungen'. In: *Sport und Recht*. Edited by ARTER & BADDELEY. Bern 2008, 161 et seq.
HAAS, Ulrich & Clemens PROKOP. 'Die Athletenvereinbarung – Der Athlet als stilles Mitglied des Verbandes'. *SpuRt* 3 no. 4 (1996): 109 et seq.
HAAS, Ulrich & Julia Jansen Julia. 'Die verbandsrechtliche Verantwortlichkeit für Zuschauerausschreitungen im Fussball'. In *Sport und Recht*. Edited by ARTER & BADDELEY. Bern 2008, 129 et seq.
HAAS, Ulrich. 'Die Überprüfung von "Spielentscheiden" in der Rechtsprechung des Court of Arbitration for Sport (CAS)'. *Causa Sport* (2007): 131 et seq.
HAAS, Ulrich. 'Die Vereinbarung von "Rechtsregeln" in (Berufungs-) Schiedsverfahren vor dem Court of Arbitration for Sport'. *Causa Sport* (2007): 271 et seq.
Halter, Fritz. Verbände und Sektionen in ihrem gegenseitigen Verhältnis nach SCHWEIZERischem Vereinsrecht, Bern 1946.
Häfelin, Ulrich, Walter Haller & Helen Keller. SCHWEIZERisches Bundesstaatsrecht. Zurich 2008.
HANDSCHIN, Lukas. 'Grenzen der Schiedsgerichtsbarkeit im Sport'. In *Sport und Recht*. Edited by ARTER. Bern 2005, 275 et seq.
HANDSCHIN, Lukas & Christoph TRUNIGER. 'Von der kassatorischen Natur'der Anfechtungsklage nach Article. 75 ZGB'. RSJ 99, no. 6 (2003): 142 et seq.
Häner, Isabelle. 'Bau-, umwelt- und verfahrensrechtliche Aspekte des Sportstättebaus'. In *Sport und Recht*. Edited by ARTER & BADDELEY. Bern 2006, 157 et seq.

Häner, Isabelle, 'Überlegungen zum Verbandsbeschwerderecht nach dem Züricher Stadion-Streit'. *Causa Sport* (2004): 121 et seq.

HANNAMANN, Isolde. Kartellverbot und Verhaltenskoordination im Sport. thesis, Erlangen/Nürnberg 2001.

HARTMANN, Heidi, 'Die Leute und die Medien erwarten halt, dass eine Frau, die boxt, auch sehr weiblich sein muss!'. *Causa Sport* (2005): 14 et seq.

HAUSHEER, Heinz & Regina AEBI-MÜLLER. Das Personenrecht des SCHWEIZERischen Zivilgesetzbuches. Bern 2005.

HAUSER, Deborah. 'Korruption im Sport', in *Jusletter (Switzerland),* 13 May 2012.

HAUSER, Robert, Erhard SCHWERI & Karl HARTMANN. SCHWEIZERisches Strafprozessrecht. Basel 2005.

HEERMANN, Peter W. 'Aktuelle kartellrechtliche Probleme im Zusammenhang mit Spielertransfers'. In *Sport und Recht.* Edited by ARTER & BADDELEY. Bern 2007, 263 et seq.

HEERMANN, Peter W. 'Der Schutz Olympischer Symbole in China'. *Causa Sport* (2008): 39 et seq.

HEERMANN, Peter W. 'Die Haftung des Sportveranstalters für die Verletzung von Verkehrs(sicherungs-)pflichten in ausgewählten Sportarten'. In *Sport und Recht.* Edited by ARTER & BADDELEY. Bern 2008, 189 et seq.

HEERMANN, Peter W. 'Haftungsrisiken des Sportverbandes bei Lizenzierungsverfahren im Ligasport'. *Causa Sport* (2004): 184 et seq.

HEERMANN, Peter W. 'Kartellrechtliche Betrachtungen zu Europa- und Weltmeisterschaften im Fussball'. *Causa Sport* (2008): 111 et seq.

HEERMANN, Peter W. 'Sport und Kartellrecht'. In *Sport und Recht.* Edited by ARTER. Bern 2005, 197 et seq.

HEERMANN, Peter W. *Verbandsautonomie v. Kartellrecht. Causa Sport* (2006): 345 et seq.

HEERMANN, Peter W. 'Schiedsrichter – Schiebung – Schadenersatz?'. *Causa Sport* (2005): 4 et seq.

HEINI, Anton. Das SCHWEIZERische Vereinsrecht. Basel 1988.

HEINI, Anton & Urs SCHERRER. 'Das SCHWEIZERische Vereinsrecht'. In *Basler Kommentar zum SCHWEIZERischen Privatrecht*, Zivilgesetzbuch I, 3rd edn. Basel 2006.

HEINI, Anton, Wolfgang PORTMANN & Matthias SEEMANN. Grundriss des Vereinsrechts. Basel 2009.

Hohl, Michael. Rechtliche Probleme der Nominierung von Leistungssportlern. Bayreuth 1992.

HONSELL, Heinrich & Nedim Peter VOGT. Kommentar zum SCHWEIZERischen Privatrecht, Zivilgesetzbuch I. Basel 2006.

Hufschmid, Daniel & Tobias Giesser. Anmerkung zum Urteil des Bundesgerichts vom 17. Juli 2007 im 'Fall Jan Ullrich'. *Causa Sport* (2008): 75 et seq.

Hürlimann, Stephan. 'Professioneller Sport und Steuern', *Causa Sport* (2004): 199 et seq.

Husting, Alexandre. L'Union européenne et le sport, l'impact de la construction européenne sur l'activité sportive. Lyon 1998.

Jacq, Patrick. 'L'organisation internationale du sport – Les structures'. In *Sport, droit et relations internationales*, Paris 1988, 1 et seq.

Jau, Martin. 'Overview of the Taxation of Non-resident Athletes and Entertainers in Switzerland'. *Causa Sport* (2006): 448 et seq.

JAQUIER, Jérôme. La qualification juridique des règles autonomes des organisations sportives. Thesis, Lausanne 2004.

Jenny, Christian. 'Arbeitsverträge von Sportlern'. In *Sport und Recht.* Edited by ARTER. Bern 2005, 175 et seq.

Jenny, Christian. 'Kein Fussball- "Erdbeben" nach CAS-Urteil im "Fall Webster"'. *Causa Sport* (2008): 26 et seq.

Jenny, Christian. 'Arbeitsvertragsgestaltung im Bereich Gesundheitsschutz und bezüglich Sportverletzungen'. *Causa Sport* (2005): 364 et seq.

Jenny, Christian. 'Der Sportvermittlungs- und der Sportlermanagementvertrag'. In: *Sportlermanagement*, Bern, Munich and Vienna 2000, 21 et seq.

Jenoure, Peter. 'doping – De quoi s'agit-il? Quelques réflexions'. In *Aspects juridiques du dopage*, Colloque de Bern, 7 novembre 1990, Lausanne 1991, 15 et seq.

Jolidon, Pierre. 'Le droit du sport en Suisse'. RSJ (1990): 389 et seq.

Jolidon, Pierre. Commentaire du Concordat suisse sur l'arbitrage. Bern 1994.

Jolidon, Pierre. La responsabilité civile et pénale des boxeurs en droit suisse. In: Mélanges Assiste 1989, 187 et seq.

Jolidon, Pierre. 'La responsabilité civile et pénale des participants à des activités sportives'. RDS I (1989): 17 et seq.

Jolidon, Pierre. 'Le droit du sport en Suisse'. RSJ (1990): 369 et seq.

Jolidon, Pierre. 'Ordre sportif et ordre juridique – A propos du pouvoir juridictionnel des tribunaux étatiques en matière sportive'. RJB (1991): 213 et seq.

Kaddous, Christine, 'L'arrêt Bosman et la libre circulation des personnes au sein de l'Union européenne'. *Droit et sport,* Coll. CIES, vol. 2, Bern 1997, 154 et seq.

Kälin, Oliver. 'Sorgfalt und Verantwortlichkeit beim Anbieten von Risikoaktivitäten'. In *Sport und Recht.* Edited by ARTER & BADDELEY. Bern 2008, 225 et seq.

Karaquillo, Jean-Pierre. *Le droit du sport.* 2nd edn. Paris 1977.

Karaquillo, Jean-Pierre. 'Les normes des communautés sportives et le droit étatique'. In *Conseil de l'Europe*, Colloque sport et droit 1988, 51 et seq.

Kaufmann-Kohler, Gabrielle. Arbitration at the Olympics, Issues of Fast-Track Dispute, Resolution and Sports Law. The Hague, London and New York 2001.

Kaufmann-Kohler, Gabrielle. 'Atlanta et l'arbitrage ou les premières expériences de la division olympique du Tribunal Arbitral du Sport'. Bull. ASA (1996): 433 et seq.

Kaufmann-Kohler, Gabrielle & Antonio Rigozzi. Arbitrage International. 2nd edn. Zurich 2010.

Keller Andreas. Die Ausschliessung aus dem Verein. thesis, Zurich 1979.

Kiener Regina. Bildung, Forschung und Kultur. In: Droit constitutionnel suisse, Zurich 2001.

Killias, Martin. Précis de droit pénal général. 2nd edn. Bern 2001.

Kleiner, Jan. 'Rechtsfragen rund um Stadionverbote'. In *Sport und Recht.* Edited by ARTER & BADDELEY. Bern 2008, 19 et seq.

Klemm, Tanja. 'Rechtsprechung zum Vereinsrecht'. *Causa Sport* (2005): 284 et seq.

Klose, Martin. Die Rolle des Sports bei der Europäischen Einigung – Zum Problem von Ausländersperrklauseln. Berlin 1989.
Kocher, Martin. 'Anmerkungen zum Urteil des Verwaltungsgerichts des Kantons Bern vom 2. Oktober 2006'. *Causa Sport* (2007): 193 et seq.
Kocher, Martin. 'Verschärfte Besteuerung der Werbeeinnahmen von Sportlern'. *Causa Sport* (2006): 512 et seq.
Krekel, Jan F. & Mirjam TEITLER. 'Urheber- und wettbewerbsrechtliche Aspekte von Public-Viewing-Veranstaltungen im Vergleich des deutschen und SCHWEIZERischen Rechts'. *Causa Sport* (2006): 156 et seq.
Kubli, Felix. Haftungsverhältnisse bei Sportveranstaltungen. Zurich 1952.
KUMMER, Max. Spielregel und Rechtsregel. Bern 1973.
Lalive, Pierre, Jean-Françoise Poudret & Claude Reymond, Le droit de l'arbitrage interne et international en Suisse. Lausanne 1989.
Lapouble, Jean-Christophe. 'L'intervention publique en matière de dopage'. *Revue française d'administration publique*, no. 97, January-March.2001, 117 et seq.
Laure, Patrick. Le dopage. Paris 1995.
Leglise, Michel. 'L'enfant et la pratique sportive de haut niveau'. *Revue Olympique*, February-March 1996, 52 et seq.
Leglise, Michel. Pour une lutte contre le dopage. Fédération International de Gymnastique, Lyss 1983.
Lob Jean. Dopage, responsabilité objective ("strict liability") et de quelques autres questions. In: RSJ 1999, 270 et seq.
Louveau, Catherine, et al. Dopage et performance sportive: analyse d'une pratique prohibée. Paris 1995.
Lüscher, Hans. Die rechtliche Stellung der Vereinssektionen nach SCHWEIZERischem Recht. thesis, Zurich 1945.
Maracci, Marco. 'Institutionalisation et "militarisation" du sport en Suisse (1914–1945)'. *Sports et formes*, Lausanne 2001, 35 et seq.
Margeat, Henri. 'Une assurance moderne pour le sportif'. In *Les problèmes juridiques du sport – responsabilité et assurance*, Paris 1984.
Martig, Christoph P.A. 'Sportyachten in Seenot – Grundsätze des internationalen Rechts über Hilfeleistung und Bergung'. *Causa Sport* (2006): 3 et seq.
Martin-Achard, Edmon. La loi fédérale contre la concurrence déloyale du 19 décembre 1986 (LCD). Lausanne 1988.
Mätzler, Eugen. Der Lizenzspielervertrag in der Nationalliga des SCHWEIZERischen Fussballverbandes. thesis, Zurich, 1985.
Miege, Colin. Le sport européen. Coll. Que sais-je? Paris 1996.
Miege, Colin. Les organisations sportives et l'Europe. Paris 2000.
Mimiague, Marie-José, Le problème du doping en droit pénal comparé. Bordeaux 1973.
Modl, Christian. 'Rechtliche Aspekte der Sportvermittlung im SCHWEIZERischen Recht'. In: *Sportvermittlung. Sportlermanagement*, Bern, Munich and Vienna 2000, 41 et seq.
Mohler, Markus H.F. 'Sicherheitsrecht und Rechtssicherheit bei Sportveranstaltungen (staatliche Sicherheitsmassnahmen, Umfang und Grenzen)'. In *Sport und Recht*. Edited by ARTER & BADDELEY. Bern 2008, 73 et seq.

Montel, Alberto. Responsabilità per danno causato in gara sportiva. In: Rep. 1955, 170 et seq.
Morandi, Jean-Pierre, Werner Altweg & Pierre Jolidon. 233; Jugement de la Cour de cassation pénale du Tribunal cantonale vaudois du 23 janvier 1990.
Moreillon, Laurent. La résponsabilité civile en cas d'accident de haute montagne. Thesis, Lausanne 1987.
Moreillon, Laurent. 'Les tendances récentes en matière d'infractions à la vie et à l'intégrité corporelle par omission et leurs conséquences en droit de la responsabilité civile'. In Recueil de travaux en l'honneur du prof. F. Gilliard, Lausanne 1897, 75 et seq.
Mottl, Ingeborg. 'Rechteverwertung im Rahmen der UEFA EURO 2008TM', *Causa Sport* 2008, 119 et seq.
Müller, Paola. 'Die Vergabe von Namensrechten an Fussballstadien in der Schweiz'. *Causa Sport* (2006): 555 et seq.
Muresan, Remus. 'Das Diskriminierungsverbot zugunsten russischer Profisportler in der EU gilt grenzenlos'. *Causa Sport* (2005): 5 et seq.
Muresan, Remus. 'Die Ausländerregelung der Eishockey Nationalliga im Lichte des Verbands- und Freizügigkeitsrechts'. *Causa Sport* (2005): 98 et seq.
NETZLE, Stefan. Sponsoring von Sportsverbänden, vertrags-, persönlichkeits-, und vereinsrechtliche Aspekte des Sport-Sponsorings. thesis, Zurich 1988.
NETZLE, Stefan. 'Immaterialgüterrechtlicher Schutz von Sportveranstaltungen im Zusammenhang mit der Werbung'. In *Sport und Recht*. Edited by ARTER & BADDELEY. Bern 2006, 67 et seq.
Nolte, Martin. 'Der Bildnisschutz von Sportlern im Lichte der Caroline-von-Hannover-Entscheidung des EGMR', *Causa Sport* (2005): 246 et seq.
Noret, André. Le doping. 2nd edn. Paris 1991.
NOTH, Michael. 'Ambush Marketing (Assoziationsmarketing) an Sportveranstaltungen – Smart oder rechtswidrig?'. In *Sport und Recht*. Edited by ARTER & BADDELEY. Bern 2006, 19 et seq.
NOTH, Michael. 'Comeback oder Stayback? Gedanken zur Durchsetzbarkeit der Comeback-Regelung im Doping-Statut der Swiss Olympic Association'. *Causa Sport* (2008): 444 et seq.
Oftiger, Karl & Emil W Stark. SCHWEIZERisches Haftpflichtrecht. Besonderer Teil, T II/2, Zurich 1989.
Orth, Mark E. 'Was hat Sport mit freiemWettbewerb zu tun?'. *Causa Sport* (2004): 195 et seq.
Oswald, Denis. A propos du dopage: les sanctions en cas de dopage, fautif ou non. *Revue juridique et économique du sport* 39 (1996): 55 et seq.
Oswald, Denis. 'Le pouvoir juridictionnel des organisations sportives et ses limites'. In *Tribunal Arbitral Du Sport*, Conférence internationale Droit et Sport, Lausanne, 13–14 September 1993, Lausanne 1994, 41 et seq.
Oswald, Denis. 'Le règlement des litiges et la répression des comportements illicites dans le domaine sportif'. In *Mélanges en l'honneur de Jacques-Michel Grossen*, Basel 1992, 67 et seq.
Pache, Jean-Jacques. La responsabilité civile en matière de sports. Thesis, Lausanne 1951.
PACHMANN, Thilo. Sportverbände und Corporate Governance. thesis, Zurich 2007.

PACHMANN, Thilo. 'Die Haftung des ehrenamtlich tätigen Vereinsvorstands und ihre Beschränkung'. in Vertrauen – Vertrag – Verantwortung, Zurich 2007, 255 et seq.
PACHMANN, Thilo & Thomas Wehrli. 'Where to go with Athletes' tax optimisation after the crack down on the Licence Box Model? Possibilities of structuring Athletes' tax in Switzerland' Global Sports and Taxation Review, September 2015, 34 et seq.
PACHMANN, Titus. CAS etabliert neue Standards für indirekten Dopingnachweis, *Causa Sport* (2013).
Parlasca, Susanne. Kartelle im Profisport, Die wettbewerbspolitische Problematik der Mannschaftssportligen Major League Baseball, National Football League und Fussball-Bundesliga, Berlin and Hamburg 1993.
Partikel, Andrea M. Formularbuch für Sportverträge. Munich 2000.
Personne, Jacques. Le sport pour l'enfant – ni records, ni médailles – Conseils aux parents. Paris 1993.
Peter, Henry. 'La forme juridique des clubs suisses: situation actuelle et perspectives souhaitables'. In *Comment améliorer la situation économique des clubs sportifs*, coll. CIES, vol. 4, Bern 2000, 7.
Peter, Henry. 'Le sponsoring sportif'. In *Chapitres choisis du droit du sport*, Etudes et recherches du GISS, Geneva 1988, 125 et seq.
Petermann, Frank Th. 'Burnout im Professional-Sport'. *Causa Sport* (2004): 70 et seq.
Pfister, Bernhard. 'Der "Fall Webster" Überlegungen nach deutschem Recht'. *Causa Sport* (2008): 29 et seq.
Pfister, Bernhard. 'Der Managervertrag des Sportlers'. In *Sportlervermittlung, Sportlermanagement.* Bern 2003, 123 et seq.
Pfister, Bernhard. 'Verbandsregelwerke als nationales Recht?'. *Causa Sport* (2005): 291 et seq.
PHILIPP, Peter. Rechtliche Schranken der Vereinsautonomie und der Vertragsfreiheit im Einzelsport. thesis, Zurich 2004.
Pieth Mark. 'Strafrecht'. In *Basler Kommentar zum Srafgesetzbuch*, Band I, 4th edn. Basel 2018.
Poll, Günter. 'Sportübertragungsrechte in der Europäischen Union aus urheberrechtlicher Sicht'. *Sport in der Europäischen Union.* vol. 19, Heidelberg 1996, 13 et seq.
Pons, Jean-François. Sport an European competition policy. Fordham Corporate Law Institute, twenty-sixth Annual Conference on International Antitrust Law & Policy, New York 14–15 October 1999.
PORTMANN, Wolfgang. Bindung von Berufssportlern an die ausbildenden Clubs. In: Causa Sport (2004) 220 et seq.
PORTMANN, Wolfgang. 'Das SCHWEIZERische Vereinsrecht'. In Tercier Pierre, SCHWEIZERisches Privatrecht, Bd. II/5, 3rd edn. Basel 2005.
PORTMANN, Wolfgang. 'Einseitige Optionsklauseln in Arbeitsverträgen von Fussballspielern'. *Causa Sport* (2006): 200 et seq.
PORTMANN, Wolfgang. Individualarbeitsrecht. Zurich 2000.
PORTMANN, Wolfgang. 'Kooperationsvereinbarung zwischen Fussballverbänden und Spielergewerkschaft – eine Etappe auf demWeg zu einem Gesamtarbeitsvertrag?'. *Causa Sport* (2006): 312 et seq.

PORTMANN, Wolfgang. 'Vereinbarung eines Handgelds im Arbeitsvertrag zwischen Fussballklub und Spieler – Qualifikation und Verjährung'. *Causa Sport* (2007): 458 et seq.

Pougin, Andreas. Die verfassungsrechtliche Bewertung des Kinderhochleistungssports unter Berücksichtigung des Jugendarbeitschutzgesetzes und des Familienrechts. thesis, Cologne 2000.

Ravi, Yasar. 'Les contrats de sponsoring sportif: notion, qualification et règles applicables'. *Droit et Sport*, coll. CIES, vol. 2, Bern 1977, 3 et seq.

Rehberg, Jörg. Verletzung beim Fussballspiel. Urteilsanmerkung zu BGE 109 IV 102, Recht 2/1984, 54 et seq.

Rehbinder, Manfred. SCHWEIZERisches Arbeitsrecht. Bern 1995.

Reinhart, Markus. Die strafrechtliche Bedeutung der FIS-Regeln. thesis, Zurich 1976.

Rempfler, Christa. 'FIFA-Reglement als anationales materielles Recht?'. *Causa Sport* (2004): 237 et seq.

RIEMER, Hans Michael. 'Beschränkung der persönlichen Haftung des Vereinsvorstandes durch Ressortverteilung'. *Causa Sport* (2005): 373 et seq.

RIEMER, Hans Michael. Die Vereine – Systematischer Teil und Kommentar zu Articles 60–79 ZGB. Berner Kommentar I/3/2, 3rd edn. Bern 1990.

RIEMER, Hans Michael. 'Neuerungen im Vereinsrecht: Mitgliederbeiträge und Haftung von Vereinsmitgliedern'. *Causa Sport* (2005): 52 et seq.

RIEMER, Hans Michael. 'Zur Frage des zwingenden Charakters von Art. 75 ZGB in den Bereichen Anfechtungsklage bei internationalen Schiedsgerichten'. *Causa Sport* (2005): 359 et seq.

RIEMER, Hans Michael. 'Sportrechts-Weltmacht Schweiz'. *Causa Sport* (2004): 106 et seq.

RIEMER, Hans Michael. 'Dopingkontrollen beim Training und im Privatleben von Sportlern'. *Causa Sport* (2008): 126 et seq.

Rinaud, Jean-Marie & René Christini. 'Le pouvoir disciplinaire des instances sportives'. In *Les problèmes juridiques du sport*, Paris 1981, 329 et seq.

Rigozzi, Antonio. L'arbitrage international en matière de sport, Basel 2005.

Rippe, Klaus Peter, 'Leistungssport oder Ethik – da müssen Sie entscheiden!', *Causa Sport* (2005): 234 et seq.

Rohner, Kurt & Adrian Wymann. 'Das Freizügigkeitsabkommen mit der EU und der SCHWEIZER Sport – Konsequenzen für die Arbeitsverhältnisse'. *Causa Sport* (2004): 5 et seq.

Roth, Robert. 'Le droit pénal du sport'. In *Chapitres choisis du droit du sport*, Geneva 1993, 101 et seq.

Rousseau, Dominique. 'Un centenaire mercantile'. In '*Le sport, c'est la guerre*'. supplément No. 30 au Monde diplomatique, 27.

Rückert, Susanne. Die ertragsteuerliche Behandlung des Sponsoring. Cologne 1999.

Ruetz-Venzin, Christian. Finanzielle Beitragspflichten der Vereinsmitglieder. Zurich 1985.

Rumphorst, Werner & Adrian Fikentscher. 'Elektronische Medienrechte an Sportveranstaltungen'. In *Sport und Recht*. Edited by ARTER & BADDELEY. Bern 2006, 99 et seq.

Ryban, Frank. Das Rechtsverhältnis zwischen dem Lizenzfussballspieler und seinem Verein. Frankfurt am Main 1999.

Sattiva Spring, Christine. Les fédérations à but idéal en droit suisse – Etude de quelques problèmes caractéristiques des structures fédératives. Lausanne 1990.

SCHERRER, Dorothe. 'Strafrechtliche Sanktionen nach Sportverletzungen'. *Causa Sport* (2006): 31 et seq.

SCHERRER, Urs & Heinz Tännler. 'Wann ist ein "Beschluss" ein Beschluss?'. *Causa Sport* (2005): 280 et seq.

SCHERRER, Urs. 'Sportlervermittlung und Sportlermanagement'. Bern, 2000.

SCHERRER, Urs. 'Aktuelle Rechtsfragen bei Sportvereinen'. *Causa Sport* (2005): 46 et seq.

SCHERRER, Urs. 'Aspects pénaux du dopage'. In *Aspects juridiques du dopage*, Colloque de Berne, 7 November 1990, Lausanne 1991, 21 et seq.

SCHERRER, Urs. 'Die Spielvermittler-Regelung des Weltfussballverbandes (FIFA)'. In *Sportlervermittlung, Sportlermanagement*, Bern, Munich and Vienna 2000, 93 et seq.

SCHERRER, Urs. 'Dopingkontrollen während der EURO 08?'. *Causa Sport* (2008): 125 et seq.

SCHERRER, Urs. 'Probleme der Lizenzierung von Klubs im Ligasport'. In *Sport und Recht*. Edited by ARTER & BADDELEY. Bern 2006, 119 et seq.

SCHERRER, Urs. 'Spielregel und Rechtsregel – Bestandesaufnahme und Ausblick'. *Causa Sport* (2008): 181 et seq.

SCHERRER, Urs. 'Sportler-Management und Sportler-Vermittlung im globalisierten Sport'. in *Sport und Recht*. Edited by ARTER. Bern 2004, 87 et seq.

SCHERRER, Urs. Sportrecht – Fälle aus der Praxis. Münsingen 1985.

SCHERRER, Urs. 'Vereinsrechtliche Anfechtungsklage und Schiedsgerichtsbarkeit im Sport'. *Causa Sport* (2008): 58 et seq.

SCHERRER, Urs. 'Wie gründe und leite ich einen Verein?'. 10th edn. Zurich 1996.

SCHERRER, Urs. 'Zur Verantwortlichkeit der Organe von Sportvereinen und Sportkapitalgesellschaften'. In *Sport und Recht*. Edited by ARTER. Bern 2005, 223 et seq.

SCHERRER, Urs & Kai Ludwig Sportrecht, Eine Begriffserläuterung. 2nd edn. Zurich 2010.

SCHERRER-BIRCHER, Dorothe. Wirtschaftliche Rezession und Sportvereine. Zurich 1994.

Schild, Wolfgang. 'Techno-Doping'. *Causa Sport* (2008): 128 et seq.

Schillig, Mark. 'Ausschluss ordentlicher Gerichte durch Verbandsvorschrift bezüglich vorsorglicher Massnahmen?'. *Causa Sport* (2005): 54 et seq.

Schillig, Mark. Schiedsgerichtsbarkeit von Sportverbänden in der Schweiz. Zurich 2000.

Schimke, Martin. Sportrecht. Frankfurt am Main 1996.

Schmid, Markus. 'Sportverletzungen und Versicherungsrechtliches'. *Causa Sport* (2006): 21 et seq.

Schnyder, Anton K. 'Rechtsbehelfe gegen Entscheide des Court of Arbitration for Sport (CAS)'. *Causa Sport* (2005): 353 et seq.

SCHWEIZER, Eva. 'Aktuelle Rechtsentwicklungen in der Dopingbekämpfung'. *Sport und Recht*. Edited by ARTER (ed.), Bern 2005, 235 et seq.

Sehling, Michael, Reinhord Pollert & Dieter Hackfort. Doping im Sport, Medizinische, sozialwissenschaftliche und juristische Aspekte. Munich, Vienna and Zurich 1989.

Sidler, Max. 'Die gesamtwirtschaftliche Bedeutung von Sportverletzungen'. *Causa Sport* (2006): 28 et seq.

Sidler, Oliver. Exklusivberichterstattung über Sportveranstaltungen im Rundfunk. Unter besonderer Berücksichtigung des Rechts auf Bericht- und Kurzberichterstattung (Article 7 RTVG). Fribourg 1995.

Siegfried, Michael. Die Fernsehberichterstattung von Sportveranstaltungen, Die Rechtsbeziehungen zwischen teilnehmenden Sportler Sportveranstalter und Sportverband. Munich 1990.

Siegrist, Robert & Daniel THALER. 'Ausnahmsweiser Entzug der Suspensivwirkung von Rechtsmitteln gegen Sportstättenprojekte – am Beispiel des Zürcher Rechts'. *Causa Sport* (2004): 132 et seq.

Silance, Luc. Les sports et le droit. Paris, Bruxelles 1998.

Simon, Gérald. Puissance sportive et ordre juridique étatique – Contribution à l'étude des relations entre la puissance publique et les institutions privées. Paris 1990, 58 et seq.

Staehlin, Adrian, Peter Gauch & Jörg Schmid. Kommentar zum SCHWEIZERischen Zivilgesetzbuch, das Obligationenrecht, Articles 331–355, Zurich 1996.

Staehlin, Adrian, et al. Kommentar zum SCHWEIZERischen Zivilgesetzbuch, Obligationenrecht. Articles 319–362 OR. Zurich 1996.

Stahlin, Adrian & Frank Vischer. Der Arbeitsvertrag: Articles 319–362 OR. Zürcher Kommentar V/2/c, 3rd edn. Zurich 1996.

Stamm, Hanspeter & Markus Lamprecht. Sportvereine in der Schweiz, Probleme – Fakten – Perspektiven. Chur and Zurich 2005.

Stark, Emil W. 'Das sogenannte Handeln auf eigene Gefahr'. RSJ 50 (1954): 21 et seq. and 40 et seq.

Steinauer, Paul-Henri, L'enfant dans le Code civil, in: 'L'image de l'homme en droit' Mélanges publiés par la faculté de droit é l'occasion du centenaire de l'Université de Fribourg. Fribourg 1990.

Stiffler, Hans-Kaspar. SCHWEIZERisches Skirecht. 2nd edn. Derendingen, 1991.

Stratenwerth, Günter. SCHWEIZERisches Strafrecht. Besonderer Teil 1, 5th edn. Bern 1995.

Streiff, Ullin & Von Kaenel, Adrian. Arbeitsvertrag. Zurich 1993.

Sutter, Thomas. Rechtsfragen des organisierten Sports, unter besonderer Berücksichtigung des Einzelarbeitsvertrages. thesis, Basel 1984.

Tännler, Heinz & Tanja Haug. 'Kommerzielle Verwertung von Sportveranstaltungen'. *Causa Sport* (2007): 138 et seq.

Tännler, Heinz. 'Der Schiedsrichter im Spannungsfeld von Sport, Recht und Ethik'. *Causa Sport* (2005): 15 et seq.

Tännler, Heinz. 'Einfluss von Verbandsregelungen auf Arbeitsverträge im Bereich Gesundheitsschutz und bezüglich Sportverletzungen'. *Causa Sport* (2005): 368 et seq.

Tarasti, Lauri. Legal Solutions in International Doping Cases – Awards by the IAAF Arbitration Panel 1985–1999. Milan 2000.

TEITLER, Mirjam. 'Rechtsnatur und Anwendung des WADA-Code'. *Causa Sport* (2007): 395 et seq.
Tercier, Pierre. Le droit des obligations. 2nd edn. Zurich 1999.
THALER, Daniel. 'Ambush Marketing mit der UEFA EURO 2008TM – Eine Standortbestimmung'. *Causa Sport* (2008): 160 et seq.
THALER, Daniel. 'Anmerkung zum Urteil des Bundesgerichts vom 17. Juli 2007'. *Causa Sport* (2007): 371 et seq.
THALER, Daniel. 'Anmerkungen zum Urteil des Bundesgerichts vom 24. Oktober 2007'. *Causa Sport* (2007): 490 et seq.
THALER, Daniel. 'Anmerkungen zum Urteil des Obergerichts des Kantons Zürich vom 23. März 2007'. *Causa Sport* (2007): 382.
THALER, Daniel. 'Anmerkungen zum Urteil des Verwaltungsgerichts des Kantons Aargau vom 23. Mai 2006'. *Causa Sport* (2007): 213 et seq.
THALER, Daniel. 'Athletenvereinbarungen und Athletenerklärungen'. In *Sport und Recht*. Edited by ARTER & BADDELEY. Bern 2007, 19 et seq.
THALER, Daniel. 'BGE 131 II 81 – Stadion Zürich, grundsätzliche Klarstellung zum Fahrtenregime beim Sportstättenbau'. *Causa Sport* (2005): 286 et seq.
THALER, Daniel. 'Der Traum vom Fussballweltmeistertitel: Wieviel Einsatz und Risiko ist zulässig, um zu siegen? Eine international-haftungsrechtliche Betrachtung des Fouls'. *Causa Sport* (2006): 172 et seq.
THALER, Daniel. 'Fussball im Dunst der Geldwäsche'. *Causa Sport* (2004): 11 et seq.
THALER, Daniel. 'Hooliganismus und Sport'. In *Sport und Recht*. Edited by ARTER & BADDELEY. Bern 2006, 245 et seq.
THALER, Daniel. 'Sportregeln und zivilrechtliche Haftung'. In *Sport und Recht*. Edited by ARTER. Bern 2004, 129 et seq.
Trachsler, Walter. Rechtliche Fragen bei der fotografischen Aufnahme. Zurich 1975.
Tribunal, Arbitral du Sport (TAS)/Comité Internationale Olympique, Recueil des sentences du TAS. Bern 1998.
Trommer, Hans-Ralph. Die Transferregelungen im Profisport im Lichte des 'Bosman-Urteils' im Vergleich zu den Mechanismen im bezahlten amerikanischen Sport. Berlin 1999.
VALLONI, Lucien. 'CAS Structure and Procedure – It is now Time for a Change!'. In *Football Legal.* (2016): 36-44.
VALLONI, Lucien. 'Doping – Auswirkungen auf den Arbeitsvertrag'. In *Sport und Recht*. Edited by ARTER & BADDELEY. Bern 2007, 203 et seq.
VALLONI, Lucien & Eric Neuenschwander. 'The role of Switzerland as host: Moves to hold sports organisations more accountable, and wider implications.' In Global Corruption Report 2016.
Vieweg, Klaus. Doping, Realität und Recht, Coll. Beiträge zum Sportrecht. vol. 1, Berlin 1998.
Vieweg, Klaus. 'Doping und Verbandsrecht'. NjW (1991): 1511 et seq.
Vieweg, Klaus. Normsetzung und – Anwendung deutscher und internationaler Verbände, Eine rechtstatsächliche und rechtliche Untersuchung unter besonderer Berücksichtigung der Sportverbände. Berlin 1990.
Vischer, Frank. Der Arbeitsvertrag. Basel 1994.

Vögeli, Hans Felix. Strafrechtliche Aspekte der Sportverletzungen, im besonderen die Einwilligung des Verletzten im Sport. Zurich 1994.

Wahrenberger, André. 'Sportsponsoringverträge'. In *Sport und Recht*. Edited by ARTER. Bern 2005, 147 et seq.

WaldHAUSER, Hermann. Die Fernsehrechte des Sportveranstalters. Berlin 1999.

Walter, Gerhard. 'Schiedsgerichtsbarkeit und Sport'. In *Sport und Recht*. Edited by ARTER. Bern 2004, 173 et seq.

Warnke, Kerstin. 'Das Hepatitis- und HIV-Infektionsrisiko im Sport – Aufklärung ist die beste Prävention'. *Causa Sport* (2005): 361 et seq.

Weber-Dürler Hans, Peter. Gesellschafterversammlung, Urabstimmung und Delegiertenversammlung als Beschlussformen des SCHWEIZERischen Gesellschaftsrechts. Zurich 1973.

Wehrenberg, Stefan. 'Polizeieinsätze bei Sportgrossveranstaltungen'. In *Sport und Recht*. Edited by ARTER & BADDELEY. Bern 2006, 183 et seq.

Wiesemann, Ulrich & Ulrich Spieker. Sport, Spiel und Recht. NJW-Schriftenreihe, Munich 1997.

Winiker, Christian & Men-Andri Benz. 'Richtige Anreizstrukturen zur Verhinderung von Klubpleiten'. *Causa Sport* (2005): 228 et seq.

Winiker, Christian. 'Die Markenführung als Determinante des sportlichen Erfolgs von Fussballklubs'. *Causa Sport* (2004): 100 et seq.

Witteler, Michael. Die Besteuerung von international tätigen Sportlern. Münster 1999.

Wohlers, Wolfgang. 'SCHWEIZERisches Strafgesetzbuch'. In *Handkommentar*. 4th edn. Bern 2020.

Wyler, Rémy. 'La convention d'arbitrage en droit du sport'. RDS (1997): 45 et seq.

Wyler, Rémy. 'Sportif blessé – Responsabilité civile, subrogation de l'assureur social et privilège de recours'. In *Sport und Recht*. Edited by ARTER & BADDELEY. Bern 2007, 161 et seq.

Zen-Ruffinen, Piermarco, Jean PHILIPPe Dubey & Gianni Infantino. 'De la titularité à la cotitularité des droits de télévision dans le sport'. *Media Lex* (1999): 154, et seq.

Zen-Ruffinen, Piermarco & Christine Guy-Ecabert. 'Installation sportives et aménagement de territoire'. *Droit et sport*. Coll. CIES, vol. 2, Bern 1997, 223 et seq.

Zen-Ruffinen, Piermarco & PHILIPPe SCHWEIZER. 'Petite Revue de Jurisprudence en Droit du Sport'. *Causa Sport* (2007): 67 et seq.

Zen-Ruffinen, Piermarco. 'De quelques problèmes juridiques posés par la minorité dans le sport de haut niveau'. In Un champion à tout prix? Les droits de l'enfant dans le sport. Institut internationale des droits de l'enfant, Sion 1999, 93 et seq.

Zen-Ruffinen, Piermarco. 'La forme juridique des clubs sportifs dans quelques Etats européens'. I\n Comment améliorer la situation économique des clubs sportifs. coll: CIES, vol 4, Bern 2000, 39 et seq.

Zen-Ruffinen, Piermarco. 'Petite Revue de Jurisprudence en Droit du Sport'. *Causa Sport* (2005): 57 et seq.

Zufferey, Jean-Bapiste. 'Les contrats du sport professionnel face aux bonnes moeurs'. RSJ (1990): 113 et seq.

Selected Bibliography

Index

The numbers here refer to paragraph numbers

Index

www.ingramcontent.com/pod-product-compliance
Lightning Source LLC
LaVergne TN
LVHW011133300926
849160LV00008B/636